Education for National Development

PRAEGER SPECIAL STUDIES IN
INTERNATIONAL ECONOMICS AND DEVELOPMENT

Education for National Development

EFFECTS OF U.S. TECHNICAL TRAINING PROGRAMS

Albert E. Gollin

PRAEGER PUBLISHERS
New York · Washington · London

The purpose of the Praeger Special Studies is to make specialized research monographs in U.S. and international economics and politics available to the academic, business, and government communities. For further information, write to the Special Projects Division, Praeger Publishers, Inc., 111 Fourth Avenue, New York, N.Y. 10003.

PRAEGER PUBLISHERS
111 Fourth Avenue, New York, N.Y. 10003, U.S.A.
5, Cromwell Place, London S.W. 7, England

Published in the United States of America in 1969
by Praeger Publishers, Inc.

Library of Congress Catalog Card Number: 76-77005

Printed in the United States of America

PREFACE

One of the most influential forces in international affairs in recent decades has been the emergence of new nations accompanied by the rising aspirations for a better life of peoples in economically backward areas. Partly in response to this, a new set of international institutions has evolved, linking old and new societies, the developed and the underdeveloped, in ways that have altered established usages and assumptions in international relations. Prominent among these are the programs and modes of assistance, bilateral and multilateral, which have served as the vehicles for meeting the development aspirations and needs of poor nations since the 1950s.

The strategic role that foreign assistance can and indeed must play in national development is a theme that is readily apparent both in the ever-expanding professional literature on the problem and in the voluminous arguments and appeals of national leaders and international agency officials. In the continuing debate over the value of foreign aid, which has been a companion of the program in the United States since its inception, much of the so-called information on programs takes the form of critical exposés and negative assertions and is usually answered by positive testimonials and counter-assertions. Careful studies and analyses of the ways in which various types of assistance have actually been employed, what has and has not worked, and why, are, by comparison, encountered much less frequently. The relative scarcity of more objective data on these issues is not surprising, given the magnitude and complexity of such programs, which makes the task of systematic research correspondingly

difficult. Other factors include the constraints on
evaluative activities common to bureaucracies, the
sometimes divergent interest in or sensitivity to the
results of such studies by the parties involved in
the aid relationship, and various problems of method,
organization, and substance intrinsic to comparative
or cross-national research.

In spite of these retarding influences, research
or evaluative studies have been conducted on the operations or effects of a number of assistance programs. The results of one such effort constitute
much of the source materials of this book, which is
devoted to a detailed examination of the character,
evolution, and selected consequences of a U.S.
technical-assistance program called "participant
training." In existence as an identifiable part of
larger aid projects for more than two decades, this
program seeks, through the education and training of
foreign nationals, to develop the human resources
needed for economic progress and the modernization
of traditional social systems. More than 100,000
people from underdeveloped countries have taken part
in this program and have received varied training in
the United States or in other countries. Simply in
terms of the number of people who have passed through
it, participant training is the most significant of
the various educational or cultural-exchange programs
sponsored by the U.S. government. However, of greater importance to the student of the development process is the fact that this program has been designed,
as a recent Agency for International Development
(AID) report states, to be "primarily a technical-
assistance effort to promote and transfer modern
technologies and skills." Thus, a study of its operation and effects can clarify a number of issues
in the problem area of guided or planned social
change, and, in particular, the role of educational-
aid strategies in national development.

The study that provided the data base for this
book, details of which are discussed in Part One,
represents one of the most successful uses of survey
methodology on a world-wide scale that has been made

to date. Undertaken on a cooperative, binational
basis in each of the developing countries that met
certain criteria of eligibility, the surveys with
returned participants that form the study's core
were carried out in more than thirty countries. The
same interview instruments and procedures were designed to ensure maximum comparability of findings.
In these days of tight budgets, there are probably
few problems of a theoretical or practical character
that could command a similar investment of time and
resources. The example this study affords, however,
should dispel doubts as to the feasibility of em-
barking on such a multinational follow-up effort
when it seems desirable to do so.

In any study of this scope and character, a
number of people deserve special mention. My first
acknowledgment of indebtedness is to AID, which
allowed me to make further use of data that required
much organizational ingenuity and human energy to
gather. The concern of its Office of International
Training (which is responsible for participant training) to know how the program is received and used
led to the launching of the research project noted
above, from which I took the survey data used in
this book. Earlier work of mine on aspects of that
study, including a number of reports and an analysis
written under a contract between AID and my employing organization, provided me with the detailed knowledge that made this secondary analysis a feasible
undertaking. Forrest E. Clements, who served as
AID's coordinator for this study, was a continuously
helpful source of information on the program and the
circumstances and conduct of the study. AID bears
no responsibility for the analysis or interpretation
of data in this work, for all of which I am solely
responsible.

Another debt that I wish to acknowledge, one
discharged imperfectly by these few words, is to
three distinguished teachers with whom I studied
sociology at Columbia University: Paul F. Lazarsfeld,
Herbert H. Hyman, and Robert K. Merton. As all whom
they have instructed can attest, their high standards

and professional achievements exert an influence upon one's own work in many useful ways. A number of former and current colleagues at the Bureau of Social Science Research have also rendered valuable assistance; I wish to acknowledge in particular the help of Robert T. Bower, Gene B. Petersen, and John M. Kert, Jr.

My final debt, the most extensive of all, is to my wife and fellow sociologist, Gillian. Her example and encouragement have been decisive in my fulfillment of a commitment of long standing. _Omnia vincit amor_.

Albert E. Gollin

Bureau of Social
   Science Research, Inc.
Washington, D.C.

CONTENTS

Page

PREFACE   v

LIST OF TABLES   xiii

LIST OF ABBREVIATIONS   xviii

PART ONE: THE TRANSFER OF TECHNOLOGY

Chapter

1   EDUCATIONAL AID FOR DEVELOPMENT   3

     Technical Assistance in Historical
       Perspective   4
     Human Resources for Development   9
     Foreign Study and the Transfer Process   13
     The Survey of Participant Training   16
     Notes   22

PART TWO: PARTICIPANT TRAINING

2   PARTICIPANTS AND THE SELECTION PROCESS   33

     The Participants: A Collective Portrait   34
         Age, Sex, and Marital Status   34
         Prior Formal Education and Training   38
         Residence and Mobility   43
         Occupational Characteristics   44
     The Selection Process   50
         Program Objectives and Selection
           Criteria   50

            Selection for Participant Training   51
            Criteria of Selection   57
      Notes   65

3   THE TRANSITION TO TRAINING   71

    Anticipatory Socialization and
      Organizational Commitments   71
    Preparations for Training   74
            Planning the Programs   74
            Participants' Role in Planning
              Programs   74
            Advance Orientation and Information   75
            Advance Commitments to Use Training   76
    Satisfaction with Training Prior to
      Departure   81
    First Steps on Arrival   84
    Notes   88

4   THE ANATOMY OF TRAINING PROGRAMS   91

    The Parameters of Training   92
            A Typology of Training Programs   102
    University Studies: A Special Case   105
            Regular and Special Students   107
            Career Value of a Degree   110
    Notes   115

5   EVALUATIONS OF TRAINING: THREE
        PERSPECTIVES   121

    Training As Seen by Participants   122
            Technical Aspects   122
            Nontechnical Aspects   131
    Supervisors' Views on Training   137
    Training As Seen by U.S. Technicians   140
    Notes   143

PART THREE: THE CONSEQUENCES OF TRAINING

6   THE AFTERMATH OF TRAINING: CAREER
         PATTERNS   151

     Placement and Career Patterns   151
             Occupational Status and Mobility   152
             Economic Sectors Then and Now   156
             Placement After Training   158
     Patterns of Occupational Mobility   161
             Value of Training to Career   164
     Work Contexts and Mission Contacts   168
             The U.S. Mission: Follow-up and
                 Assistance   172
     Notes   179

7   TRAINING INTO PRACTICE   184

     The Concept of Program Effectiveness   184
             The Uses of Training   187
             Types of Use at Work   190
             Barriers to Use   191
             Plans for Future Use   194
             Training Others: The Role of
                 Communicator   197
     A Criterion Measure of Use   201
             Index of Utilization   201
     Notes   206

8   PATTERNS IN THE USE OF TRAINING   210

     Use and Attributes of Participants
         and Programs   210
     Use and Evaluations of Program
         Processes   221
     Use and the Aftermath of Training   234
     An Epilogue on Three Themes   245
     Notes   251

Page

SELECTED BIBLIOGRAPHY   259

ABOUT THE AUTHOR

LIST OF TABLES

Table   Page

1.1.   Participants in the Surveys and Their
       First Recorded Year of Departure,
       by Country of Origin   21

2.1.   Age of Participants Entering Training
       in Selected Years up to FY 1967   35

2.2.   Prior Formal Education: Type of
       Degree by Location of University   40

2.3.   Residential Mobility Patterns of
       Participants at Selection and
       Interview, by Country   45

2.4.   Occupational Status of Participants
       at Selection and Interview   48

2.5.   Participants' Views of Selection Agent
       by Their Prior Work Contacts with
       U.S. Mission (USOM)   55

2.6.   Participants' Beliefs About Importance
       of Five Criteria for Their Selection   58

2.7.   Beliefs About Importance of Personal
       Contacts and Needs of Job As
       Selection Criteria, by Country
       of Participants   62

3.1.   Organizational Plans for the Use of
       Training, by Supervisors' Prior
       Involvement, Obtained from
       Supervisors About Specific
       Participants   78

Table   Page

3.2.   Proportion Well Satisfied with Program
       Arrangements and Duration Prior to
       Departure   83

4.1.   The Distribution of Participants by
       Training Fields   95

4.2.   Major Training Fields of Surveyed
       Participants by Period of Departure,
       and of All Non-European Participants
       to 1967   96

4.3.   Typology of Training Programs and the
       Distribution of Participants in Each   103

4.4.   Proportion of University-Trained
       Participants Who Were Regular
       Students and Median Duration of
       Training by Program Type   108

4.5.   Career Value of a Degree for University-
       Trained Participants by Their Student
       Status and Receipt of a Degree in
       Training   111

5.1.   Desired Length of Training Program and
       Actual Duration of Dissatisfied
       Participants   125

5.2.   Absence of Language Difficulty During
       Training by Scores on Oral and
       Written English Tests   128

5.3.   Difficulty with English During Training
       by an Index of English Language
       Proficiency   130

5.4.   Supervisors' Evaluations of Importance
       of Participants' Training Programs
       by Duration   139

xiv

Table   Page

5.5.   Technicians' Evaluations of
          Contribution of Participants'
          Programs by Duration   142

6.1.   Patterns of Mobility in Occupational
          Status, from Selection to Interview   154

6.2.   Classification of Economic Sectors
          by Two Measures of Participants'
          Job Mobility   157

6.3.   Patterns of Occupational Mobility   162

6.4.   Career Value of Training by Site
          of Program and Earned Degrees   166

6.5.   Career Value of Training by
          Participants' Patterns of
          Occupational Mobility   167

6.6.   Organizational Setting of Participants
          Trained Abroad, by Country of Origin   171

6.7.   Supervisors' Helpfulness in Using Foreign
          Training, As Seen by Participants   173

6.8.   Postprogram Contacts with USOM by
          Availability of a U.S. Technician
          to Participant and Frequency of
          Contact   176

7.1.   Extent of Participants' Use of
          Training in Current Jobs   189

7.2.   Major Difficulties in Using Training   193

7.3.   Plans for Future Use of Training by
          Time Since Program Completion and
          by Use of Training   196

7.4.   Extent to Which Participants Conveyed
          Training to Others   199

Table   Page

7.5. Construction of an Index of Utilization
      with Definition of Categories and
      Proportion of Participants in Each   202

7.6. Index of Utilization, Categories, and
      Distribution of Participants   203

7.7. Cross-Validation of the Utilization
      Index: Very High and Low Use Compared
      on Items from Three Sources of Data   205

8.1. Utilization of Training by Participants'
      Age and Prior Education at Selection   211

8.2. Utilization of Training by Current
      Occupational Status   214

8.3. Utilization of Training by English-
      Language Problems and by Country
      (Site) of Training   216

8.4. Utilization of Training by Type of
      Program and by University-Earned
      Degree   218

8.5. Utilization of Training by Duration
      and Field of Training   220

8.6. Utilization of Training by Views on
      Three Selection Criteria and on
      Participants' Roles in Program
      Planning   223

8.7. Utilization of Training by Sources of
      Advance Information About Program
      and by Satisfaction Prior to Training   225

8.8. Utilization of Training by Supervisors'
      Prior Involvement in Program and by
      Prior Organizational Plans for Use   227

Table   Page

 8.9.   Utilization of Training by Participants'
        Evaluations of Selected Program
        Aspects   229

8.10.   Utilization of Training by Indices of
        Satisfaction with Technical and
        Nontechnical Aspects of Training   231

8.11.   Utilization of Training by Time Since
        Completion of Program and by Index
        of General Satisfaction with Training   235

8.12.   Utilization of Training by Career Value
        of Training and by Patterns of
        Occupational Mobility   238

8.13.   Utilization of Training by Aspects of
        the Organizational Setting   241

8.14.   Utilization of Training by Pattern of
        USOM Contacts After Training   244

LIST OF ABBREVIATIONS

AID   Agency for International Development

ASPAU   African Scholarship Program of American
         Universities

FY   Fiscal Year

ICA   International Cooperation Administration

LASPAU Latin American Scholarship Program of
         American Universities

UNRRA   United Nations Relief and Rehabilitation
         Administration

USOM   United States Operations Missions

PART ONE

THE TRANSFER OF TECHNOLOGY

CHAPTER **1** EDUCATIONAL AID
FOR DEVELOPMENT

Education has long had a somewhat ambiguous
status in U.S. government programs in the international field. It has been seen and used as a
convenient vehicle for the exchange of citizens
with other countries in order to promote greater
mutual understanding through teaching, scholarship,
or professional and academic contacts. Education
and specialized training have also been employed
for more narrowly defined purposes, including the
achievement of some political impact upon various
elite groups in other nations or the facilitation
of some economic or military-assistance project.
However, it is difficult to classify specific programs by their purposes, as there is considerable
overlap in the goals enunciated by sponsors, and
one also finds some shifts in emphasis among goals
in the history of many of these programs.

This work attempts to describe and analyze one
of these educational programs, evaluating its mode
of operations and some of its short- and long-range
consequences relative to its explicit and implicit
goals. The program, in existence as a part of U.S.
technical assistance for more than two decades, has
carried a variety of titles, but for the longest
stretch it has been known as "participant training."
Our study has a broader objective as well: to clarify certain aspects of the general problem of bringing about technological change and modernization,
through the use of education and training to diffuse
requisite skills, knowledge, and techniques. The
program's stress upon the training of selected professional and administrative elites to take on the
role of change agents in their own milieus also will

3

enable us to examine the question of the individual's strategic role in national development.

Because participant training has received little attention in the literature on international education or foreign aid, despite its scale and longevity, it may be helpful to indicate how it has evolved relative to its changing foreign-policy context. After sketching its history, we will discuss some implications of two critical processes intrinsic to the program--human-resources development and the transfer of technology--and describe the study from which our survey materials were drawn.

TECHNICAL ASSISTANCE IN
HISTORICAL PERSPECTIVE

Like many innovations in U.S. foreign policy, technical assistance emerged in an identifiable form as a stepchild of World War II. Its origins can be traced to a small program initiated in 1942 by the Institute of Inter-American Affairs.[1] Assistance projects were launched in a few countries with goals of improving agricultural productivity, health and sanitation, and other fields vital to the hemispheric war effort. U.S. advisors and specialists provided direct assistance through their work on these projects and engaged in some local training activities. Several hundred Latin Americans were sent to the United States on inspection tours, for practical experience and, in some cases, for extended periods of study. A few aid projects in the field of education were also begun in several countries. In addition, State Department grants were made to Chinese students (caught in the United States by the war) and to several Middle East institutions (e.g., Robert College in Istanbul, Turkey) for special training programs. Educational assistance also played a minor role in the programs of the United Nations Relief and Rehabilitation Administration (UNRRA), begun in 1943 with U.S. support and personnel.

A new phase in foreign assistance began at the close of the war and lasted until around 1950. In

this period, the focus of attention was Western
Europe, suffering from the dislocations and devasta-
tion of war and from the presence of communist power
within and on its countries' borders as a major
threat to its political stability. The initial
response of the United States was primarily economic
rather than military.

> The recovery of Western Europe . . . was
> regarded as essential to world recovery.
> . . . Although Congress and the Adminis-
> tration were heavily motivated by secu-
> rity considerations, military action was
> subordinated to economic assistance.
> . . . The emphasis, particularly during
> the first two years of the Marshall Plan,
> was entirely on economic means.[2]

The renaissance of European economic life that
was stimulated by capital supplied through the Marshall Plan was so impressive that it affected economic planning and thinking for a long time afterward.[3] The model of the development process it
fostered centered on the role of capital formation
and investment. "Economists and educators alike
evidenced the belief that capital was a cure-all to
the problem of development."[4] This emphasis was slow
to undergo change; it was not until the attention of
planners turned to the special problems of economically backward nations that some of its limitations
became apparent.

As part of Marshall Plan aid, programs of training that had industrial productivity as their focus
were developed.

> At the outset the /Economic Cooperation
> Administration7 accorded scant recogni-
> tion to the educational phase of the
> economic assistance enterprise. But it
> was not long before it was engaged in
> technical training of the personnel
> needed to assure continuing development
> of the agricultural and industrial pro-
> jects it was supporting.[5]

"Productivity teams" made up of two categories of
older participants--managers and technicians, shop
stewards and trade-union leaders--were sent to the
United States on brief visits to observe industrial
practices and to learn about techniques for increasing productivity. Groups of younger workers came
for periods of intensive work experience in factories,
sometimes lasting for as long as one year. Practical
training was usually supplemented by discussions on
problems of supervision and lectures on labor-
management relations. (A few years later, this mode
of productivity training was again employed with
participants of similar status from Japan and other
Asian countries.) The training of European participants continued during the next decade; by 1960,
almost 20,000 had come to the United States for study
or training.

A second turning point in the postwar era was
the outbreak of the Korean War which ushered in a
new direction in assistance policies that lasted
until about 1955. "Foreign assistance was increased
rather than diminished as had been expected at the
end of the Marshall Plan. The motivation became
overtly and almost solely security considerations;
and security came to be rather narrowly interpreted
in military terms."[6] This period witnessed a pro-
liferation of bilateral- and regional-security agreements, a tendency in policy making that was called
"pactomania" by its critics. Economic assistance
to some underdeveloped nations was part of these
agreements; given largely in the form of "defense
support," it permitted them to enlarge their military
forces without completely disrupting their weak
economies.

Just before the start of this period, however,
a new note was struck--the enunciation of Point Four
in President Harry S. Truman's Inaugural Address in
1949.

> Fourth, we must embark on a bold new
> program for making the benefits of our
> scientific advances and industrial

> progress available for the improvement
> and growth of underdeveloped areas.
> More than half the people of the world
> are living in conditions approaching
> misery. . . . For the first time in
> history, humanity possesses the knowl-
> edge and the skill to relieve the
> suffering of these people.
>
> The United States is pre-eminent
> among nations in the development of
> industrial and scientific techniques.
> The material resources which we can
> afford to use for the assistance of
> other peoples are limited. But our
> imponderable resources in technical
> knowledge are constantly growing and
> are inexhaustible.
>
> I believe that we should make
> available to peace-loving peoples the
> benefits of our store of technical
> knowledge in order to help them real-
> ize their aspirations for a better
> life. . . .[7]

This was the first clear mandate for technical
assistance to assume an independent status as part
of U.S. foreign operations. In fact, when this major
change in U.S. assistance policy was announced, no
concrete plans for its implementation existed. A
close observer of the way in which a casual suggestion became high public policy remarked: "It was
only . . . after the Inaugural Address had been
delivered and the 'bold new program' acclaimed all
over the world that machinery was set up to . . .
make plans. The . . . actual program was not to
come until twenty-one months later."[8] In the period
that followed, technical-assistance programs assumed
two forms: an expansion in the numbers of U.S.
advisors sent to underdeveloped countries, and a
growth in the numbers of foreign nationals who came
to the United States for technical training. In the
years prior to 1950, less than 2,000 people from a

handful of countries came for training; the numbers
increased sharply thereafter, from 1,710 in 1950 to
almost 5,000 from 59 nations in 1955.[9]

A third period that can be identified, which
ran from 1955 to 1961, represented a consolidation
of the trends noted earlier. The International
Cooperation Administration (ICA) was founded as a
central coordinating agency for all the programs of
economic, military, and technical assistance that
had been launched in preceding years. A new element
was added in the same year by the Soviet Union's
decision, in the post-Stalin era, to enter into com-
petition with the United States for the support and
favor of the "third world" by launching programs of
economic and technical assistance, including low-
interest loans. One U.S. response was to increase
funds for technical cooperation and development
grants and, in 1957, to institute a new program of
development loans whose expenditures quite rapidly
outstripped the relatively modest ($111-$180 million)
sums being spent on the former types of assistance.[10]
Technical assistance assumed a more important role
in the totality of U.S. programs as a means for providing aid to new or neutral nations and, toward the
close of this period, it took on added importance as
a means for restoring the foundering position of the
United States in Latin America.

As aid to Europe dropped off, the proportion of
Europeans sent to the United States for technical
training declined sharply. In 1952, they accounted
for 90 per cent; three years later, 41 per cent; and,
by 1960, they made up only 10 per cent of all participants in the program. In that year, almost
6,800 foreign nationals from 84 countries arrived
in the United States for training, pushing the total
trained in the succession of programs since 1942 to
more than 50,000. Although this was the largest
nonmilitary, governmentally sponsored program for
the education and training of foreign nationals, its
scope remained modest in comparison with the total
U.S. foreign-assistance effort, and small even with
respect to the provision of technical training.

Within roughly the same period (1951-61), the U.S. military-assistance program provided formal instruction in U.S. installations to more than 130,000 men from foreign nations; it continues to train almost half again as many annually as its nonmilitary counterparts.[11]

With the founding of the Agency for International Development (AID) in 1961, technical assistance received added emphasis in the foreign-aid programs of the incoming Kennedy Administration. The character of the participant-training program was altered by the addition of contingents from new African nations and an increase in trainees from countries in the Alliance for Progress. At the present time, about 6,000 foreign nationals from 70 countries arrive in the United States annually for training; several thousand more are offered training in their own countries or at other sites outside the United States. By 1967, more than 100,000 trainees had arrived in the United States for technical training--three times as many as have come to the United States under the sponsorship of the better-known Fulbright Program.[12]

HUMAN RESOURCES FOR DEVELOPMENT

The interest in the role of education and training in the development process is of comparatively recent vintage. The economic theories that successfully guided assistance policies in the Marshall Plan years, and for a while afterward, viewed foreign aid primarily as a stimulus and supplement to domestic-capital formation. But even in the case of Europe, as many have pointed out, insufficient attention was paid to other prerequisites for economic reconstruction, such as Europe's long history of developing a wide range of functionally relevant skills and institutions among its population. In James A. Perkins' succinct phrase: "Europe did not have to be invented; it only had to be remembered."[13]

Many influences converged in the decade of the 1950s to encourage a reconsideration of the primacy

of capital formation and investment as the well-
springs of economic development. One was a revival
of interest in the concepts of investment in education and human capital on the part of economists
dealing with the problem of a lagging U.S. economic
growth rate.[14] Perhaps the most significant influence was the emergence of new nations and the rising
international clamor for development assistance.
First, it produced a quickening stream of literature
written by students of the development process whose
perspectives differed considerably from those adopted
by most economists. A long and growing list of noneconomic prerequisites was one byproduct of their
work.[15] Second, the prevailing conception was badly
dented by several years of practical experience with
assistance programs for underdeveloped countries.
Quite often, capital assistance could not be produc-
tively employed because of deficiencies rooted in
the social, political, and cultural structures of
these countries. Increasingly, reference was made
to the problem of "absorptive capacity," connoting
among other things: lack of knowledge, lack of
skills, lack of management experience, institutional
limitations (e.g., political disorder), and cultural
and social constraints.[16]

As aid strategies and the concepts on which they
were based were revealed to be decidedly less relevant to underdeveloped areas than to Europe,[17] technical assistance, particularly in the field of education, assumed greater importance. Its main value
lay in the help it promised in the solution of the
first three problems of absorptive capacity noted
above.

The function of technical assistance and
other forms of foreign help with human
resources is twofold. It can help fill
gaps between the skill requirements implicit in development programs and the
domestic stock of skills. But it is
also needed to strengthen and supplement
a country's capacity to produce new
skills via its education system. Thus

foreign help can supplement both the
stock and the flow.[18]

The concept of human resources has provided a
useful bridge between the theoretical concerns of
the student of the development process and the practical requirements of the assistance planner. The
literature on the relationship of human resources to
the process of development, reflecting influences
suggested earlier, has quickly grown to such proportions that a bibliography listing 1,150 items warned
the reader that "this present volume is far from
exhaustive."[19] The concept has the useful property
of being broadly inclusive with respect to its implications for development, as one authoritative definition indicates.

> Human resource development is the process
> of increasing the knowledge, the skills,
> and the capacities of all the people in
> a society. In economic terms, it could
> be described as the accumulation of human
> capital and its effective investment in
> the development of an economy. . . .
> /Politically it7 prepares people for
> adult participation in political processes.
> . . . /Socio-culturally it7 helps people
> to lead fuller and richer lives, less
> bound by tradition. In short, the pro-
> cesses of human resource development un-
> lock the door to modernization.[20]

The participant-training program clearly falls
into the category of technical assistance for human-
resources development. But it has only recently
formulated its objectives in terms of this overarch-
ing concept. As we have seen, in the early years,
education and training were viewed largely as an
adjunct (or afterthought) to massive programs of
economic and military assistance oriented mainly to
other issues than the economic progress of underdeveloped areas. One of the first clear statements
of the high priority attached to human-resources
development appeared in the enabling legislation
that established AID in 1961.

In countries and areas which are in the
earlier stages of economic development,
programs of development of education and
human resources through such means as
technical cooperation shall be emphasized,
and the furnishing of capital facilities
for purposes other than the development
of education and human resources shall
be given a lower priority until the requisite knowledge and skills have been
developed.[21]

As European participants were replaced by
trainees from underdeveloped countries, the scope
of the program's objectives began to widen. Earlier,
the goal of the program was more narrowly seen as
the limited transfer of ideas and techniques that
would increase productivity in on-going enterprises.
The tasks of development and modernization, as opposed to reconstruction and growth, involve the
building of new institutions, the transforming of
traditional social patterns, and the induction of
new motivations and commitments.[22] An official
statement of the program's objectives gives evidence
of these fundamental goals.

The objectives of the AID training programs are not only to improve the technical, professional, and managerial
skills and knowledge of participants,
but also to introduce attitudes and
values essential to developmental activities, and to inculcate an appreciation of the need for social as well
as economic growth and to demonstrate
insofar as possible that these are in-
separable. Conscious effort is made,
therefore, to assure exposure to the
thinking and living processes possible
only in a free and democratic political
society.[23] /Italics added./

FOREIGN STUDY AND THE TRANSFER PROCESS

The help provided by technical assistance, especially through education, in solving the human-resources problems of underdeveloped countries, essentially takes three forms. It contributes to the building of a nation's indigenous educational and training capacities; it sends advisors or supports the importation of expatriate teachers and skilled personnel; and it supports the migration of foreign nationals abroad for training or advanced education.

All of these modes of assistance have certain disadvantages. For example, building up local educational facilities is slow, costly, and raises serious issues of priorities to be granted to various educational levels and to differing curricular emphases.[24] Especially in the case of higher education, problems of selection and control of access to scarce openings that will serve as bases for the formation or recruitment of new elites or cadres of technical experts become pressing issues.[25] The use of expatriates, often in short supply and thus costly, tends to arouse negative sentiments from their counterparts, less technically competent superiors, or those they supervise.[26] And, study or training abroad, an option taken by increasing numbers as opportunities multiply in economically advanced countries, is often alleged to be dysfunctional in its character for later application and to have led in recent years to the phenomena of the nonreturning foreign student and the brain drain.[27]

All of these forms of assistance have important implications for the transfer of technology to the developing countries, a fact that has recently received growing attention in the literature on development. In economics, theoretical work has been concentrated mainly on entrepreneurship or other sources of technical progress; the problems of the transfer of technology from innovators to imitators --whether internally or across national boundaries-- attracted little interest.[28] A closely related

formulation, the diffusion of innovation, has been a
stock topic in sociology and anthropology, in which
it is seen as one of a number of general sociocultural processes determining the content or structure of social systems. Much of the research on
this topic has been focused on aspects of the system
undergoing change, rather than on mechanisms or elements of the process of diffusion or transfer.[29]

The conception of the diffusion process by which
technology, skills, and knowledge are transferred
through the training of individuals and which we
shall employ to guide our analysis distinguishes two
levels at which this process operates. At the individual level, it involves the acquisition of a body
of knowledge and techniques necessary for performing
critical occupational roles. This can be seen primarily as a process of cognitive learning whose outcome hinges mainly upon the interaction of those who
take training with the quality and substance of instruction. A more complex aspect of the process at
this level is the "resocialization" of those undergoing training. The values and motives of trainees
must be articulated closely with the performance of
their development-related tasks. Sociologically
viewed, the attitudes and commitments of those undergoing training cannot be taken for granted. Where,
for example, concepts of community are narrowly defined or work discipline is variably adhered to, new
dispositions must be internalized, or added incentives gained by those who will serve as innovators,
to harness their role performance more dependably
to a wider collective effort.

Implicit in the idea of foreign study, and explicit in the rationale of this program, is the view
that through an exposure to the values, norms, and
practices of economically advanced societies, the
trainees may come in time to change their perspectives on their own society, their work roles, or
themselves in ways which will strengthen their later
effectiveness as change agents. Thus, the process
of "enskilling people"[30] from developing nations
operates in two realms--that of substantive knowledge

and skills, and of attitudes and values which can
shape future conduct. In parallel with this distinction, the thrust of training may be seen as having
both technical and social aspects; it seeks not only
to effect the transfer of specific, occupationally
relevant techniques or skills but also to convey an
awareness of the wider social system, especially its
organizational arrangements, within which such work
roles are performed in modern societies.

At the institutional level, two complexes may
be identified as crucial for the transfer process.
One is the context and structure of training programs, the institutional arrangements that define
the environment for learning and resocialization.
The other is the social and cultural setting to
which trainees return and the forces impinging upon
the work place that shape their innovative acts and
determine the reception given to them. The reduc-
tionism implicit in the notion of an individual being
trained to serve as a change agent needs to be qualified by a consideration of the organizational context within which his efforts are made. As has been
argued, "The diffusion of innovations has been con-
ceived primarily as an educational process, with
little recognition of the necessity of establishing
an organizational base and an institutional vehicle
for fostering the acceptance of the innovations."[31]

This conception of the diffusion process differs
in its perspective from that taken in other sociological analyses. Our data come from and in large
part reflect the perspective of the carriers of innovation. Characteristically, prior research and
theory on diffusion have centered on the process of
adoption: The focus is on the problem of acceptance
by a system of an innovative item. At certain points
these two perspectives fuse; both are concerned with
the time dimension, the idea or practice being diffused, the channels employed, and aspects of the
social structure or cultural values which influence
the process. But the main difference lies in the
nature of the dependent variable; for us it is the
extent of utilization of training by these change

agents, while in most diffusion research it has been
the degree of acceptance of an item by some social
system or its members.[32]

This sketch of some conceptual issues involved
in training individuals to carry out the process of
technological transfer contains three main elements
--the characteristics of the participants, the nature
and structure of training, and the environments in
which they perform their occupational roles. Taken
together, they define the nature of this educational
venture in technical assistance and, in varying degrees, determine the outcome of the process. Data
from the surveys will be used to describe their inter-
relationships and to analyze their differential consequences for the transfer process.

THE SURVEY OF PARTICIPANT TRAINING

As the focus of technical training shifted from
Europeans to participants from underdeveloped areas
after 1955, several studies were undertaken to assess the operations and results of the program in
each of a number of countries.[33] These studies
varied greatly in method, scope, and mode of analysis; little cumulative value could be derived from
them. Late in 1959, responding primarily to a Congressional inquiry, the International Cooperation
Administration (now AID) decided to conduct a world-
wide study of its participant-training program. The
policy memorandum that launched the study of returned
participants made these key points.

The participant-training program is a
training and educational program of major
magnitude. It is an integral component
of the ICA-host countries' economic development programs, whose broad objectives it is designed to serve. . . . Is
/it/ succeeding in its objectives? . . .
A careful study of the results of the
participant-training program /by means
of/ a systematic evaluation employing

> standardized content and methodology in
> all countries . . . will permit the col-
> lection and analysis of uniform and mean-
> ingful information, and its use as a
> management tool in guiding the conduct
> of future training activities.[34]

Each U.S. Operations Mission was responsible
for the conduct of the survey in its host country.
Comparability of findings was sought through the
preparation in Washington of common procedures for
sampling, guidelines for interviewing and coding,
standard interview schedules and code books, and so
on.[35] Personal interviews were conducted in the
language most appropriate to the participant's cultural setting. The standard English-language version of the schedule was translated into Spanish,
French, and Arabic; on occasion, one of these was
used as the basis for translation into local dia-
lects by multilingual interviewers.

Work began in a few countries in 1960 and continued up to 1967; studies were completed in 32
countries, the bulk of them having been done in the
period 1961-63. The results were punched into IBM
cards following a predesignated format, and a dupli-
cate set of cards was sent to AID in Washington.
Data from the 23 countries which had sent results by
the end of 1963 comprise the empirical materials for
our secondary analysis.

The inclusion of a country's participants was
determined primarily according to whether their number was large enough to warrant the cost of the survey and whether the concurrence of the host country's
government could be obtained. The study was treated
as a cooperative enterprise, with as full an involvement of local officials as was possible. European
countries were deliberately excluded, as the program
was no longer active there.

All participants in a country who had been back
from training for at least six months were considered
eligible for interviewing; in a majority of the 23

countries whose data are examined below, samples of
former participants were taken because of the large
numbers of eligible participants. In such cases, a
sample size of 500 interviews was suggested; this
goal was overachieved in several countries because
of local decisions or misunderstanding of the study's
guidelines. As another aspect of the study design,
interviews were also conducted with samples of the
participants' current work supervisors, and with U.S.
technical advisors and training-program personnel in
each of the countries. These supplementary sources
of information served as a means for checking on the
accuracy of participants' responses at several points
in our analysis.

The principal units of analysis in this work
are the individual participants: their judgments,
perceptions, actions, and experiences relating to
their training episode and its aftermath. This
choice of analytical strategy was shaped by several
considerations of a conceptual and practical nature.
First, the survey from which our empirical materials
were drawn, in line with the program's underlying
assumptions, was focused on the specific character
and consequences of training for each individual
participant. This emphasis, built into the study
design, sets limits on the extent to which one can
readily or properly reorient the survey data to
address problems at a different level of analysis,
such as inter-nation comparisons.

Only occasional reference will be made in this
work to inter-nation differences. The number of
countries whose participants were interviewed is too
great to handle conveniently by parallel analyses of
findings, until recently the most commonly used
strategy in analyzing multinational survey data.[36]
To have done so would have been costly, cumbersome
in presentation, and in many respects redundant.[37]
More significantly, systematic data were not collected as part of this study on these countries as
units--as social, political, economic, and cultural
entities. Such detailed information could serve as
a data base for interpreting inter-nation differences

in the survey findings, for bridging the gap between the sheer descriptive fact of observed differences and the interpretation of their significance. Without such data, one must consider "country" to be a contextual variable of indeterminate scope and character.[38]

One might have employed data on these countries from other sources, for example, from some recent compilations that have stimulated a good deal of comparative, cross-national research.[39] After a few tentative explorations along this path, we reverted to our original strategy of focusing on individual differences. The set of countries included in this survey are selective and rather homogeneous, compared with the more inclusive and heterogeneous set contained in these data sources. On most of the dimensions and typologies used in such works as a means of classifying countries, our set tended to form a cluster. For example, almost all were at the low end of the scales and indicators of economic development. Moreover, the available measures tend to be both crude and time-bound in nature. (Countries are characterized at a single point in time, and the adequacy and reliability of information and classificatory judgments, as both authors and critics of these works have affirmed, are in varying degrees open to question.) Because the programs and events about which our samples of participants were questioned took place over a considerable span of time, it is impossible to match the country conditions reflected in these measures with the participants' experiences, thus rendering the drawing of inferences about the relationship of the former to the latter more an exercise in ingenuity than a procedure rooted in sound methodological principles.

Weighty problems of inference and interpretation thus attend the use of such supplementary country-level measures as a basis for inter-nation comparisons of these surveys' findings. In our view, such considerations argued for a more conservative, analytical approach, one which focuses on individuals and on those specifiable social facts or circumstances

measured in the survey. Other approaches to the comparative analysis of these data exist, of course,
and some examples of how they might extend the scope
of future studies of this type will be noted in subsequent chapters.

In order to combine the national contingents of
surveyed participants, some of the data had to be
upweighted to compensate for different sampling
ratios used in many countries as well as certain
other minor technical problems. As a result, the
total weighted sum of 19,025 respondents represents
the universe of eligible participants in the 23
countries; it is estimated that this total comprises
about two thirds of all non-European participants
during the period in which the surveys were conducted.[40] The results of our analysis cannot of
course be generalized beyond this set of countries.

In most of the analysis that follows, the
weighted total of 19,025 participants forms the
basis for our presentation and discussion of findings. When lesser numbers or unweighted figures
are used, e.g., when data from U.S. technicians or
supervisors are reported, the reason for doing so
is specified. The countries and their contingents
of respondents, before and after the weighting process, are shown in Table 1.1, which also indicates
the first year in which a trainee's departure was
recorded.

The organization of this book corresponds with
the typical pattern of movement of the participants,
beginning with their selection and following them to
their current situation. Part Two is heavily descriptive in nature; its chapters deal with characteristics of the participants, the structure and
processes of training, and participants' reactions
to their training experiences. Variables that are
expected to bear significantly upon the transfer
process are introduced, and their empirical interrelations are traced. We also seek to link our
study clearly to a wider substantive context by
showing how these data relate to certain issues in

TABLE 1.1

Participants in the Surveys and
Their First Recorded Year of
Departure, by Country of Origin

| Country | First Year | Participants | | |
		Interviewed Number	Weighted Number	Weighted Per Cent
Brazil	1940s	538	2,045	10.7
Philippines	1951	510	1,734	9.1
Thailand	1951	512	1,690	8.9
Taiwan	1951	619	1,610	8.4
India	1951	1,449	1,594	8.4
Turkey	1949	1,207	1,569	8.2
Pakistan	1951	610	1,281	6.7
Korea	1955	524	1,153	6.1
Chile	1940s	427	1,153	6.1
Vietnam	1954	402	804	4.2
Greece	1950	372	781	4.1
Jordan	1951	254	508	2.7
Ecuador	1940s	390	507	2.7
Costa Rica	1952	388	504	2.7
Israel	1951	369	443	2.3
Egypt	1951	217	434	2.3
Ethiopia	1951	197	315	1.7
Nicaragua	1952	182	309	1.6
Morocco	1958	147	191	1.0
Jamaica	1953	122	122	.7
British Honduras	1953	78	101	.5
British Guiana	1954	81	97	.5
Surinam	1954	73	80	.4
Total		9,668	19,025	100.0

international education and comparative research on
the modernization process.

The concluding chapters in Part Three are devoted to an analysis of the diverse consequences and
uses of training. In them, the conditions affecting
the use of foreign study, examined in the light of
our model of the transfer process, are a central concern. The significant role of three processes--pro-
fessionalization, institutionalization, and human-
resources development--in determining the outcome of
this assistance strategy is explored in a brief epi-
logue.

NOTES

1. This historical review draws upon a number
of accounts of U.S. educational- and cultural-
exchange programs. The most valuable work for our
purposes is Charles A. Thomson and Walter H. C.
Laves, Cultural Relations and U.S. Foreign Policy
(Bloomington: Indiana University Press, 1963),
especially Part I. Also see Robert Blum, ed.,
Cultural Affairs and Foreign Relations (Englewood
Cliffs, New Jersey: Prentice-Hall, Inc., 1963);
U.S. Congress, House, Committee on Government Opera-
tions, Government Programs in International Education:
A Survey and Handbook, 85th Congress, 2d Session,
House Report 2712 (Washington, D.C.: U.S. Government
Printing Office, 1959); John P. Powelson, "Educa-
tional Assistance, Economic Development and United
States Foreign Policy," in Don C. Piper and Taylor
Cole, eds., Post-Primary Education and Political
and Economic Development (Durham: Duke University
Press, 1964), pp. 128-52; and Institute of International
Education, Committee on Educational Interchange
Policy, Twenty Years of United States Government
Programs in Cultural Relations (New York: Institute
of International Education, 1959).

2. Edward S. Mason, "Competitive Coexistence
and Economic Development in Asia," International

Stability and Progress, Background Papers for the
Eleventh American Assembly, Arden House, Columbia
University, May 2-5, 1957 (New York: The American
Assembly, Graduate School of Business, Columbia Uni-
versity, June, 1957), p. 60.

   3.   Between 1948, the starting point of Marshall Plan aid, and 1958, the participating countries had an average annual rate of increase in per
capita gross national product of 8.5 per cent; this
was more than twice the rate achieved by the United
States in the same period. See U.S. Congress, Senate, Committee on Foreign Relations, United States
Foreign Policy: Compilation of Studies, 87th Congress, 1st Session, Document No. 24 (Washington,
D.C.:   U.S. Government Printing Office, 1961), p.
289.

   4.   Powelson, op. cit., p. 136.

   5.   Thomson and Laves, op. cit., pp. 91-92.

   6.   Mason, op. cit., p. 61.

   7.   The full text of Point Four is printed in
Halford L. Hoskins, ed., "Aiding Underdeveloped
Areas Abroad," The Annals of the American Academy
of Political and Social Science, Vol. CCLXVIII
(March, 1950), p. 183.

   8.   Louis J. Halle, The Society of Man (New
York: Harper and Row, 1965), p. 23. His account
of this episode is a delightful example of what
can really be involved in "an idea whose time has
come"; see pp. 20-30.

   9.   International Cooperation Administration,
Office of Participant Training, Participant Training
Operations: Statistical Report--June 30, 1960
(Washington, D.C.:   International Cooperation Ad-
ministration, 1961), p. 5.

   10.   Agency for International Development, Statistics and Reports Division, U.S. Foreign Assistance

and Assistance From International Organizations, Obligations and Loan Authorizations, July 1, 1945- June 30, 1962 (Washington, D.C.:   Agency for International Development, April, 1963), p. 1.

11.   Institute of International Education, Committee on Educational Interchange Policy, Military Assistance Training Programs of the U.S. Government (New York: Institute of International Education, July, 1964), p. 6.

12.   See Walter Johnson and Francis J. Colligan, The Fulbright Program: A History (Chicago: University of Chicago Press, 1965), pp. 343-46.

13.   James A. Perkins, "Foreign Aid and the Brain Drain," Foreign Affairs, Vol. XLIV, No. 4 (July, 1966), p. 609.

14.   Among many writers who could be cited in this connection, one of the most influential was Theodore Schultz.   A number of his papers contributed to a great debate during this period on the sources of economic growth and on the process of development.   One of these can serve as a point of entry; see his AEA presidential address, "Investment in Human Capital," American Economic Review, Vol. LI, No. 1 (March, 1961), pp. 1-17.

15.   For some tart comments on this proclivity, see Albert O. Hirschman, "Comments on 'A Framework for Analyzing Economic and Political Change,'" Development of the Emerging Countries: An Agenda for Research (Washington, D.C.:   The Brookings Institution, 1962), pp. 39-44.   More recently, Hirschman carried his skeptical analysis of the stultifying effects of an excess of foreknowledge even further; see his Development Projects Observed (Washington, D.C.:   The Brookings Institution, 1967).

16.   These were drawn from a useful discussion by John H. Adler; see his Absorptive Capacity: The Concept and Its Determinants (Washington, D.C.:   The Brookings Institution, 1965).

17. See Bert F. Hoselitz and Ann R. Willner, "Economic Development, Political Strategies, and American Aid," in Morton A. Kaplan, ed., The Revolution in World Politics (New York: John Wiley and Sons, 1962), pp. 355-80.

18. Angus Maddison, Foreign Skills and Technical Assistance in Economic Development (Paris: Development Centre of The Organisation for Economic Cooperation and Development, 1965), p. 12.

19. Marian Crites Alexander-Frutschi, ed., Human Resources and Economic Growth (Menlo Park, Calif: Stanford Research Institute, 1963), p. ix.

20. Frederick Harbison and Charles A. Myers, Education Manpower and Economic Growth: Strategies of Human Resource Development (New York: McGraw-Hill Book Company, 1964), p. 2. In their first chapter, the authors sketch the history of the concept in economics.

21. Quoted by Howard E. Wilson, "Education, Foreign Policy, and International Relations," in Robert Blum, ed., Cultural Affairs and Foreign Relations (Englewood Cliffs, New Jersey: Prentice-Hall, Inc., 1963), p. 95.

22. See "Motivational Patterns for Modernization," International Social Science Journal, Vol. XX, No. 3 (1968), pp. 397-484. On the general theoretical significance of motives, see David C. McClelland, The Achieving Society (Princeton: D. Van Nostrand, 1961); and Everett E. Hagen, On the Theory of Social Change (Homewood, Illinois: The Dorsey Press, Inc., 1962).

23. U.S. Congress, House, Subcommittee on International Organization and Movements, Committee on Foreign Affairs, Ideological Operations and Foreign Policy: Report No. 2, 88th Congress, 2d Session, House Report 1352 (Washington, D.C.: U.S. Government Printing Office, 1964), p. 35.

24. The literature on educational planning is vast; for an orientation to the basic issues and guidelines for choice of strategies, see Bert F. Hoselitz, "Investment in Education and Its Political Impact," and William J. Platt, "Conflicts in Educational Planning," in James S. Coleman, ed., Education and Political Development (Princeton: Princeton University Press, 1965), pp. 541-65, 566-82; W. Lee Hansen, "Human Capital Requirements for Educational Expansion: Teacher Shortages and Teacher Supply," in C. Arnold Anderson and Mary Jean Bowman, eds., Education and Economic Development (Chicago: Aldine, 1965), pp. 63-87; C. Arnold Anderson, "The Impact of the Educational System on Technological Change and Modernization, in Bert F. Hoselitz and Wilbert E. Moore, eds., Industrialization and Society (The Hague: UNESCO and Mouton, 1963), pp. 259-78; Policy Conference on Economic Growth and Investment in Education, The Challenge of Aid to Newly Developing Countries (Paris: Organisation for Economic Cooperation and Development, 1962); OECD Study Group on Education, Social Objectives in Educational Planning (Paris: Organisation for Economic Cooperation and Development, 1967); and C.E. Beeby, ed., Fundamentals of Educational Planning (in six booklets; Paris: UNESCO, International Institute for Educational Planning, 1967).

25. See James S. Coleman, ed., Education and Political Development, op. cit., Part III, passim

26. See Maddison, op. cit., p. 13, pp. 17-40; C. Arnold Anderson, "Economic Development and Post-Primary Education," in Don C. Piper and Taylor Cole, eds., Post-Primary Education and Political and Economic Development (Durham: Duke University Press, 1964), pp. 1-26. The Peace Corps represents a partial exception at best to this generalization; see R. Freeman Butts, American Education in International Development (New York: Harper and Row, 1963), pp. 48-92; Robert B. Textor, ed., Cultural Frontiers of the Peace Corps (Cambridge, Mass.: The M.I.T. Press, 1966); and David Hapgood and Meridan Bennett, Agents of Change (Boston: Little, Brown and Co., 1968).

27.   See Walter Adams, ed., <u>The Brain Drain</u>
(New York: The Macmillan Company, 1968), for a recent summary of research and arguments on this phenomenon.

28.   See Daniel L. Spencer and Alexander Woroniak, eds., <u>The Transfer of Technology to Developing</u>
<u>Countries</u> (New York: Frederick A. Praeger, 1967).
For a discussion of the problems of "domesticating"
science and technology in the United States, see
National Science Foundation, <u>Proceedings of a Con-</u>
<u>ference on Technology Transfer and Innovation</u>, NSF
67-5 (Washington, D.C.:   U.S. Government Printing
Office, 1967).

29.   See Everett M. Rogers, <u>Diffusion of Inno-</u>
<u>vations</u> (New York: The Free Press of Glencoe, 1962);
and Homer G. Barnett, <u>Innovation: The Basis of Cul-</u>
<u>tural Change</u> (New York: McGraw-Hill Book Company,
1953).   Other examples of "systems-oriented" approaches may be found in papers in a work dealing
with innovation in education; see Terry L. Eidell
and Joanne M. Kitchel, eds., <u>Knowledge Production</u>
<u>and Utilization in Educational Administration</u> (Eugene,
Oregon: Center for the Advanced Study of Educational
Administration, University of Oregon, 1968).

30.   See Albert Lepawsky and Rosalind Lepawsky,
"Enskilling People," <u>International Development Re-</u>
<u>view</u>, Vol. III, No. 3 (October, 1961), pp. 16-22.

31.   Milton J. Esman and Fred C. Bruhns, "Institution Building in National Development: An Approach to Induced Social Change in Transitional
Societies," in Hollis W. Peter, ed., <u>Comparative</u>
<u>Theories of Social Change</u> (Ann Arbor, Michigan:
Foundation for Research on Human Behavior, 1966),
pp. 318-42.

32.   This distinction is clearly illustrated
by two excellent reviews of diffusion research.   In
his "accounting scheme" of the diffusion process,
Elihu Katz fails to include any mention of the role
of change agents; presumably he sees the change agent

as a channel through which an item is diffused rather than as a prime determinant of the rate of acceptance. See Elihu Katz et al., "Traditions of Research on the Diffusion of Innovation," American Sociological Review, Vol. XXVIII, No. 2 (April, 1963), pp. 237-52. Everett M. Rogers, on the other hand, devotes a chapter to the role of the change agent but views him as an outsider to the system undergoing change; in our study, the change agent is a member of the system; see Everett M. Rogers, Diffusion of Innovations, op. cit., pp. 254-84.

33. Ralph B. Spence, Technical Training of Pakistanis in the United States: An Evaluation of the I.C.A. Program, 1951-1955 (Karachi, Pakistan: United States Operations Mission, 1956); John B. Stabler and E. Theodore Mogannam, Followup and Evaluation Study of Returned I.C.A. Participants in Egypt (Cairo, Egypt: United States Operations Mission, 1956); Cameron F. Bremseth, Followup Evaluation Study of Iranian Participants Who Received Training in the United States Under I.C.A. Sponsorship (Teheran, Iran: United States Operations Mission, 1956); Instituto de Pesquisas de Opiniao e Mercado, An Evaluation of Selected Returned Participants in the Point IV Labor Training Program, Brazil, Report prepared for the United States Operations Mission (Rio de Janeiro, Brazil: Instituto de Pesquisas de Opiniao e Mercado, 1957); Cameron F. Bremseth, An Evaluation of the Participant Training Program in Taiwan (Taipei, Taiwan: Mutual Security Mission to China, 1957); International Research Associates, A Study of Reactions to the I.C.A. Exchange Program Among Returned Mexican Grantees (Vallarta, Mexico: International Research Associates, 1959); United States Technical Cooperation Mission, Indo-American Participant Training Program: An Evaluation Study (New Delhi, India: U.S. Technical Cooperation Mission, 1959); and Hollis W. Peter and Lawrence E. Schlesinger, Using U.S. Training in the Philippines: A Follow-up Survey of Participants (2 vols.; Ann Arbor: Institute for Social Research, University of Michigan, 1959).

34. International Cooperation Administration, _Evaluation of Participant Training Program_, ICATO Circular A 175, November 5, 1959. (Mimeographed.)

35. A description of the survey's principal instruments is provided in the bibliography. Schedules are available upon request, from the Evaluation Staff, Office of International Training, Agency for International Development, as are copies of individual reports for most of the countries in which the survey was completed.

36. Many studies could be cited; for one of the earliest and one of the more recent examples, see Eugene Jacobson and Stanley Schachter, eds., "Cross-National Research: A Case Study," _The Journal of Social Issues_, Vol. X, No. 4 (1954); and Hadley Cantril, _The Pattern of Human Concerns_ (New Brunswick, New Jersey: Rutgers University Press, 1965).

37. As noted earlier, a separate report was prepared and published on the survey's findings for almost all of the countries in which it was completed.

38. For a similar point of view and some suggestions on how the deliberate choice of countries according to certain criteria can overcome this ambiguity, see Johan Galtung, "Some Aspects of Comparative Research," _Polls_, Vol. II, No. 3 (Spring, 1967), pp. 1-19.

39. See, for example, Bruce M. Russett _et al._, _World Handbook of Political and Social Indicators_ (New Haven: Yale University Press, 1964); and Arthur S. Banks and Robert B. Textor, _A Cross-Polity Survey_ (Cambridge, Mass.: The M.I.T. Press, 1963). For useful critiques of this and other approaches to comparative research, see Michael Haas, "Aggregate Analysis," _World Politics_, Vol. XIX, No. 1 (October, 1966), pp. 106-21; Stein Rokkan, ed., _Comparative Research Across Cultures and Nations_ (Paris and The Hague: Mouton, 1968); and Celso Furtado, "Intracountry Discontinuities...," Bruce M. Russett, "The _World_

<u>Handbook</u> As a Tool in Current Research," and Mattei
Dogan and Stein Rokkan, "Quantitative Ecological
Analysis: Contexts, Trends, Tasks," <u>Social Science
Information</u>, Vol. VI, No. 6 (December, 1967), pp.
7-16, 17-33, and 35-47.

40. Each country was assigned a weighting factor, which was applied to the data for its participants during the computing of tabulations. Weighting
factors ranged from 1.0 (no weighting of data) to
3.8 (data multiplied 3.8 times before being added in
with the rest); their use had the effect of doubling
the number of interviewed participants. This methodological procedure made little substantive difference; a detailed, comparative analysis of the weighted
and unweighted samples' responses across several hundred items showed variations which rarely exceeded 1
per cent.

PART TWO

PARTICIPANT TRAINING

CHAPTER **2** PARTICIPANTS AND
THE SELECTION
PROCESS

Before exploring some consequences of training
and their relation to the diffusion of modernizing
skills and knowledge, we will review empirical data
on participants and the programs which they were
offered. Knowledge of the kinds of people who were
selected, their preparation for training, and the
program sequences through which they moved is essential in defining the specific character of this international educational enterprise. In our earlier
discussion of the diffusion process, three key elements were isolated: The personal and social attributes of the agent of change; his training experience,
seen as both an occasion or environment for learning
and in terms of the substance that is conveyed and,
in varying degrees, acquired; and the social and
cultural setting to which the change agent returns
and in which his innovative efforts have taken place.

The surveys which are our sources of information covered these three compound elements in our
diffusion model in a descending order of specificity
and completeness. From available data, we can learn
much about who and what the participants were, a
good deal about the forms their training took, less
about the actual substance of their training, and
only a little about salient aspects of their post-
training environments. In our descriptive accounts
of these matters, a certain asymmetry will be observ-
able in the space allotted to each, therefore, and
inferences will replace evidence when data are lacking.

THE PARTICIPANTS: A COLLECTIVE PORTRAIT

Age, Sex, and Marital Status

Compared to many better-known programs of
international-educational exchange, participant
training is exceptional in its focus on mature individuals. The largest number were in their 30s when
selected, with a median age of 35. The age range
of 30-50 would, until quite recently, have included
about two thirds of all trainees at the time of
their departure. Twenty-seven per cent were under
30, with about a third under 25 years of age in the
time periods covered by the survey.

More recent AID statistics on the age of participants, while not strictly comparable, nevertheless clearly show that the proportion of younger
selectees is much higher and reflects the growing
numbers of African and Latin American participants
being chosen under newer policy directives which emphasize the selection of potential leaders (Table 2.1)

The age of the participants was, of course,
associated with other aspects of their status at
selection. Younger men tended to have had less
experience in their work specialties; they were
lower in occupational status, more frequently single,
and so on, but these relationships will be omitted
in this portrait. We will refer to age fairly frequently, because it was closely related to the types
of training programs that were devised and to participants' evaluations of training. Age has a strategic value too, as it is an attribute of participants which is partly under the administrative control of the donor of technical training, through
the selection process.

Participant training has been largely a man's
world: Men accounted for 89 per cent of all respondents, and proportions over the years covered by the
survey ranged from 84 to 100 per cent. Figures for
the most recent year, fiscal year (FY) 1967, show

TABLE 2.1

Age of Participants Entering Training
in Selected Years up to FY 1967
(In Percentages)

Age	All Participants[a]		U.S. Arrivals[b]			
	Before 1955	1955 to FY 1961	FY 1962	FY 1964	FY 1966	FY 1967
Under 30	24.4	27.7	34.2	46.5	42.0	32.3
30-39	45.3	41.9	39.5	37.0	37.6	40.9
40-49	24.2	24.2	19.1	13.7	16.3	21.3
50 and over	6.0	6.2	7.2	2.7	4.0	5.5
Total[c] %	99.9	100.0	100.0	100.0	99.9	100.0
(N)	(4,207)	(14,596)	(5,000)	(5,764)	(4,647)	(4,878)

[a]Data from surveys of returned participants in 23 countries. Not all were U.S. arrivals; about one in six never
came to the United States for training.

[b]Data from Annual Report on Participant Training: Fiscal Years 1960-67 (Office of International Training, Agency
for International Development); the age categories used there-
in are combined as: up to 30, 31-40, 41-50, 51 and over.

[c]Excludes those whose age was not ascertained (NA).

that men constituted 92 per cent of all U.S. arrivals.
This preponderance is not surprising; the status of
women, especially in the realms of technical and specialist work, is even less elevated in the underdeveloped world than in our own country; women would be
less likely, therefore, to be deemed eligible for
advanced training by virtue of their occupational
status and prospects.[1]

What can be said about the women participants?
First, their employment is concentrated primarily in
two fields--in education, particularly as teachers,
and in health, mainly in nursing, public health, and
as laboratory aides. Other occupational areas from
which women participants were drawn were such public
services as librarians, social welfare workers, and
also as home economists. As could be expected, wom-
en participants were strongly clustered at the professional and technical levels; over two thirds had
attained this occupational status compared to just
over half of the men participants. More women than
men were directly employed by their government when
selected (86% vs. 74%); although few in numbers,
twice as many were not employed (or were students)
when selected.

Another set of characteristics which distinguish women from men participants is their age,
prior education, and marital status. They were
younger and had less often been university trained;
over a third (38%) had never attended a university.
But the sharpest difference is in their marital
status; almost four in five of the men were married,
compared to only one third of the women.

The nature of the training that women received
dovetailed neatly with their backgrounds. Because
they were single, they could more readily be programed for longer periods of training which would
in turn further enhance their professional skills.
Training in such professional and technical subjects
is most often taken in academic settings. Three
quarters of the women had some form of university
training as part of their programs, over a third of

whom earned a degree. By comparison, only 44 per
cent of the men were sent for any academic training,
just over a quarter of whom earned a degree. The
duration of their training reflects this pattern:
more than half of the women were in training longer
than a year, compared to less than a third of the
men.

   We conclude this brief review of the contingent
of female trainees with the observation that they
have been less mobile in their careers after their
return home than their male counterparts. Currently,
two in five are in exactly the same job they held
when selected, and fewer have changed jobs at any
time since their return. Their occupational fate,
even as professionals with foreign, specialized
training, still has been determined primarily by
their social status as women.

   Marital status is of course associated with age,
as we have noted. Those who were single tended to
go on longer programs of training. Further, one can
expect that marital status would have implications
for participants' reactions to a number of aspects
of training. For example, those with greater family
obligations might be expected to show greater concern with the adequacy of their training allowance.
Each participant is given an allowance by AID to
cover his travel and living expenses, but no adjustment in this stipend is made on the basis of marital
status. Foreign governments usually agree to continue to pay the trainees' salaries while in training and provide some form of support for their de-
pendents.[2] Married men who leave their wives and
family at home might feel more concerned over their
allowance because of objective need (e.g., if their
government were remiss in paying their families) or
for more subjective reasons. If accompanied by
their families (a practice which is discouraged by
AID), the married participants would face substantially greater expenses that might represent a serious drain on their resources, one that could not
have been adequately foreseen. Thus, married men
could be expected to express dissatisfaction with

their training allowance more frequently than single participants, and indeed this was the case. Thirty per cent said their allowance proved to be "too little," compared to 25 per cent of those who were single; though small, the difference is a significant one. Differences in marital status had little bearing on other aspects of the study and can be disregarded in subsequent analysis.

Prior Formal Education and Training

The participants' education and training prior to selection can be seen both as an indicator of their personal achievements and status, relative to the spread of higher education in developing nations, and as a criterion used in their selection. Among the items of information on education gathered from records and during the interview were years of formal education, special schooling, university training, types of earned degrees, and fields of study.

One difficulty in analyzing these materials, a point with which researchers in international education are painfully familiar, is the fact that the great diversity of educational systems around the world renders comparisons treacherous. This problem is severe enough when research is restricted to people from countries whose systems are patterned after English or continental European models; in our case, Chinese, Indian, and Arabic systems are also represented in some participants' backgrounds. Serious problems exist, for example, in locating comparable points in total years of education which divide elementary, secondary, and higher education, or in equating first degrees with more advanced or professional ones. Moreover, how advanced degrees function as prerequisites for entry into certain occupations is not always self-evident; in many underdeveloped countries, a degree in law or medicine serves as a ticket of admission to high-level administrative positions unrelated to these specialties. As a result, our analysis will deal with roughly comparable, less-refined aspects of educational achievement: the earning of a degree, some

university work, or none; training at some specialized school or institute, or none. Other facets of
the participants' educational histories will be discussed more briefly.

As might be expected, they are extraordinarily
well educated; prior to selection, two thirds (65%)
held a university or college degree, and another 8
per cent had done some university work.[3] Five sixths
of this group had attended universities in their own
country; those who had been educated abroad tended
more often to earn degrees at postgraduate levels.
The principal countries in which overseas degrees
were earned, in order of magnitude, were the United
States, India, Japan, Great Britain, Pakistan, France,
Germany, and Lebanon. Taken together, degrees earned
in these eight countries accounted for three quarters
of all those that had been acquired abroad. Two
thirds of all earned degrees were at the Bachelor's
level (Table 2.2).

A distinct trend exists in the data on the education of participants over the years covered by the
survey. The proportion of participants who had not
earned a degree prior to selection has more than
doubled, from 19 per cent of all who left prior to
1951 to 41 per cent of those who left for training
in 1959 or later, with the proportion increasing consistently during the years in between. This finding
may indicate a substantial lessening in the importance of formal education as a selection criterion.
Some changes that will be shown in the nature of
training programs over the years are presumably associated with the declining levels of participants'
formal education, because the need for training of
certain kinds will vary with the prior education and
existing skills of the trainees.

Those who had no prior university training were
younger; at selection, more than a third were under
30. (Conversely, only among the under-25 age group
of participants does the proportion without earned
degrees differ significantly from those in other age
groups: Two thirds had no university training, compared with only one third of older participants.)

TABLE 2.2

Prior Formal Education: Type of
Degree by Location of University
(In Percentages)

| Type of Degree | Attended University | | Total[a] |
	At Home	Abroad	
Bachelor's level	70	50	67
Master's level	10	24	12
Ph.D. level	2	8	3
M.D.	9	10	9
Law	7	6	7
Other professional	2	2	2
Total per cent	100	100	100
(N)	(10,389)	(1,817)	(12,206)

[a]Excludes those NA on either or both items (N =
189), those who did not attend a university (N =
5,061), or those who attended but earned no degree
(N = 1,569).

A compensatory element in the educational background of nonuniversity-goers is the greater extent to which they had taken specialty training in their occupational areas. (Such training was defined in the survey as "of an advanced vocational or technical character, but not given at a college or university.") The subject-matter areas reveal their vocational character: industrial trades, agricultural trades, normal school teaching, business and commercial skills, and the like. More than half (57%) of nonuniversity-trained people had attended some course of a specialized character, while only one in six who held degrees had also done so. Only 11 per cent of the entire sample had had neither sort of formal preparation.

A few implications of the participants' prior educational achievements can be mentioned at this point. First, their high levels of attainment should be kept in mind when considering the issue of how "degree minded" they were in their evaluations of training. In discussions of foreign students, one frequently hears the comment that earning a degree is a primary goal for most of them, and other values of the foreign experience are often heavily compromised if they are not permitted to earn one. This is not surprising; no less (and usually far more) than in the United States, advanced education and the degrees earned in the process confer special prestige and marketable advantages. This is especially true in countries where access to higher education is sharply restricted both by a small number of academic openings and by differences in social privilege that facilitate the entry of the elite's children. One's life chances are, as a result, often largely fixed at an early stage.

Educational differences can be expected to be associated with participants' judgments about aspects of their training. Those who were younger or less well educated might be expected to express a particular satisfaction at having been selected, because this training program offered them the hope of compensating for serious deficiencies in their

educational attainments as well as a chance to learn
specific, job-related skills.

For others, with credentials for entry into
some desired career already secured, this program
may have somewhat different attractions. It might
confer some added authority or personal stature upon
them and thus prove useful when they seek to introduce change or be promoted. But they can also be
expected to show more discerning or critical reactions to the program. For them, training may have
a marginal occupational utility, or it may be less
exciting an experience because they have already
been abroad, or in other ways exposed to a wider
range of foreign influences and communications. The
gains to be derived from training may not compensate
them adequately for the disruptions in routines of
life and work that a trip abroad entails. Moreover,
the change in social role from that of practicing
professional or administrator to that of student or
trainee can be unsettling or experienced as a loss
in status. We will examine findings on such expected
differences in a later chapter.

A final comment can be made about one implication of the trend toward selecting people with less
education. In most nations receiving technical assistance, the layer of high-level or middle manpower
--managers, professionals, technicians, or, more
generally, people with postsecondary training--is
rather thin. A prolonged program of assistance of
any size that seeks to develop human resources will,
at some point, need to stimulate the growth in the
numbers of such people, perhaps by supporting an
expansion of local or regional educational institutions as an adjunct to the provision of advanced or
special training for special purposes. If not, some
dilution in the level of educational preparation of
later groups of participants is likely to occur,
making necessary a chain of adjustments in the goals
and substance of training in later years. As with
most issues in the theory and practice of development assistance, one usually has to adopt a strategy
embracing a range of mutually supportive programs

rather than concentrating on any one tactic. The
problem of human-resources development is particularly resistant to single-program educational solu-
tions.

Residence and Mobility

The data on participants' places of residence
at two points in time, at selection and interview,
can be scrutinized for their bearing on the process
of selection and as indicators of the concentration
or dispersion of the rather scarce stock of trained
manpower which these people represent in their countries. We will briefly report on where participants
were and are and the main patterns of geographic
mobility reflected in these data.

A majority of participants (59%) came from their
capital cities and have remained there; of those living there when selected, just over nine in ten still
do. Lesser proportions of the 29 per cent who had
been living in provincial cities when selected, or
of the 12 per cent selected from rural towns and vil-
lages, were still there at the time of interview.
The main drift was, in general, <u>away</u> from the countryside and, in particular, <u>to</u> the capital. Over
one half of all who changed locales were, when interviewed, found in their capital cities; most of them
came from provincial urban centers rather than directly from rural settlements. The flow of trained
manpower to the countryside was minimal; provincial
cities and rural areas together lost twice as many
participants as they gained.

The concentration both of selectees and of those
who have been geographically mobile in the capitals
of their countries reflects the fact that most of the
participants were relatively senior government employees, and governmental administration in most of
the surveyed countries is highly centralized. No
special characteristics were found to distinguish
those in any of the three residential settings except for a tendency that older, more experienced,

and higher-level participants were residents of their capitals even more often than their counterparts.

The most striking contrasts in the data on residence and mobility were found among the <u>countries</u> in the survey. The tendency for the capital to loom large in the selection and retention of participants varied markedly. In some countries, India and Israel for example, the dispersion of participants among the other locales has been quite high. In others such as Egypt, Surinam, or Thailand, participants were and are predominantly concentrated in their capitals, while a few, Brazil and Ethiopia for example, are distinguished primarily by the residential mobility of their participants.[4] The patterns revealed in these data can only be interpreted properly in the context of labor-force data on mobility of such people for each country. Reliable data on this topic are not available. In their absence, all we can do is demonstrate the intriguing fact that such differences exist (Table 2.3).

A few implications of training for various patterns of geographic mobility can be found in the survey data. For example, those who moved from the capital city to rural areas after training tended to see their training as detrimental to their careers more often than others, and in a few cases this suggests that being sent for training was a means of easing someone out of office. But those who came from rural areas and returned to them did not differ from others more "strategically" located in their assessments of the worth of their training. Finally, those who migrated to the capital city were the most enthusiastic of all groups about the consequences of training. The training program may have given them access to career opportunities they would otherwise have been denied.

Occupational Characteristics

Data on the participants' occupational status when selected for training and in its aftermath are

TABLE 2.3

Residential Mobility Patterns of Participants
at Selection and Interview, by Country
(In Percentages)

| Country | Residentially Stable (Same at Both Times) | | | Residen-tially Mobile | Total[a] Number (=100%) |
	Capital City Area	Provincial Centers	Rural Area		
Egypt	94.0	1.4	3.3	1.4	(430)
Surinam	91.6	2.8	1.4	4.2	(79)
Thailand	87.9	7.2	1.6	3.3	(1,686)
Chile	76.8	12.9	1.6	8.7	(1,150)
Vietnam	76.2	11.5	--	12.3	(780)
Korea	75.2	12.0	0.4	12.4	(1,153)
Costa Rica	67.4	13.2	10.1	9.3	(502)
Br. Honduras	65.4	--	21.8	12.7	(101)
Ecuador	64.5	21.1	2.8	11.8	(506)
Greece	59.4	23.4	3.8	13.5	(781)
Nicaragua	58.2	26.9	1.1	13.7	(309)
Jordan	56.2	30.3	2.8	10.7	(508)
Philippines	54.4	8.1	20.9	16.6	(1,707)
Ethiopia	53.9	8.4	2.1	35.6	(306)
Jamaica	51.6	16.4	12.3	19.7	(122)
Pakistan	49.2	14.6	13.2	23.0	(1,277)
Br. Guiana	48.7	7.5	30.0	13.8	(96)
Taiwan	47.1	21.2	12.8	18.9	(1,607)
Brazil	41.3	10.9	5.8	42.1	(2,025)
Turkey	38.7	34.4	3.5	23.4	(1,559)
Morocco	33.1	51.4	14.8	1.0	(185)
Israel	18.0	69.3	5.9	6.8	(426)
India	9.6	51.6	22.1	16.7	(1,585)
All Countries	54.3	20.1	8.3	17.3	(18,880)

[a]Excludes those NA on places of residence at either or
both points in time (N = 145).

essential to an understanding of their needs and
their evaluations and uses of training. In large
measure, the limits on what training can achieve are
defined by a few occupational dimensions. For example, the amount of a participant's work experience
prior to selection or his occupational status (or
level) will have a direct bearing upon the kind of
training that will be deemed most relevant. And a
crucial prerequisite for effective use of training
is an adequate fit between the substance of training
and a participant's job. We will briefly review
some basic occupational data on participants; the
analysis of occupational mobility and of occupation-
related influences on attitudes or effects of training will be discussed in later chapters.

   In most countries of the underdeveloped world,
the national government has assumed the primary (or
sole) responsibility for development planning and
programs. Because participant training is a facet
of broader, government-to-government development programs, it is not surprising to find that a large number of participants came from the public sector.
The locus of employment of three out of four participants was some government agency; an additional 6
per cent were working in a nationalized industry.
Thus, four out of every five participants were selected from the public sector; half of the remainder
came from private business or industry. Smaller
numbers were chosen from trade unions, the free professions or, as students, from the ranks of the
economically inactive. Although the public sector
has remained the single largest source of participants, a distinct trend toward selecting more people
from the private sector set in after 1955, when ICA
was established during the Eisenhower presidency.
The proportion of trainees in private business more
than tripled over the years covered by our survey,
from about 5 per cent in the earliest period to over
17 per cent at the time AID was initially founded.
Since then, the proportion has declined and a larger
number of students has been selected; the government
remains the employer of the great majority of participants.[5]

The occupational _status_ that each participant held when selected sheds a good deal of light on the strategic focus of this training program. The occupations of these participants ranged from cabinet minister to cabinet maker; selectees at these status extremes were relatively rare.[6] The typical participant has held some professional or middle-level administrative position in his work organization. The single largest group, over one third of the total, consisted of teachers and scientists; if engineers are added to their ranks, the category of "professionals" includes almost one half of the participants. The next largest group, almost 30 per cent, were drawn from the stratum of managers or administrative officials. Less than 1 per cent were from the topmost occupational rank in the nation (defined officially as positions having "national impact"), but about 7 per cent came from the level immediately below the top. A closer examination of this elite group reveals that their jobs were largely outside the political system of legislators, ministers, and judges; officials such as these usually come to the United States under the auspices of other governmental exchange programs, such as the State Department's Foreign Leader Program.

There have also been relatively few trainees from the low end of the occupational status structure, and very few (less than 2%) who were classified as "students." Participant training is aimed primarily at the crucial layer of middle-level manpower: the professionals, technicians, and officials now in positions with authority and responsibility for carrying out development programs and projects or who will become the senior civil servants and trained cadre for future development work. Participants from the private sector (i.e., business, industry, or the trade unions) included a higher proportion of high-level administrators and correspondingly fewer from the ranks of professionals than those from the governmental sector. (Table 2.4 shows the occupational status of the participants at selection and at the time of interview.)

TABLE 2.4

Occupational Status of Participants at
Selection and Interview (In Percentages)

At Time of Selection	Occupational Status	At Time of Interview
0.7	Top policy makers, executives and administrators, e.g., university heads; directors of national organizations	1.0
6.9	Second-level policy makers, etc., e.g., deputy directors of national organizations; heads of regional institutions; business executives	10.0
28.7	Administrative officials: line and staff, e.g., production managers; education inspectors; personnel, finance, welfare officers	33.2
34.8	Professionals: scientists and teachers, e.g., university, other teachers; agricultural, physical, or social scientists	31.3
10.8	Engineers, e.g., civil, electrical, agricultural, or mechanical engineers	9.4
9.0	Subprofessionals, technicians, e.g., nurses, health technicians; surveyors, draftsmen; research, technical aides	7.6
2.9	Supervisors, inspectors, and foremen	2.7
1.5	Artisans and craftsmen	1.0
1.8	Workers and others, e.g., clerical, semiskilled	1.5
2.8	Inactive and not ascertained, e.g., students	2.4
99.9	Total Participants	100.1

(N) = 19,025

From the data presented so far, we would also expect the participants to show rather extensive amounts of <u>specialized work experience</u>, and this was the case. Omitting the students, at selection about one in eight had worked in some specialized capacity for less than two years, while three in eight had more than ten years of experience. The median for the group was 7.8 years of specialized-work experience; those of higher and lower status had more experience than the middle strata of professional and subprofessional trainees. A minimum of two years of specialized work has been a requirement for selection for some time, one that appears to have been fairly consistently met.

The seniority in age, work experience, and occupational status of these trainees sharply distinguishes participant training from other educational exchange programs. These data, which delineate the participants' strategic positions in their countries' occupational systems, are crucial in forming a composite image of the otherwise diverse nature of the people who enter training. Occupational status also will play a central role in our analysis of participants' reactions to training.

Another aspect of the participant's work setting was the <u>area of economic activity</u> or economic sector. Even after combining individual fields of work into broad categories, participants were found to be widely distributed across the various economic sectors. The educational area, primarily at the university level, was the single largest sector, containing one fifth (21%) of all participants, followed by government administration (17%) and agriculture (16%). Manufacturing and mining accounted for almost 10 per cent of the participants, and medical services accounted for another 8 per cent. The rest were widely scattered among a half dozen other areas: transportation, communications, engineering, utilities, banking, and so forth. The survey yielded data on this aspect of their occupations both at selection and interview and thus made it possible to see which areas gained and lost participants in

the interim. We will discuss this later, as part of
an analysis of patterns of occupational mobility.

THE SELECTION PROCESS

Ideally, in order to assess the operation of a
selection or screening process, one needs information
about those who dropped out or were rejected as well
as those who passed through it successfully. By comparing these groups, one can identify critical junc-
tures in the process and assess the importance of
various criteria or circumstances in selection or
rejection. We have data only on those who went
through the process, received training, returned
home, and were located and interviewed. This group
is inadequate for carrying out a full analysis of
the dynamics of the selection process. Nevertheless,
their answers can be used as evidence of some prevailing beliefs about selection; they provide clues
as to departures from the official norms as well.
Information from other sources will also be cited
to place the selection process in its administrative
context.

Program Objectives and Selection Criteria

The problem of selection has been a perennial
one in the operation of exchange programs and in discussions about foreign students, primarily because
it raises the issue of objectives in an insistent
way. (At this point, we will deal with its implications for government-sponsored exchange programs;
the broader issue of the selection or admission of
foreign students will be discussed in a later chapter.) However vaguely defined the objectives of
exchange programs (e.g., "to enhance mutual understanding" or "to promote better cultural relations"),
at some point they must be translated into specific
guidelines for choice. These take the form of criteria for the selection of individuals who possess
certain desired qualities. In defining objectives
and criteria, proponents and planners of exchange

programs seem constrained to be imprecise, in part
for fear of offending foreign governments' sensibil-
ities or of arousing their sponsors' displeasure.
Each program tends to lay stress upon a different
set of qualities, in line with its emphasis on special target groups or potential clientele. For one,
emphasis is placed on choosing "leaders . . . /from
abroad with/ significant influence over important
organizations and institutions or substantial seg-
ments of public opinion."[7] Another tries to find
"American scholars . . . /willing to serve/ in certain fields of high demand in the less developed
countries."[8] More recently, through the efforts of
an interagency Committee on Youth, the selection of
"young and potential leaders" has been given a high
priority in all government-sponsored exchange programs with developing nations.[9]

Once established, selection criteria have a
dual significance for the conduct of exchange programs or for organizational programs in general.
First, they exert some pressure for the clarifica-
tion of a program's objectives, and in so doing they
occasionally contribute to their alteration. Second,
in a related vein, they provide a means by which an
evaluation of the conduct of the program can be made.
Who are the "right" people to reach in the light of
a program's formal objectives? Are they being
reached? If so, a minimum condition has then been
met for appraising the program's effects. If not,
changes either in the program's objectives or in
its methods of implementation may be required.[10]

Selection for Participant Training

As the objectives of participant training
shifted, from the upgrading of European trainees'
skills to the cultivation of the developing nations'
human resources, the criteria for selection altered
and were defined more sharply. Criteria and procedures for selecting trainees have remained essentially the same since 1955, although some changes
in emphasis have occurred as a result of broader

policy directives or local exigencies. An operational study in 1966 summarized the official norms governing the selection process; this description can
serve as a useful prelude to our analysis of the survey data.

> Crucial fields of activity are identified
> in which training would make a significant
> impact on the economic and social develop-
> ment of the cooperating country. Next an
> analysis is made of the manpower require-
> ments in each activity field . . . and an
> assessment of the kinds and levels of skill
> needed . . . /as well/ as the priorities
> among competing manpower requirements. . . .
> The next step is a determination, also
> in cooperation with the host government,
> of the qualifications for candidates at
> various levels and for various kinds of
> training. . . . Candidates are then re-
> cruited. . . . The Mission gives final
> approval to those candidates meeting its
> general and technical criteria.
> Ideally each candidate should have
> the following qualifications:
> 1. be a citizen of the country and
> of good moral character and not a member
> of unlawful organizations;
> 2. possess sufficient maturity to
> provide proper representation for his
> country in his associations abroad; he
> should show ability to understand a for-
> eign culture and to benefit from educa-
> tional and observational experiences
> abroad;
> 3. be in good health as indicated
> by a satisfactory medical examination;
> 4. display an adequate understand-
> ing and utilization of English, unless
> he is to undergo training in a group
> large enough to justify an interpreter;
> 5. show that he has utilized all
> appropriate and practical training avail-
> able in his own country in his field of
> study or training;

    6.   possess an ability to work with
others in order that the multiplying effect of the training can be reasonably
assured after his return;

    7.   be employed at the time of his
nomination in the field of training for
which he is proposed or be assured of
assignment in such field after his return;
the candidate should have had several
years of work experience in his own or
related fields; and

    8.   be technically and educationally
qualified for the training proposed.[11]

The first step in the selection process was
usually <u>not</u> one initiated by the participants. Only
one in six (16%) made an application to be sent for
training; the rest were invited or selected to go by
others. Among those who applied, <u>personal contacts</u>
were the principal channels through which they first
heard about participant training. Over a third mentioned their work supervisor or some work colleague
as the initial source of information, and half that
number mentioned a U.S. Mission official; friends
or former participants were also cited, but much
less frequently. The rest mentioned some formal
announcement.

Participants were asked to name the person or
agency who had actually selected them for training.
Few mentioned more than one; in the opinion of a
majority (51%), the key person in the process was
their <u>work supervisor</u>. (The critical role of a participant's work supervisor in the program, noted
here for the first time, will be a recurrent theme
in our analysis.) The patterning of opinions varied
substantially when the participant's locus of employment was taken into account. For example, half of
those employed by labor unions believed that the
final decision was made by their union, rather than
by supervisors, the Mission, or their government.
(As will be shown, labor is a field that differs
markedly from others in the programing of training;
these selection differences in the data reflect the

use of an independent, nongovernmental channel for
many labor trainees.) About a third of the students
claimed they had won a scholarship rather than having been selected; this finding suggests that the
program's focused, occupation-related objectives may
not have been entirely obvious to all. (In some
countries, such as Thailand, with a long history of
sending people abroad for advanced study, all training opportunities are viewed as scholarships.)

Most participants made no mention of a Mission
role in their selection, a fact which may well be a
function of their very limited awareness of the activities of U.S. personnel. Some hints of the role
that the Mission had in a minority of instances can
be gleaned from a finding that participants who
worked for or with USOM[12] prior to their selection
were much more likely than others to cite their work
supervisor as a selection agent. One can surmise
that they were selected by someone who was also a
Mission employee or counterpart (Table 2.5).

Data from two other sets of interviews can also
be drawn on to supplement the views of the participants. The work supervisors of a majority of participants were questioned about their perceptions of
the selection process and the role they played in
choosing their subordinates. Some U.S. technicians
were asked about the selection of participants they
had known at that early point in their programs.
Information pertaining to the selection of every participant is not available from both sources. Their
answers cannot be compared systematically with those
given by the participants; however, as views on the
selection process from two sharply contrasting vantage points, they are of some interest.[13]

Supervisors agreed quite closely with their subordinates on the first step taken in entering the
program; only 11 per cent were said to have applied
on their own. According to them, "someone in our
organization" actually initiated the process of
training for two thirds of the participants. Supervisors said they had recommended four fifths of

TABLE 2.5

Participants' Views of Selection Agent
by Their Prior Work Contacts
with U.S. Mission (USOM)
(In Percentages)

| Selection Agent | Prior USOM Contacts at Selection | | | |
	Worked for/with USOM	Had Any Other Contacts	Had No Previous Contacts	Total
rk supervisor	65	57	44	51
nistry, government official	13	16	21	19
S. Mission	12	11	9	10
l others	10	16	26	20
Total per cent[a]	100	100	100	100
(N)	(4,001)	(3,426)	(11,354)	(18,781)

[a]Excludes those NA on prior USOM contacts (N = 224).

those about whom they were asked and helped to <u>plan
the programs</u> of one half. Their claims of having
been involved in either or both of these preliminary
activities encompass all but 18 per cent of the programs of their subordinates.[14]

At another point in the interview, the supervisors were asked to express their satisfaction with
six general aspects of the program as a whole, one
of which was "selection procedures." They were divided into two groups--those who had previously been
participants and those who had not. One third of
both groups (69%) said they were dissatisfied with
the way selection was being carried out.[15] (Only
the "duration of programs" received a higher proportion of dissatisfied judgments.) The reasons given
for dissatisfaction fell into three categories: Competitive examinations or the opinions of supervisors
should be given greater weight; the knowledge or
past experience of candidates or the existence of
genuine, job-related needs for training should be
more rigorously applied criteria; and the selection
machinery operates too slowly or carelessly. (These
criticisms are echoed in another AID study, an excerpt from which is given at the end of this chapter.)

The depiction made by U.S. technicians of their
role in selecting candidates is, as might be expected,
quite different from that which emerged from the
answers of participants. They asserted that they
had helped to select, plan the program, and secure
employers' interest and consent for over two thirds
of the small (10%) group that they had known at that
early stage of programing. (The short-term hiring
and rotation in assignments of technical-assistance
personnel necessarily made for this shrinkage in
data on participants' selection from this source.)
Incidental comments made by U.S. technicians lend
further support to an image of unevenness in apply-
ing the criteria discussed earlier. In the judgment
of about one third, the selection process could be
improved by stressing the factors of work experience,
ability, and language facility, and by eliminating
political or family influence.

In general, both supervisors and technicians
saw themselves as more active and influential in the
selection process than they were seen to be by the
participants, and their general observations were
consonant with a view that selection is being made
in conformity with norms in a great majority of cases.

One minor aspect of the selection of participants is the auspices under which they are sent.
Almost all were jointly sponsored by a ministry of
their government and by AID or its predecessor agencies. A small but growing number has been sponsored
by U.S. universities under contracts with AID.[16]
Seven per cent of the surveyed participants were programed directly by universities; by 1967, this proportion had risen to over 20 per cent, channeled
largely through the African Scholarship Program of
American Universities (ASPAU),[17] and a similar con-
sortium for the education of students from Latin
America (LASPAU).[18] As could be expected, this group
of participants resembled other foreign students who
come to the United States for higher education more
than they do other participants. All but 14 per cent
attended universities, and over one half of them
earned degrees while in training. (By contrast,
among AID-sponsored participants, 48 per cent attended a university, only one in four of whom earned
a degree.) The conjunction of these two facts, university training and the earning of a degree, will
be shown to have an important bearing on the consequences of training.

Criteria of Selection

In the absence of evidence from other sources
on the relative importance of criteria used in their
selection, the participants' opinions were sought.
However, their answers cannot be taken at face value;
the criteria about which they were asked involve
normative issues that are in varying degree personally or politically sensitive. We will use them
merely as indicators of importance, relative to one
another, in order to explore circumstances affecting
the judgments about each.

Each participant was asked:

How important was each of these factors in
deciding if you would go on the training
program? Your personal ability? The needs
of your job? Your personal contacts? Your
language ability? Your professional and
educational qualifications? /For each, an
answer was recorded as "very important,"
"not very important," or "don't know."_7

The way in which the participants evaluated each of
these criteria is shown in Table 2.6.

TABLE 2.6

Participants' Beliefs About Importance of
Five Criteria for Their Selection
(In Percentages)

Criteria	Degree of Importance			
	Very	Not Very	Don't Know, NA	Total Per Cent[a]
Professional and educational qualifications	88.6	8.2	3.2	100.0
Needs of the job	88.0	9.7	2.3	100.0
Personal ability	87.8	7.2	5.0	100.0
Language ability	64.4	32.0	3.6	100.0
Personal contacts	35.5	58.5	6.0	100.0

[a]Percentages in each row are based on all participants (N = 19,025).

Of the five, only personal contacts[19] would seem, from a normative perspective, to be a retrogressive or questionable basis for selection. Foreign-language ability can have greater or lesser importance depending upon the country of training and the trainee's level of skill. The other three are generally pertinent and unexceptionable criteria in light of the program's professed objectives. It is not surprising that almost nine in ten believed them to have been "very important" in their selection. We will explore the correlates of three of these criteria in greater detail, reserving personal contacts until last.

Needs of the Job. All training is meant to be directly related to an existing or anticipated set of work tasks, yet one trainee in ten rated job needs as relatively unimportant. There are only slight hints in the data of what was involved in the selection of this group. They tended to be younger, less experienced, lower in status, more insulated from Mission contacts, and less involved in the preparation of their programs. This cluster of attributes suggests that they were sent for training on a more casual, less purposive basis; the differences are, however, quite small.

Language Ability. Three interrelated influences on the extent to which language ability was deemed very important by participants were discovered. One is a set of personal attributes, mainly age and work experience. The younger or less-experienced trainees cited it more often than others; this was true also of those with more formal education. These personal characteristics set limits upon the type of training which can be usefully devised; both of the other factors to be discussed will serve to amplify this point.

The single, most powerful circumstance was whether a program required a knowledge of English, and if it did, how confident or capable one felt in his command of the language. Seventy per cent of participants who were sent on programs requiring English felt their language ability was a very important criterion; among the rest, only about half as many (37%) deemed it important. Among those needing English, the more confident one felt about his English skills, the more often was his language ability cited as an important criterion for his selection.[20] (This latter finding may have the status of a self-confirming judgment: i.e., "Because I am proficient in the language, it must have been important in my being chosen." All these judgments, it should be remembered, were retrospective.)

The third factor, related to the others, was the type of program in which participants were involved. Observation tours and special-group tours make the least demands upon language skills; interpreters often accompany such programs. Those who went on either type of program solely were, therefore, less likely to have judged language ability as an important criterion.

Personal Contacts. At first glance, a participant would seem unlikely to acknowledge that his personal contacts were important in his selection for training. To be chosen because of "who you know" represents a departure from impartial, objective selection criteria, such as achievement, ability, and proven need. Few participants considered these approved criteria unimportant, but more than a third (36%) also believed that personal contacts had been "very important." How can we account for this small but still sizable pattern of response? Are there any implications of personal contacts other than corruption or favoritism?

One observation relates to the broader social and cultural setting in which personal relationships affect goal achievements or the gaining of career advantages. Societies or organizations vary in the extent to which the play of personal factors is minimized or controlled, permitting merit or other more objectively assessed qualities significantly to shape the distribution of social rewards. They also vary in the extent to which advantages bestowed on the basis of kinship, caste, or politics are seen as

legitimate and discussed without resentment or negative connotations. An equalitarian or openly competitive model of a process of selection for foreign
training has little empirical relevance in societies
where traditional or hereditary distinctions of status and power are decisive. In such cases, to say
that personal contacts were important is less a commentary on lapses of objectivity in selection than
it is on the prevailing norms of the social system
within which the process operates. Personal contacts
might, therefore, not necessarily have the one familiar
implication of favoritism or "pull" but a variety of
meanings intimately associated with the cultural and
social structures within which selection for training is carried out.

Following this line of sociological speculation,
one would expect to find that the citing of personal
contacts as important varies across countries because
of cultural, social, or political differences, inde-
pendently of other considerations. Moreover, such
variations should be greater, for example, than variations in the mention of "job needs," a criterion
which is more universally pertinent. The findings
on this point are unequivocal. Variations in citing
personal contacts range between 12 and 74 per cent
across the countries in the survey, while for job
needs the range is much narrower, between 84 and 100
per cent. Let us assume further that a desire to
please the interviewer or AID, or cautiousness in
giving what might be thought to be an unacceptable
answer, may have affected the participants' judgments
about these criteria. This tendency, termed a
"courtesy bias," has been noted in cross-cultural
research.[21] From this perspective, the range of difference across countries in the participants' views
that personal contacts were important takes on added
weight as evidence of the play of powerful sociocultural forces (Table 2.7).

Selection for participant training also depends
in large part upon personal knowledge of candidates
in their present or anticipated work setting; impersonal agencies or procedures, as we saw, were rarely

TABLE 2.7

Beliefs About Importance of Personal Contacts
and Needs of Job As Selection Criteria,
by Country of Participants

| | Selection Criteria: | |
| | Per Cent Saying: "Very Important" | |
Country	Personal Contacts	Needs of Job
Morocco	74%	92%
Ecuador	68	91
British Guiana	62	94
British Honduras	62	99
Philippines	57	96
Ethiopia	56	84
Jordan	56	100
Brazil	55	85
Chile	54	84
Greece	53	85
Costa Rica	50	91
Egypt	45	97
Vietnam	43	92
Jamaica	42	97
Surinam	36	94
Turkey	33	87
Pakistan	26	92
Nicaragua	26	100
India	25	91
Israel	22	91
Korea	17	85
China (Taiwan)	14	90
Thailand	12	88
	37%	90%

[a]Base for percentages excludes those NA and "don't
know" responses; see Table 2.6.

believed by participants or their supervisors to have
played an important role. Personal contacts, especially those arising from work on development projects with or for the U.S. Mission, can be a means
by which candidates come to the attention of selection agents. Personal acquaintance arising from
work relationships renders such people more "socially
visible."[22]

Some data can be used to document this point.
One half of those who said a U.S. official had selected them gauged personal contacts as very important; those with any prior Mission contacts were
also more likely to deem them important than those
with none at all. Higher-status participants generally had closer ties with USOM prior to their selection or had some work contacts, as did those lowest
in status; both groups more often cited their personal contacts as significant in their selection. An
analysis of a small group who went for training more
than once showed them to be distinguished from others
chiefly by their close ties with the Mission; these
people were clearly more "visible" than others. For
the relatively few craftsmen and workers selected
for training, these personal relationships were probably crucial, because there are so many to choose,
and so few who have been chosen, from this occupational stratum.

Finally, there remains the more familiar, pejora-
tive implication of personal contacts. And one can
identify a set of correlates of those who mentioned
personal contacts which evokes an image that their
selection involved a relaxation of more stringent
criteria. Participants who were much older, especially those over 55, who were selected by unions,
trade associations, or other nongovernmental agencies, who went primarily for brief observation tours
or as members of special-group tours, were all more
likely to view their personal contacts as having
been significant. Political objectives may have had
more relevance in their selection.

In the absence of other data which could pin-
point their significance more precisely in individual

cases, one can only explore the role of personal contacts in this inferential fashion. Personal contacts
rarely seem to be the sole basis for selection; they
can be decisive in bringing people more prominently
into consideration or in choosing among candidates
who for the most part were also adjudged qualified
on the grounds of need or ability.

Another study that dealt with this topic yielded
an image of selection as a much more "political"
process. To balance off our analysis, we shall
quote an excerpt from it. It is an exceptionally
candid, compact discussion of the problems that
arise in cooperative development projects.

> The standard selection procedure cannot
> be followed fully and meaningfully in some
> countries where the host governments lack
> or fail to provide personnel able and
> willing to cooperate in it. Insufficient
> numbers of efficient and honest government
> officials are part of the problem to which
> the Participant Training Program is often
> addressed . . . .
> Sometimes the host government may
> insist on selecting candidates entirely
> by itself, often without a preliminary
> manpower assessment or a careful screen-
> ing on the basis of standard criteria.
> This insistence usually results in some
> unqualified candidates nominated by a
> host government for political reasons or
> through misunderstanding of the nature
> of American training institutions or
> through misunderstanding of the objec-
> tives of the training program or of a
> project's objectives. In these cases
> the Mission is faced with, at the least,
> protracted argument, and occasionally
> with the dilemma of either choosing the
> best of several improperly qualified can-
> didates or having no training program at
> all--with resulting delay or failure of
> important projects . . . .

In some countries officers of the
host government lack appreciation of the
value of technical education in contrast
to the type of education they themselves
have received . . . . Trained in literature or art, or /as7 military officers
. . . . they have never understood nor
concentrated upon the techniques and dis-
ciplines required to achieve economic
development . . . . nor is the scientific
attitude a concept they have encountered.
Often these officials come from a
cultural tradition in which status, wealth
and family connections determine prestige
and position. They have been taught to
look down upon the knowledge and techniques
associated with agriculture, engineering
and industry. Although officially com-
mitted to economic development, they are
emotionally antipathetic both to acquiring
technical skills themselves and to permitting members of other castes or classes
in the social structure of the country to
acquire such training. The result can be
candidates for training who are not seriously desirous of learning new skills but
who perhaps have stated a desire for training in order to enjoy the experience of a
trip to the United States and such prestige
as it confers upon them.[23]

NOTES

1. Recent statistics show a similar preponderance of men among all foreign students in the United
States, although not as heavy as in our sample of
AID-sponsored participants. Of all foreign students
in 1967-68, three out of four were men. See Institute of International Education, Open Doors 1968:
Report on International Exchange (New York: Institute of International Education (July, 1968), p. 3.

2.   See Agency for International Development, Office of International Training, Horizons Unlimited: A Statistical Report on Participant Training: 10th Annual Edition (Washington, D.C.:   Statistical Control Branch, Agency for International Development, November, 1968), p. ix.

3.   As noted above, the act of earning a degree or attending a university does not imply equivalent preparation for occupations or professions. But in all of these countries, only a fraction of the population has such opportunities; these figures can be taken as indicators of the high relative achievement of these participants.

4.   These data underestimate the true extent of rural residence; in a few countries, a tendency existed to concentrate interviewing near the capital or major urban centers because of the greater cost and difficulty of reaching more distantly located participants.

5.   The survey's omission of the very substantial numbers of European participants from private industry during the Marshall Plan years should be recalled here. The trend holds only for selection patterns among the underdeveloped countries' participants.

6.   Classifications of occupational status were based on a very detailed AID coding system. Our analysis used broader categories derived from that scheme, because the information was classified in too much detail to be used in cross tabulations.

7.   This is one of the key criteria used in the Foreign Leader Program of the Department of State. See Robert E. Elder, The Foreign Leader Program: Operations in the United States (Washington, D.C.: The Brookings Institution, 1961), p. 16. Elder provides some evidence of the varied interpretations to which this criterion has given rise. From his and others' accounts, the definition of "opinion leaders," a category which most programs seek to reach, appears to be an elusive as well as an elastic one.

8. This criterion and the objective which gave rise to it have created a small but thorny problem for the Fulbright Program. See Francis A. Young, "The Conference Board of Associated Research Councils in the United States, A Brief Historical Account with Special Reference to National and International Manpower Problems," Social Science Information, Vol. IV, No. 2 (June, 1965), pp. 111-27.

9. The work of this committee, set up in the wake of then-Attorney General Robert Kennedy's trip to Japan, India, and Indonesia in 1962, is carried on partly in the gray area of U.S. foreign operations. Some idea of its concerns can be gotten from papers and remarks delivered at two conferences held in Washington in 1964 and 1966; see U.S. Department of State, Bureau of Educational and Cultural Affairs, Changing Roles of Youth in Developing Nations: A Conference Report (Washington, D.C.: Policy Review and Research Staff, August, 1964); and Bureau of Social Science Research, Inc., Youth and Leadership in the Developing Nations: Summary Report on a Conference (Washington, D.C.: Department of State, September, 1967). Also indicative of the orientation of this effort were the disclosures early in 1967 of C.I.A. involvement in the activities of various student groups and cultural organizations with international ties.

10. When objectives are translated into selection criteria, a set of standards is created by which the performance of program administrators can be assessed. If departures from these standards are too widespread to be hidden or overlooked, then either the criteria and their underlying objectives must be altered or efforts must be made to secure adequate compliance. The former action involves the familiar pattern of the succession of goals in organizations; see David L. Sills, The Volunteers (Glencoe: The Free Press, 1957). The latter is a problem of social control, one that is intensified by the establishment of procedures which serve as a means of assessing role performance in the light of a program's objectives. On the functions of the establishment of performance criteria for the goals of a

public agency, see Peter M. Blau, The Dynamics of
Bureaucracy (Chicago: University of Chicago Press,
1955). For a general theoretical discussion of the
relation of norms to role performance, see Robert K.
Merton, Social Theory and Social Structure (rev. and
enlarged ed.; Glencoe: The Free Press, 1957), pp.
341-53.

11. Harley O. Preston, Operations of the Participant Training Program of the Agency for International Development (Washington, D.C.: Office of
International Training, AID, November, 1966), pp.
30-32.

12. "USOM" is government jargon for U.S. Operations Missions, set up by ICA in countries whose assistance programs required separate administration.
The term used more recently to designate these entities is "USAID"; for the sake of historical accuracy we will use "USOM" or refer simply to "the Mission" in our discussion.

13. Twenty per cent of the participants said
they had no supervisor, and 2 per cent refused per-
mission to have him interviewed. Depending upon the
item of information and estimates of the number whose
supervisors might have been interviewed, we have comparative data on participants from between 50 and 80
per cent of their supervisors. The corresponding
proportions for data on participants obtained from
interviews with U.S. technicians are far lower, between 10 and 40 per cent. The possibilities for
cross relating answers from the three sources are,
therefore, rather limited with respect to selection
but somewhat better for other issues in participant
training.

14. This finding is based on data relating to
the programs of under half of all participants.

15. The identical proportions of both groups
who rated this program aspect as satisfactory give
one grounds for assuming that "sour grapes" (at not
having been selected themselves) did not enter into
the judgments of those who hadn't been participants.

16. For a review of the operations of U.S. universities in the field of technical assistance made at the time of this survey, see Edward W. Weidner, The World Role of Universities (New York: McGraw-Hill Book Company, 1962), especially pp. 134-287. See also Education and World Affairs, The University Looks Abroad (New York: Walker, 1965). The recurring strains in the relationship between the universities and the federal government in technical-assistance ventures are succinctly and ably analyzed in John W. Gardner, AID and the Universities (New York: Education and World Affairs, 1964). A more recent analysis of the "troubled partnership" is contained in Richard A. Humphrey, ed., Universities . . . and Development Assistance Abroad (Washington, D.C.: American Council on Education, 1967).

17. On the operations of ASPAU, see Education and World Affairs, The Foreign Student: Whom Shall We Welcome? (New York: Education and World Affairs, 1964), pp. 22-24. Recent cuts in the foreign-aid program have radically affected both programs, as well as those of other agencies engaged in educational and cultural exchange.

18. These statistics were drawn from AID's annual report, Horizons Unlimited, op. cit., p. 5, p. 13.

19. This term was translated in the French version of the interview schedule as vos relations, and in the Spanish version as sus contactos personales.

20. A participant's confidence in his linguistic skills was measured by an index based on answers to two questions: whether or not he had taken special training in English, and whether or not some (more) would have been helpful. Those who neither had such training nor wanted it were adjudged as most confident; other combinations reflected lower levels of confidence.

21. A good treatment of courtesy bias is that by Robert Edward Mitchell, "Survey Materials Collected

in the Developing Countries: Sampling, Measurement, and Interviewing Obstacles to Intra- and International Comparisons," <u>International Social Science Journal</u>, Vol. XVII, No. 4 (1965), pp. 665-85, especially p. 681. This form of bias is one of a more general class, termed "interviewer effects" in studies using the method of personal interview. See Herbert H. Hyman <u>et al.</u>, <u>Interviewing in Social Research</u> (Chicago: University of Chicago Press, 1954).

22. The concept of social visibility used in this context is adapted from a more general theoretical formulation of its significance in and for social groups. See Merton, <u>op. cit.</u>, pp. 319-22.

23. Preston, <u>op. cit.</u>, pp. 32-34.

CHAPTER **3** THE TRANSITION
TO TRAINING

ANTICIPATORY SOCIALIZATION AND
ORGANIZATIONAL COMMITMENTS

Prior to their departure, and in part concur-
rent with their selection, participants undergo a
good deal of formal preparation for training. This
is designed to orient them to the program's character and to smooth the transition from work to study
and from their own country to another. One major
goal of preparatory activities is "to focus the
trainee's thoughts on the experience he is about to
undergo and to impress upon him the seriousness and
intensity of effort expected of him."[1]

Language training may be offered or intensified
in this period. Opportunities may be given for participants to enter actively into the planning of
their programs in conferences with Mission officials,
and publications are distributed for private study.
Participants are sometimes asked to prepare a work-
book containing statements of their past training
and experience, the relation of their background to
training and in turn its relation to future work,
their perceptions of how their work is related to
national development, and so on. A final conference,
held shortly before departure, is held to "reassure
the participant and his family, to ease his first
days of adjustment, and to lay a foundation for a
relationship with the USAID which should continue
after his return."[2]

The orientation process is designed to carry
over into the period of arrival for training. Participants are met at airports; meetings are arranged

71

between them and AID program managers or other program coordinators; special orientation courses are offered at various sites to enlighten them further about life in the country of training. Visits and hospitality tours are arranged.[3] The manifest functions of these elaborate procedures are to facilitate cross-cultural adjustment and learning,[4] to establish and strongly reinforce the idea of the purposive character of training, and to create a firm communication link between participants and the U.S. agency that is sponsoring their training.

A respecification of the social-psychological concept of anticipatory socialization can help to clarify some additional functions of these activities. As originally formulated, it referred to a process by which individuals "take on the values of the non-membership group to which they aspire, find readier acceptance by that group and make an easier adjustment to it."[5] The point of view is that of the aspirant who is motivated to seek group membership. Our respecification is made from the standpoint of the group that seeks to affect the individual's future course of action. His motivation to change cannot be assumed; instead, it is considered as problematic in its strength, direction, and constancy.

In our conception, anticipatory socialization is a process by which groups strive to use information and inducements in an attempt to alter an individual's role definitions and institutional attachments. At a minimum, it can lead to greater readiness to learn the content of new or altered roles; at a maximum, it can lead to a radical restructuring of group loyalties and the acquisition of new values and self-images. The latent functions of preparatory activities directed at participants, therefore, are to induce or refocus motivation in order to enhance the prospects for learning new skills and techniques and to establish the preconditions for attitude change and resocialization.[6]

Another focus in this preparatory phase is the securing of commitments from employing organizations

and foreign governments to the aims and purposes of
training for those they have nominated and helped to
select. In principle, not only is the consent of
such groups sought, but they must also demonstrate
an awareness of the need for training their employees
and show a willingness to make appropriate use of
them upon their return. The primary concern of the
Mission's programers is with the issue of <u>placement</u>.
Certification must be made not only so that each participant has obligated himself to serve his country
for a minimum of two years[7] but also that his work
will be on a project or in a field for which his
training is essential.

The soliciting of such commitments may be seen
as an attempt by AID to create a necessary condition
for the effective use of the foreign trainee's newly
acquired skills and knowledge. It is the social
structural complement to the effort made to prepare
individual participants for optimal learning. Attention is paid not only to manpower training but to
its utilization. Because training is invariably
only one small strand in a network of assistance-
program agreements, the amount of leverage available
to the Mission for establishing this vital precondition is probably at a maximum in this period. Agreements made in advance of training have a binding
character that attempts made to persuade employers
subsequently cannot readily achieve, especially when
(as is usually the case) it is the foreign government itself with which the Mission must deal.

Having analyzed the theoretical rationale for
various pretraining procedures, showing their functions for learning and for utilization, we turn now
to some survey findings on how often or how well
they have been discharged.

PREPARATIONS FOR TRAINING

Planning the Programs

Participants were asked about the sources, substance, and adequacy of the information they received about the plans for their programs and the part they played in determining what kind of training they were to get. From their replies, one could more accurately call them "hit-or-miss recipients" rather than "participants" at this stage of training. Fewer than one half heard anything about their training program at their place of employment; the key informant for a majority of this group was their work supervisor. Only one in three was supplied with any planning information by the ministry that acted as their formal sponsor. Thus, two participants in five received no information from either source prior to their departure.

Most of the information about plans for training dealt with substantive details of the program. Significantly, only one in five of those who were informed at all about training plans recalled any references to the post-training work they would be called upon to do. This picture of a meager and uneven flow of information, derived from responses to two questions about its sources, will be altered and sharpened substantially when we review answers to questions dealing with a number of specific topics of advance information.

Participants' Role in Planning Programs

Only about one third of the participants took an active part in planning their training program. The main factor which determined whether a participant was afforded such an opportunity was his seniority or high status. Almost half of those older, more experienced, or better educated (especially those highest in occupational status) helped to plan their training. Even among those who entered into

the planning process, about one in five felt they
did not participate to the extent they would have
wished. Thus, over one half (55%) of the entire
group expressed serious misgivings about the opportunity they had to help plan their own training program.

One of the more well-documented findings of
research on people's reactions to a novel or changing social situation is that a sense of participation in making decisions facilitates subsequent
personal adjustment and leads to more effective
performance.[8] If active participation has a moti-
vating effect, its use is hardly being exploited
in this program. There are, of course, realistic
limits to the role trainees can play in an assistance program of this scope and variety; changes frequently must be made at the last minute. Because a
planning role has been denied to most participants,
the formal orientation they receive subsequently
becomes all the more fateful in building or main-
taining a positive attitude toward training.

Advance Orientation and Information

As we have seen, many participants received
only minimal information about plans for their training. They were also asked about the advance information they received on a few key aspects of their
future programs and countries of training. Whenever
they expressed dissatisfaction, they were asked what,
in retrospect, they would have found useful to know.
The topics about which they were asked lie at the
core of any attempt to prepare people for foreign
study. From the responses that were elicited, one
can identify some deficiencies in the flow of information.

Participants were asked if they had gotten
enough information about several concrete aspects
of their training program. Because people's definitions of "enough" will vary according to personal
needs, an affirmative answer is an indicator of only

a roughly comparable level of individual satisfaction. By this standard, advance information on the length and timing of training was conveyed satisfactorily with greater consistency than on other topics, including the substance of their programs. About one third of the participants expressed dissatisfaction in answers to two or more questions relating to program details.

As noted earlier, much of the rationale for any orientation process relates to the "culture shock" that can arise when the social and cultural distance between the social patterns in the participants' own lands and those prevailing in the country of training (for most, the United States) becomes too great. Participants were asked how satisfied they were with several items of information of the type needed to facilitate their adjustment to the country of training, e.g., customs, religious practices, use of money, and so forth. In general, these aspects of the orientation process were evaluated more favorably than those relating to the training program. More than three fourths felt that such topics had been adequately treated. Only with respect to "colloquial speech and idioms" did as many as one quarter of the participants express dissatisfaction with their orientation. This was clearly part of a larger problem: The use of a foreign (English) language during training and in daily life.

Advance Commitments to Use Training

As noted earlier, certain steps concerning the placement of participants, if taken early, can subsequently yield large dividends. The full utilization of a participant's training depends upon a host of unpredictable contingencies; a firm commitment or plan to place the trainee appropriately is, however, one clearly specifiable prerequisite. Where such a commitment does not exist, training is more likely to prove to be a pleasant but irrelevant interlude.

To discover whether or not plans for the use of participants existed prior to their departure, we

turn to interviews held with their supervisors, the
people most likely to have known about such advance
organizational commitments. We have data on this
issue from the supervisors of only 27 per cent of
the participants in our survey.[9] As they remembered
it, the employing organizations of seven out of eight
trainees "had plans as to how his training would be
utilized after he came back." The one variable which
was most closely associated with the existence of
such a plan or commitment was the supervisor's own
early involvement in his subordinate's program of
training. The more extensive the involvement, the
more likely was it that claims for the existence of
an organizational commitment were made (Table 3.1).

No clear time ordering of these two variables
is possible; their positions in the statement of the
finding could, with equal justification, have been
reversed. We incline to the view, however, that a
supervisor's degree of involvement is a variable of
a more general order than the more specific question
of whether or not a plan existed.[10] It also seems
quite likely that he was the official from whom such
a commitment would have been sought. However the
relationship is viewed, the finding clearly demon-
strates the crucial role of a trainee's work supervisor in establishing a link between his training
and his organization's commitment to its use. This
relationship is particularly interesting, because
one might have expected supervisors to claim that
plans had existed, regardless of their prior degree
of involvement, simply as a matter of verbal conformity to an established norm.

Whether or not participants returned to a "prepared" occupational setting, one in which training
had a pre-established function, was unrelated to their
characteristics or to the types of training they
took. It was also unrelated to their views on whether training had been of value to their careers. Its
sole important association, as we will show, is with
the extent to which training was used, a neat illustration of how the utilization of training can be
affected by early attention to the postprogram work
environment, irrespective of the character of trainees

TABLE 3.1

Organizational Plans for the Use of Training,
by Supervisors' Prior Involvement
Obtained from Supervisors About
Specific Participants (In Percentages)

| Existence of Prior Plan | Degree of Supervisor's Involvement[a] | | | |
	Recommended and Helped Plan Program	Did Either Activity	Did Neither Activity	Total
Plan for use existed	97.1	85.4	65.2	87.4
No plan existed	2.4	12.3	33.6	9.4
Don't know	.5	2.3	12.2	3.2
Total per cent[b]	100.0	100.0	100.0	100.0
(N)	(1,263)	(921)	(474)	(2,658)

[a]Based on answers by supervisors to two questions about each participant: "Did you recommend that /X̲7 be sent on a training program?" "Did you help in planning /X̲'s̲7 training program?"

[b]This table is based on the unweighted number of participants whose supervisors were interviewed. It excludes participants whose supervisors did not know them prior to training (N = 2,912), or who were NA on either item (N = 30), and those who had no data from a supervisor (N = 4,068).

or programs. And the most significant actor in the
process of preparing a trainee's occupational setting
was his immediate work supervisor.

Participants rarely mentioned the Mission as a
prime source of information, and few believed that
it played an important role in their selection. But
prior association with the Mission, as employees or
on a cooperative development project, might have provided them with an indirect means of learning what
was ahead or expected of them. They were asked:

At the time you were selected to go abroad,
were you employed by USOM or on a project
run jointly by USOM and your government?

/If Yes/ Full-time, part-time or
occasionally?
/If No/ Before you were selected,
had your work ever brought you into contact with any USOM project?

Three out of five had never had any previous
contacts with U.S. Mission development work. Just
over a fifth of the participants had been working
(mostly full time) for or with USOM on a development
project; the remainder had some prior contacts but
were not associated with Mission-sponsored activities when selected. In our analysis of the role of
personal contacts, this variable was used to show
how closer association with the U.S. Mission might
have rendered a participant more socially visible as
a candidate for training. Its relationship to the
orientation process, however, was slight: Those who
were closely associated with USOM at selection were
only marginally more likely to have been satisfied
with information about their program or country of
training than those who had had no prior contacts.

These answers cannot be taken as adequate indicators of the full extent of Mission involvement in
the selection and preparation of participants. Much
of the actual work in this period is hidden from the
view of participants; if we consult data from another

source, a different picture emerges. The small number of U.S. technicians interviewed who claimed that
they were active in the early stages of these participants' programs asserted that:

> they had prior work contacts with 79 per
> cent;
> they gave predeparture information to 75
> per cent;
> they helped plan the programs of 68 per
> cent;
> they helped select 65 per cent;
> they coordinated the programs with employ-
> ers of 64 per cent.

The disparity in the views of participants and
U.S. technicians as to the scope or extent of involvement of Mission personnel is not surprising, as
the questions were dissimilar in wording and
their replies, also reflect the different vantage
points of each group. The technicians were under an
additional normative constraint: They would not want
to admit to little responsibility for or control over
such vital aspects of programing.

If one views the participants' answers as indicators of their personal knowledge rather than of
objective reality, one finds a situation sharply at
variance with official doctrine. The general picture is one of Mission inactivity, of a distance
between it and the individual selectee. There seem
to be only faint traces in the data of any imprint
made upon them by the Mission at this early stage.
And this picture holds across all categories of participants, with the significant exception of those
at the highest occupational level. Presumably their
national prominence caused more attention to be paid
to them by the Mission during the predeparture period. In sharp contrast, those lowest in occupational
status and the youngest, least-experienced selectees
seem to have been at the periphery of Mission attention even more frequently than others.

SATISFACTION WITH TRAINING
PRIOR TO DEPARTURE

We argued earlier that intensive advance planning and orientation can do more than serve the in-
formational needs of the participants. It can also
shape their initial perspective on training; good
preparation can induce a more favorable attitude,
one of greater satisfaction with the approaching program. In a retrospective attempt to measure trainees'
predeparture attitudes, the participants were asked:
"Before you left to go abroad, how satisfied were
you with your training program? Were you well satisfied, not very well satisfied, or didn't you know
enough about it /to form a judgment7?"

The time referent of this question gives rise
to ambiguities in the interpretation of replies,[11]
as does the wording of the response categories. For
example, those who were coded as giving an indeterminate response (the third alternative) may have
been indirectly giving vent to a dissatisfied mood.
But this category also includes a group who honestly
couldn't remember how satisfied they felt at the
time. The responses to this retrospective question
do not faithfully reproduce the degree of satisfaction these participants felt about their training.
We can, however, use the proportion who were "well
satisfied" as a crude standard or criterion for assessing the extent to which preparatory activities
influenced early attitudes toward training. (Those
who gave other answers can be assumed to be less
satisfied, although precisely how much or on what
grounds cannot be known.) Over-all, 55 per cent
remembered themselves as having been "well satisfied"
before going abroad.

What kinds of circumstances affected the satisfaction with which training tended to be viewed?
The most significant set of determinants was related
to the flow of information that participants received
from a variety of sources. On almost every comparison which was made, those who received more information or who adjudged more aspects of their program

or training country as having been adequately covered during orientation were consistently more likely to have been "well satisfied" with their program before going abroad than those less fully informed.   These findings tend to confirm our argument that sheer information giving, by fulfilling the trainees' cognitive needs, can appreciably shape the mental set or mood with which they enter training. Conversely, of course, serious shortcomings or failures in preparing them for training can have potentially damaging consequences for learning and adjustment during the training period.

Satisfaction in advance of training was also related to two program attributes that were settled during this early phase of programing: How fully arranged they were and how long they were to last. The more complete the program arrangements, the larger the proportion who remembered themselves as having been satisfied. In a related vein, shorter programs tend to be more thoroughly planned in advance, because they operate on an administratively tighter schedule. The shorter the duration of training, the larger the proportion who were well satisfied (Table 3.2).

The interpretation of all these sets of findings hinges, we believe, on a common intervening factor: the predictability of a training program. Greater prior exposure to plans and information, it is hypothesized, can increase the participants' ability to predict the character of their training sojourn more accurately. Personality differences can also intervene: Exposure to the same information can lead one man to see his planned program as fairly chaotic and another to perceive it as essentially complete, depending upon the need for certitude or tolerance of ambiguity. We cannot test this proposition empirically by introducing such personality variables; no measures of personality were incorporated in the survey instruments.

Two other findings can help to clarify the grounds for considering predictability as an

TABLE 3.2

Proportion Well Satisfied with
Program Arrangements and Duration
Prior to Departure

Attribute of Program as Planned	Per Cent Well Satisfied	Total Number[a]
Program Arrangements		
Arranged in complete detail	60	(10,736)
Arranged in partial detail	51	(6,382)
Not set up at all	40	(1,602)
Duration of Training		
Less than two months	61	(1,493)
Two to six months	55	(4,773)
Six months to one year	55	(6,006)
One to three years	53	(6,331)
Three years and over	48	(175)
All participants	55	(18,931)

[a]Those who were NA on these items are omitted
from each row in the base for percentaging.

important intervening variable. Those who were more
satisfied with the advance information they received
and those who took a more active part in planning
their program both tended to perceive their programs
as fully arranged more often than their less well-
oriented or actively involved counterparts. It seems
highly likely that in both cases a participant would
have thereby acquired a clearer image of what to expect. Thus, the conclusion seems at least tenable
that greater predictability leads to a more favorable
initial perspective on training.

No other variables linked with the predeparture
phase of the program were associated with participants' prior satisfaction. The importance they ascribed to various selection criteria was unrelated
to it; those who felt their personal contacts, job
needs, and so forth, were important were not more
often satisfied than those who felt these criteria
were unimportant. Thus, the two elements which seem
to have been crucial for the creation of a positive
mental set were the scope and quality of orienting
information and the completeness with which program
plans were drawn. (These findings, with their ra-
tionalistic flavor, may disappoint believers in the
proposition that information campaigns have little
use with heterogeneous audiences. They seem suffi-
ciently clear cut to us to suggest a reappraisal of
such convictions.) The empirical data show that the
elements in this process have been successfully combined in only a bare majority of the cases we have
examined.

FIRST STEPS ON ARRIVAL

When they arrive in the country where all or
most of their training is to take place, participants often have another chance to become more fully
informed about the aims of participant training and
the substance of their own programs. Additional
orientation is provided which deals with practical
problems and life situations that they are about to
encounter. (From the data on their predeparture

orientation, we suspect that for many this may have
been their first real occasion to learn something
about these matters.) During this initial period,
participants also have an opportunity to request
changes in their programs or to take an active role
in completing arrangements, if details have remained
unsettled.

Once they had arrived, two thirds of the participants entered into a formal program of orientation
which lasted longer than one day. The proportions
varied widely by country of training: Three out of
four U.S.-trained participants attended, while only
one fifth to one half of those trained at various
third-country sites attended. (Training taken outside the United States tends to be briefer; a formal
intake program would absorb a significant share of
the time available.)

The institution that has figured most prominently as a site for orientation sessions in the United
States was and is the Washington International Center.[12] One half of all trainees and 60 per cent of
U.S.-trained participants attended some formal session prior to training. Those who had attended found
them to be of great assistance in a number of specifiable ways, and only 11 per cent would have liked
to use the time for other purposes. This finding
suggests that at least some of the previously unmet
needs of participants for adequate preparation are
met through this medium.

The actual details of the participants' programs
varied considerably in their finality even at the
time of arrival. As they recalled it, 57 per cent
said their programs were arranged in complete detail,
34 per cent said they were only partially arranged,
and 9 per cent said they had not been set up at all.
A less than completely planned program does offer a
participant an opportunity, perhaps for the first
time, to shape the nature of his program directly.
As one might expect, however, given the official
character of this program, almost five sixths of
the trainees followed their programs as originally

planned. Only a minority of the rest were given an
opportunity to alter their programs in some way.

Before the participants are launched on their
programs, an effort is made to see that they meet
with an official who bears some responsibility for
their program, to establish a personal bond and to
review in detail their next steps. Upon arrival,
nine out of ten participants met someone who discussed their training with them. In most cases,
this initial contact was with a project manager or
program specialist, someone who may have been actively involved in the participant's program from
the time of its initial proposal.

The availability of someone to whom a participant could refer problems arising during his sojourn
might be thought of as having primarily a symbolic
value (i.e., showing greater personal concern) or as
having mainly an administrative use (i.e., providing
a focus of responsibility). The consequences of his
absence were, however, real and unfavorable. Those
who either had none or didn't remember whether they
had gave lower ratings to their training and made
relatively poorer use of it. One can suggest that
individuals sent on a program which fell between
stools, administratively speaking, were likely to
have had training that was seriously deficient in
other respects as well. As a result, it is not surprising that they were less effective after their
return.

As we have shown, there exists an intricate set
of procedures to be followed in programing participants, designed to prepare them both for their training program and for later application of their lessons to their work on development projects. Findings
from the survey indicate considerable variation in
carrying out these procedures. The AID operational
study, quoted from earlier, noted a few additional
sources of difficulty in following established regu-
lations:

Then there are disorderly governments,
changing governments, and changing goals

within ministries. In addressing this
group of problems Missions have often discovered that there may be no real or lasting understanding between them and the
host country's officials as to the objectives of the program. Changes in project
goals and in participant training programs
may be insisted on by the other government
at any stage in the training procedure,
with consequent frustration for the trainees as well as for the USAID officers. . . .

Other complications requiring devia-
tions from the standard procedure may stem
from acceleration of programs to increase
political impact at a crucial period; the
development by the Washington staff of
special group programs involving participants from several countries, which may
accelerate or delay the timing of a training program that has been set up in an
individual country; the problem of timing
in relation to U.S. Congressional appro-
priations action, which may have delayed
the availability of funds; and the built-
in high workload-peak on AID/W and universities just prior to the beginning of the
American "school year."[13]

It is a mark of the difference between head-
quarters, where policies and procedures are drafted,
and the field, where they must be carried out under
circumstances unanticipated by the policy makers,
that the closer trainees come to Washington the
closer the fit between the norms governing the training process and the experiences they undergo. We
can expect, therefore, that events in the period of
training will conform more closely to plans and intentions than those either in the period prior to
their arrival, discussed in preceding sections, or
in the aftermath of training when the trainees return home.

NOTES

1. Harley O. Preston, Operations of the Partici-pant Training Program of the Agency for International Development (Washington, D.C.: Office of Interna-tional Training, AID, November, 1966), p. 40.

2. Ibid.

3. Ibid., pp. 44-52. On this topic, as in his treatment of other matters, Preston states the norms governing procedures and then analyzes the sources of departures from them. Also see Agency for Inter-national Development, Horizons Unlimited: A Statis-tical Report on Participant Training: 10th Annual Edition (Washington, D.C.: Statistical Control Branch, Agency for International Development, Novem-ber, 1968), pp. ix-x.

4. The concept of "culture shock," a mixture of metaphor and behavioral illustrations, has strong-ly influenced training in the Peace Corps, AID, and other organizations in the international field. See Kalervo Oberg, "Culture Shock and the Problem of Adjustment to New Cultural Environments" (unpublished manuscript). For an anthropological analysis of how the concept has been applied to Peace Corps training, see Thomas Maretzki, "Transition Training: A Theo-retical Approach," Human Organization, Vol. XXIV, No. 2 (Summer, 1965), pp. 128-34.

5. Robert K. Merton, Social Theory and Social Structure (rev. and enlarged ed.; Glencoe: The Free Press, 1957), p. 265.

6. A further distinction between Merton's con-ception and this adaptation of it needs to be made. His formulation involves a transfer of an individual's loyalties from one group to another. The manifest function of the process we have outlined is not to strip away a trainee's national loyalty and acquire him as a group member, i.e., U.S. citizen, but rather to shake the individual loose from his traditional preoccupations.

Many individuals in underdeveloped countries give lower priority to obligations to their nation, compared with those associated with kinship, ethnicity, caste, or community. Participant training is in part oriented to the broadening of trainees' commitments and ultimately to a closer identification with their nation. As a cooperative undertaking with other governments, it could hardly do otherwise. The predilection of sizable numbers of foreign students and visitors to extend their stay in the United States or to seek permanent residence has become a source of chagrin rather than satisfaction to the U.S. government. See Albert E. Gollin, ed., The International Migration of Talent and Skills: Proceedings of a Workshop and Conference (Washington, D.C.: Council on International Educational and Cultural Affairs, Department of State, October, 1966).

7. Preston, op. cit.

8. The most often-quoted reference on this point is Lester Coch and John R. P. French, "Overcoming Resistance to Change," Human Relations, Vol. I (1948), pp. 512-32. For a sour look at this tradition of research, see Clark Kerr and Lloyd H. Fisher, "Plant Sociology: The Elite and the Aborigines," in Mirra Komarovsky, ed., Common Frontiers of the Social Sciences (Glencoe: The Free Press and Falcon's Wing Press, 1957), pp. 281-308. Criticism has been made of the gospel of industrial democracy through worker participation which this research celebrates, because it overlooked the social setting within which participation was sought, i.e., non-union plants, retention of full managerial powers, low status of the workers, and so forth.

9. Just over half of the interviewed supervisors did not know the participants (about whom they were questioned) at the time of their selection.

10. For a discussion of the problem of interpreting causal sequences among variables whose time ordering is unclear or not ascertainable, see Patricia L. Kendall and Paul F. Lazarsfeld, "Problems of

Survey Analysis," in Robert K. Merton and Paul F.
Lazarsfeld, eds., <u>Continuities in Social Research:
Studies in the Scope and Method of "The American
Soldier"</u> (Glencoe: The Free Press, 1950), pp. 133-
96. Also see Herbert H. Hyman, <u>Survey Design and
Analysis</u> (Glencoe: The Free Press, 1955), pp. 275-
327, especially pp. 321-27.

11. Retrospective questions about a mood or
attitude which existed some years earlier yield
answers or judgments that are heavily influenced by
the passage of time; memories about such matters
fade or are inaccurately recollected. Answers may
also be subtly affected by one's current evaluations
of the experience or its consequences. Such questions cannot be treated analytically in the same way
as questions that tap current sentiments or that
deal with factual matters.

12. The Washington International Center was
founded in March, 1950, at the request of the U.S.
government, by the American Council on Education.
In July, 1961, the responsibility for its operations
was assumed by the Meridian House Foundation. Among
the earliest recipients of orientation programs were
German and Japanese visitors, sent to the United
States by the occupation authorities. Since 1950,
more than 100,000 visitors have participated in its
orientation programs, which usually last from three
to five days and include side trips to historic
sites.

13. Preston, <u>op. cit</u>.

CHAPTER **4** THE ANATOMY OF
TRAINING PROGRAMS

Having carried the participants up to the point
of their arrival for training, we turn now to an
analysis of their training programs. In the survey,
the training sojourn was broken up into a number of
elements which represented the dimensions along
which programs can vary. This analytical approach
necessarily fragments the experience as seen from
the perspective of those who underwent training. We
have formulated a capsule description which depicts
a program as an integral entity, to serve as a starting point for our analysis; its elements comprise
the structural and substantive dimensions on which
we have data.

At some point a participant was sent to a
training site, in the U.S. or in a third
country, where he spent a period of time
studying or working in some field closely
linked with his occupational specialty.
The program he took fell into one of several types; threaded around its educational ("technical") aspects was an assortment
of other ("nontechnical") activities,
which not only helped him to pass the time
more agreeably but were meant to give the
experience a deeper personal significance
and to promote mutual understanding.

Only the more broadly comparable aspects of the
participants' diversified experiences can be treated
in this analysis. Inevitably, at such a level much
interesting data are hidden from view; qualitative
information, which can be used to illustrate quantitative findings and lighten the somewhat severe

tone of analytical treatments of survey data, was
not available to us. (To ensure confidentiality,
interview schedules were kept in the files of each
U.S. Mission and then destroyed after a report was
written on the findings.) Our secondary analysis of
these survey materials must, therefore, be pursued
at a fairly general level. We will deal with each
of these dimensions in turn.

THE PARAMETERS OF TRAINING

In most of the countries in our survey, U.S.
technical-assistance programs were initiated in the
1950s. A few trainees came earlier, from several
Latin American countries during World War II, and
from Greece, Turkey, and Iran just prior to 1950.
For analytical purposes, we grouped the calendar
years of departure for training of these participants into four time periods, partly on the basis
of the number of trainees but also to highlight the
character of participant training during these relatively distinct periods in the history of U.S. technical assistance:[1]

Up to 1950. The period prior to the launching of programs of technical cooperation
and assistance under Point IV agreements--
founding of the first formal programs
through the Institute of Inter-American
Affairs (1942); aid to Greece and Turkey
(1947); establishment of the Economic Cooperation Administration to administer
the Marshall Plan (1948); President Harry
S. Truman's Inaugural statement of Point
IV concept (1949).

1951-54. A period of rapid gyrations in
the character of U.S. assistance programs--
creation of the Technical Cooperation Administration (1950) that marked the end
of the Marshall Plan; founding of the
Mutual Security Agency (1951), replaced
in turn by the Foreign Operations

Administration (1953) during the first
administration of President Dwight D.
Eisenhower. (Most of the bilateral
participant-training agreements with
the countries in this study were made
in this period.)

1955-58. A period of consolidation of
aid programs, with the formation of the
International Cooperation Administration
(1955); period also witnessed a further
expansion of assistance programs through
U.S. Operations Missions to newly independent nations of the underdeveloped
world; participant training reorganized
and new procedures established at the
start of this period.

1959-61. A period of transition to the
formation of the Agency for International
Development (1961); period chosen primarily to isolate ICA participants who had
left for training and returned closest to
the time that the study was conducted and
to provide a fourth point in time for the
analysis of trends.[2]

One could make use of data from the surveys to
trace the changing character of participant training
during its long history. These data are especially
valuable for the study of the pre-ICA period, since
records and statistics prior to 1955 were not com-
piled on a routine or standardized basis.[3] We have
followed another path, guided by our primary concern
with the consequences of training. The time dimension is used only when it illuminates a trend in the
data that is important for the interpretation of a
finding rather than for descriptive purposes.

In earlier sections, occasional references were
made to findings linked in some way with the participants' fields of training. Participant-training
programs are administratively classified into several dozen subspecialties of fewer than a dozen

principal "training fields of activity." Our cross-tabular analysis dealt with nine major (and one minor) training fields, each of which contained 1 per cent or more of the surveyed participants. Only six, however, were "major" in the cumulative numbers who have been trained: agriculture (27%), industry and mining (15%), education (14%), health and sanitation (12%), public administration (11%), and transportation and mass communications (10%). (Some of the special areas in the major training fields are shown in Table 4.1.)

This classification of training fields was originally developed for budgetary purposes, as a means of uniformly categorizing large-scale ICA assistance projects. Technical-training programs usually are only a minor component of these projects. Having been devised for a purpose other than the classification of the subject matter of training programs, this scheme is an imprecise tool for use in interpreting the survey data. Its categories are less specific in content than they might appear at first glance; some overlap with others to a considerable degree. They can be employed primarily as a means of defining the broad substantive contexts of the participants' programs; the precise subjects that they studied cannot always be clearly ascertained from these categories.

Two general considerations enter into the balance among the training fields shown in these and other AID aggregate statistics. One is changes in the distribution of participants over time. Proportions trained in each of these fields, influenced by changing emphases in U.S. assistance policies and by variations in supply and demand for certain kinds of training, have risen or fallen appreciably over the years. Programs in industry, public administration (especially public safety[4]), and labor have grown in volume; fields such as health have experienced a corresponding decline in relative terms, although the absolute numbers trained in it yearly may have remained about the same or even increased slightly (Table 4.2).

TABLE 4.1

The Distribution of Participants by
Training Fields (In Percentages)

Training Field	Number	Per Cent
Agriculture and natural resources 　Research, extension; crop and livestock; 　land and water resources; agriculture 　economics, etc.	5,043	26.5
Industry and mining 　Industrial management; power and communi- 　cations; manufacturing; mining and 　minerals, etc.	2,811	14.8
Education 　Professional; technical; elementary; 　vocational; etc.	2,692	14.2
Health and sanitation 　Health training and education; health fa- 　cilities; environmental sanitation, etc.	2,320	12.2
Public administration 　Public budgeting, finance; police adminis- 　tration; government organization, man- 　agement; statistics, etc.	2,093	11.0
Transportation and mass communications 　Air transport; highways; railways; mass 　communications	1,847	9.7
Labor 　Labor and trade union leadership; appren- 　ticeship training; legislation and wel- 　fare services	1,040	5.5
Community development, social welfare, and 　housing	432	2.3
Peaceful uses of atomic energy	259	1.4
Trade and investment	59	0.3
All other, miscellaneous	429	2.3
All participants	19,025	100.2

TABLE 4.2

Major Training Fields of Surveyed
Participants by Period of Departure,
and of all Non-European Participants
to 1967 (In Percentages)

Training Field	Period of Departure				Combined Total up to 1967[b]
	Up to 1950	1951- 1954	1955- 1958	1959- 1961	
Agriculture	17.3	33.0	25.3	24.4	20.0
Public administration	1.3	9.3	11.8	11.6	17.7
Industry and mining	6.2	14.6	13.1	20.7	16.4
Education	1.2	11.1	16.7	11.5	15.0
Health and sanitation	56.3	15.7	11.3	6.5	9.0
Labor	2.0	4.4	5.1	7.8	7.7
Transportation and communications	14.2	8.9	9.8	10.0	6.1
Community development	-- [a]	1.3	2.3	3.4	1.8
Atomic energy	--	-- [a]	1.9	1.2	1.4
All others, NA	1.0	1.5	2.8	3.0	5.0
Total Per Cent	99.9	99.9	100.0	100.1	100.1
(N)	(410)	(3,887)	(10,814)	(3,898)	(71,902)

[a]Less than .5 per cent.

[b]Europeans were excluded to render the data more comparable
to our survey data.

Source: Agency for International Development, Office of
International Training, Horizons Unlimited: A Statistical Report
on Participant Training: 10th Annual Edition (Washington, D.C.:
Statistical Control Branch, Agency for International Development,
November, 1968).

Differences in the distribution of each country's participants are another source of variation
within the over-all findings. Ideally, the allocation of a country's participants to various fields
of training should be based upon a preliminary survey of manpower needs and resources for development;
decisions should also reflect the priorities among
fields that have been established in a national economic plan. In the initial period of participant
training, this requirement would have amounted to a
counsel of perfection: National plans and manpower
assessments were rarely available as a basis for programing in non-European countries. Nor do we know
the extent to which they are being used more recently. There is reason to be skeptical, especially because evidence from the AID study cited earlier suggests that selection decisions continue to be made
without reference to comprehensive manpower development plans.[5] One would have to study the problem of
rationality in the allocation of participants on a
country-by-country basis; without systematic information on their manpower needs and priorities, we cannot explore this problem with the data at hand.

Since the program's initiation, the vast majority (82%) of participants have been sent to training
sites in the United States. American training facilities are more numerous and better known to the officials responsible for program development. Then,
too, organizational "know-how," an American inven-
tion in the eyes of most people, is best studied and
acquired at the source. And the program's political
objective of widely diffusing a greater understanding of U.S. institutions can be achieved more directly (though not invariably better) by a sojourn in
the United States.

These considerations do not always dictate the
choice of training sites: The personal needs and
circumstances of the individual and the resource
base of his nation must also be taken into account.
The gap between the social, educational, and occupational conditions in a trainee's country and in the
United States may be so wide that attempts to bridge

it in training can create stresses which leave him
disoriented, disaffected, and ultimately ineffective
upon his return. In some cases, U.S. techniques and
practices are inappropriate models for home-country
use because they require too heavy a capital investment, too many complementary facilities, or too high
a general level of technological sophistication.

Obviously, a training site which creates problems or erects barriers to learning or to utilization by trainees upon their return home should be
avoided. In recognition of this fact, training programs were subsequently offered at third-country
sites[6] where educational facilities were adequate,
where social conditions were more congenial to the
learning of pertinent work skills, and where participants were at the same time offered opportunities
for an exposure to modernizing principles, techniques, and social norms. There is a continuing debate over the relative worth of an investment in
training participants in these settings, compared
to U.S. sites or to institutions in their own countries. (This was one of the issues toward which the
AID evaluation study was specifically oriented.)
Among the surveyed participants who were trained
prior to 1950, all came to the United States. Since
1955, only about three quarters have taken most of
their training in the United States. The ratio of
3:1 between U.S.- and third-country-trained participants has held fairly steady since 1960.[7]

The relevant data on where training was taken
were recorded in a rather unwieldy fashion; countries were classified as primary, secondary, and
tertiary training sites according to the length of
time each trainee spent in them. We have reduced
the large number of site patterns in the careers of
participants by classifying each trainee's program
in two ways: Was it in one country or more than one?
Was it solely or primarily in the United States or
in another country?[8] The resulting patterns were
finally reduced to five broad categories:

1. Mainland U.S. sites only. This was by far
the most prevalent pattern of training. Almost three

out of four (73%) participants are included in it.
By sheer weight of numbers, it set the standard for
the entire sample in the character of its participants, programs, and evaluations of its training.

2. Mainland U.S. sites primarily. This was
the second most prevalent pattern of training; one
in ten (10%) spent a brief period of time elsewhere,
usually after completion of the major stay in the
United States. Participants in this category are
almost always indistinguishable from those in the
preceding group in terms of their programs and evaluations; for analytical purposes, the two groups
will often be combined.

3. Offshore U.S. sites only. This phrase has
been adopted to cover a group of sites in former and
current territories, such as Puerto Rico, Hawaii,
Canal Zone, Alaska, Virgin Islands, and so forth.
Almost 3 per cent were trained there. Frequently we
treat Puerto Rico separately, because more trainees
were trained there alone than in most other third
countries.

4. Other third-country sites only. This group
of countries accounts for about one in ten of the
returned participants. They are further separated,
in later analysis, into countries with sizable numbers of past trainees--Lebanon (3.5%), Japan, Philippines, and Taiwan--and "all other" countries used as
sole sites for participant training.

5. All other patterns of site selection. Included here are a small number of trainees who received most of their training elsewhere but also
spent very brief periods in the United States, and
those who were trained in two (or more) countries
other than the above-specified major sites. This
catch-all category accounts for less than 4 per cent
of the participants; as could be expected, their programs were extremely diverse in character.

Among the countries that entered the survey,
all but four small ones sent a majority of their
trainees to the United States mainland for their

primary-training stay. At the other extreme, countries such as Turkey, Greece, and Egypt sent almost
all solely to the United States. For the four whose
trainees mainly went elsewhere and for others as
well, training centers in their immediate region
served as alternate sites. (We will treat Puerto
Rico as a third country in this context.) For example, most of the trainees sent to Taiwan came from
Vietnam, while a majority of those sent to Japan for
their primary-training stay came from Taiwan. The
Far Eastern nations seem to have served as a series
of stepping stones for each others' participants,
sending and receiving them in accordance with their
value as demonstration models in certain training
fields. Taiwan's strong areas appeared to be transportation and agriculture, Japan's was agriculture,
and the Philippines' were education and community
development.

In the Middle East, Lebanon (The American University of Beirut, principally) was the chief alternative to the United States for training; it served
in this role for many participants from Ethiopia,
Jordan, Pakistan, and Morocco and offered programs
in health and sanitation and in education relatively
more often than other alternate sites. Puerto Rico
was a strong alternative as a sole- or primary-
training site for participants from Latin America,
in particular for those from the nations of Central
America and the Caribbean. Among its more prominent
fields of training were education, industry and mining, and labor.

Many of the persistent problems in the education of foreign students faced by this training program and, more generally, by U.S. academic institu-
tions--their poor language skills, need for orientation and special counseling, the difficulty of
evaluating their academic records to place them
properly--could be minimized by a reduction in the
flow of students and trainees who seek entry or are
sent for training to the United States. Given the
program's subsidiary objective of promoting greater
understanding of U.S. policies and institutions, it

is unlikely that a trip here will cease to be the
core experience for a great majority of participants,
even if (as is equally unlikely) equivalent technical training could be offered to them elsewhere with
U.S. financial support.

Training programs offered over the years have differed widely; a few types of programs, used fairly consistently, served as a basis for our analysis. Each
participant was offered the following set of definitions prior to being asked about his own program:

> Now I'd like to ask you about your actual
> training program. There are several kinds
> of things that participants do in their
> training, and I'd like you to tell me
> which kinds you did in your program.
> There are observation tours which usually
> last between three and eight weeks; there
> is on-the-job training where the partici-
> pant has actual work experience; there is
> attendance at a university; and there are
> programs designed especially for groups
> of participants, not at a university and
> not observation tours.
> Was any of your time spent on an
> observation tour? In on-the-job train-
> ing? In attendance as an individual or
> a member of a group? In a special group
> program not at a university?[9]

The observation tour has been by far the most
widely used type of training: Seven out of ten
(71%) participants went on some version of one, as
individuals or in groups or teams. University
studies was the type cited next most often, by over
one half (52%) of the trainees. (As we will see,
the university served and continues to serve more
often as a locus for training than as a distinct
type: Fewer than one half were enrolled as regular
students.) Opportunities for on-the-job-training,
involving placement in work settings within private
industry, governmental agencies, or other organizations and associations, were provided to more than

two fifths (42%) of the trainees. And finally, a
small proportion of participants (21%) made the
special-group character of their program the central
element in describing it.[10]

The amount of time trainees actually spent in
each of these program types varied considerably. In
general, observation tours and programs devised for
special groups or teams were the shortest; only relatively small proportions spent as much as four months
in them. On-the-job training typically ran for somewhat
longer periods, although one half of these programs
lasted less than four months. Most of those sent to
academic settings for training spent the equivalent
of between one and four semesters on course work or
study (longer when participants were regularly enrolled students than otherwise).

One important determinant of the length of
training programs of each type was whether or not a
participant's program was comprised of more than one
type. A majority of trainees (55%) had programs
which combined two or more types. The time spent on
each type in a program consisting of one solely was
invariably longer than if that type were an element
of a "mixed" program.

A Typology of Training Programs

In order to gauge the relative merits of each
formal type, both in isolation and in combination,
we developed a program typology. Evaluations of
training could then be related more clearly to the
structure of the program being discussed. Each participant's description of the character of his program served as a basis for locating it in this
typology. Its categories and the number of trainees
whose programs were included in each are shown in
Table 4.3.

Over the years, the number who took programs
composed of two or more types declined; of the pre-
1951 trainees, 62 per cent had such programs as

TABLE 4.3

Typology of Training Programs and the
Distribution of Participants in Each

Typology of Programs[a]	Participants	
	Number	Per Cent
Observation only	4,180	22.0
University and observation	4,000	21.0
University, OJT, and observation	2,676	14.1
OJT and observation	2,616	13.7
University only	2,151	11.3
OJT only	1,664	8.7
University and OJT	1,146	6.0
Special (nonuniversity) group only[b]	592	3.1
Total	19,025	99.9

[a]Observation tour = "Observation"; On-job training = "OJT"; University studies = "University."

[b]This category includes 52 participants not
elsewhere classified. Participants who had special-
group programs combined with other types are included
in the observation tour and university studies categories.

opposed to 45 per cent of those sent more recently.
The decline was associated with a sharp increase
during the 1950s in the use of observation tours
solely, to meet the growing demand for training
within the limits of available resources.

Earlier we noted that the educational level of
selectees has been declining. These two trends may
be interrelated: In developing programs, one must
start "where the trainees are," and more intensive
or longer programs of training make greater demands
upon prior skills and knowledge. Less well-educated
selectees have to be programed differently from
those holding degrees; e.g., university graduates
were far more likely than others to have received
university-based training and were more likely to
have been enrolled in degree programs.

Other patterned differences in the use of these
program types were related to a cluster of participant attributes. The oldest trainees, those with
the most work experience and, especially, those holding the highest-status jobs, more often went solely
on observation tours. Longer, more complex programs
were (and are) scheduled less often for them, because they lack the time or because the primarily
administrative character of their work renders practical training or academic studies less relevant.
Conversely, the youngest and least-experienced trainees more often entered some sort of university program, as did scientists and others of professional
status. Engineers and technicians more often took
practical, on-job training.

Training sites were differentiated in the types
of programs offered. Puerto Rico, for example, was
often used to give trainees practical, on-job experience; university studies also appeared with some
frequency among their offerings. The main third-
country sites in the Far East were used heavily or
almost exclusively for observation tours or on-job
training. Lebanon and the U.S. mainland were the
sites for most of the programs that were wholly or
in major part university based. Each of the third-

country sites seems to be limited and specialized in
fields and types of programs. Training in the United
States, on the other hand, runs the gamut of programing possibilities, a fact that severely limits analysis of the issue of the relative merits of the United
States and third countries. They are not interchangeable program options, judging from these participants'
training careers.

The main fields of training display contrasting
mixtures of program types. Those which are of a more
technical or professional character generally show
a more diversified program structure that usually
has university training at its core. Thus, programs
in atomic energy, education, agriculture, and health
were distinguished by one or more of these hallmarks:
heavy use of universities, lesser reliance on observation tours, more programs of the mixed type. Conversely, trainees in fields such as community development or labor had programs that made greater use
of observation tours and far less use of university
settings.

UNIVERSITY STUDIES: A SPECIAL CASE

The impressive growth in the numbers of foreign
students on U.S. campuses, stimulated only in small
measure by governmental exchange programs, is a postwar phenomenon that has provoked much study and debate. Although participant training has not figured
prominently in this development, because its academ-
ically based programs were shorter term and more
specialized, its participants and cooperating institutions share some of the focal problems of these
investigations.[11] Initially, discussions and
research on "the foreign-student problem" were concerned mainly with such issues as problems of personal adjustment or favorable attitudes toward the
United States.[12] More recently, perhaps as a reaction to the increasingly close ties between the U.S.
government and universities in international education, the debate has centered around broader institutional and normative issues: the proper role of

universities in foreign programs (and vice versa),
the maintenance of scholarly standards and purposes,
the place of foreign-student training within the
total educational mission of the university, the
value of foreign vs. local education, the institutional and policy implications of nonreturning students, and so on.[13]

University studies have been shown to be one of
the two main building blocks of participant training,
whether used alone or, more frequently, as the principal element in a mixed program. An appraisal of
trainees' reactions to this type of training and its
consequences has significant implications for both
AID and the academic community. For AID, university
training is perhaps an inherently riskier or more
speculative venture: It requires a relatively greater per capita expenditure of trainee time and agency
money; it is less directly controlled by AID officials; and it can give rise, in boomerang fashion,
to trainee discontent arising from "degree-minded-
ness." What have been the experiences of trainees
who have confronted, usually for fairly extensive
periods, the complex challenges and lures of the
more permissive U.S. academic environment? How do
they react to the possibility of gaining a degree,
with its prestige or market value, as a tangible
symbol of their stay abroad, a prospect which is
raised most sharply by this training context? How
do they evaluate their academic sojourn, and how
pervasive is their interest in degrees, gotten or
foregone, as a goal or end product of training?
Answers to these questions form the subject matter
of this section, after a review of a few basic facts
about university training.

Earlier we saw that 52 per cent of all participants spent some time in university training, usually for six to twelve months; they spent more time
when enrolled as regular students and much shorter
periods if they were special students or members of
a group program. Almost four in five (78%) went to
one institution; an additional 15 per cent spent
time at two; and the rest went to more than two

colleges in the course of their training. Although
over 250 universities and colleges were mentioned,
during the years covered by the survey, 24--a relative handful in the United States, together with the
University of Puerto Rico and The American University of Beirut--accounted for a majority (51%) of
all who were sent for university training. Statistics for 1964-65 show a similar concentration, although different institutions are involved. Out of
almost 300 institutions, 27 accounted for more than
47 per cent of all AID-sponsored university trainees.[14]

Most of the more prominent training centers are
part of the land-grant college and state university
network, whose explicit goals of public service permit them to maintain greater institutional flexibility in fitting novel training programs into their
curricula and schedules. Course offerings often are
closely attuned to the practical or applied aspects
of given subject-matter areas; a large number of
self-sponsored foreign students are already on cam-
pus in most cases. Their size, the diversity of
their student body, special educational or tactical
advantages that might inhere in certain geographic
locations, and previous experience with programs of
international assistance and exchange are the major
factors that account for their great prominence as
sites for training.

Regular and Special Students

Trainees were sent to universities as regularly
enrolled students or in some special, nonacademic
status, often as members of a group program; two
fifths (42%) fell into the first category. This
distinction is a crucial one, because it bears on
the chances of earning a degree while in training.
Some participant attributes were closely related
with student status. For example, the younger the
trainee was when selected, the more likely was he
to have gone to a university and to have attended
as a regular student. Those who already held a
university-level degree were more likely to have

been sent as regular (graduate) students than those
who were less well educated. A program's structure
was also correlated with this status distinction:
Three fifths of trainees whose programs were taken
solely at a university were regular students, compared with about one third who went to one as part
of a composite type of program. The duration of
training was, therefore, also necessarily related
with student status: The university programs enroll-
ing the greatest number of regular students had the
longest duration, as Table 4.4 indicates.

TABLE 4.4

Proportion of University-Trained
Participants Who Were Regular Students
and Median Duration of Training
by Program Type

Typology of Programs[a]	Regular Students (Per Cent)	Median Duration (Months)
University only	59	16.9
University and OJT	40	13.8
University, OJT, and observation	37	11.8
University and observation	37	11.6

[a]This table is restricted to participants whose
programs consisted solely or in large part of university studies; the numbers in each category are
given in Table 4.3.

The main significance of the distinction lies
in the larger proportion of regularly enrolled students who returned home with a degree as an end product of training. Just over one quarter (26%) of
those sent on university programs (13 per cent of
all surveyed participants) earned a degree in training. But more than one half (52%) of those who were
regular students did so, compared with only 6 per
cent of other university-trained participants. Most
degrees whose character was ascertained were at the
advanced (M.A.) level, a preponderance that is true
of more recent trainees as well. The relatively
tight administrative control over the process of
acquiring a degree in training which has been exerted
in the past is reflected by the fact that five sixths
of all the degrees were earned by trainees deliberately enrolled as regular students. There seems to
have been little slippage from the more limited objectives of most university training programs toward
the individual pursuit of a degree, unless it was
originally planned as an end product of the university stay.

A lesser token of a period of training at a
university was the award of a nonacademic certifi-
cate or formal citation. About one third of university trainees received one. Adding this to the
proportion who earned degrees further emphasizes
the difference between regular and special-student
status. For, while less than one quarter (23%) of
the former went home empty-handed, almost twice as
many of the latter (43%) did so.

These findings help to bring into sharper focus
the two main patterns of relationship between participant training and the universities. In one, individual foreign nationals are sent to a university
and supported by the U.S. aid program but are otherwise on their own; for them, the university can play
its traditional role of transmitting knowledge and
bestowing degrees as symbols of successful status
passage. In the other, the university serves mainly
as a setting or facility for limited programs of
instruction. Does this contextual difference in the

functions served by university-based programs have
any impact on the trainees' opinions as to the worth
of a degree? How helpful do they believe a degree
is, or might have been, as an end product of training, and in what ways?

Career Value of a Degree

Those whose programs included any university
studies were asked about the effects of a degree on
their future careers. If they had earned one, they
were asked about its future impact; if they hadn't,
they were asked what its effect would have been.
Both groups were also asked to give reasons for
their expressed beliefs.[15] As expected, most of the
trainees evaluated the impact of a degree upon their
career in very favorable terms. Two thirds or more
of those who attended a university during training
saw at least some career benefits accruing to themselves. Their degree of certitude depended upon the
context of their program, that is, whether they had
been regular or special students. Among special
students, whether they earned a degree or not made
little difference in their views, but among regular
students, those who ended training in possession of
an earned degree were far more enthusiastic than
others about its likely impact on their careers
(Table 4.5).

Prior educational achievements also affected
trainee attitudes to some extent. While all university trainees were generally enthusiastic, the two
groups with even more positive views on the career-
enhancing effects of a degree were those who already
held one and those who had never attended a university. For the former, the advanced degree that participant training enabled them to earn represented a
welcome means of augmenting an already high level of
achieved competence and status, while for the latter
the degree that training may have permitted them to
acquire opened a range of opportunities that might
otherwise have bypassed them entirely.

TABLE 4.5

Career Value of a Degree for University-
Trained Participants by Their Student Status
and Receipt of a Degree in Training
(In Percentages)

| Career Value of a Degree[a] | Regular Student | | Special Student | | |
	Earned Degree	No Degree	Earned Degree	No Degree	Total
Very helpful	72	58	46	48	57
Somewhat helpful	19	16	25	18	18
Not at all helpful	6	20	23	26	19
Don't know	3	6	6	8	6
Total Per Cent[b]	100	100	100	100	100
(N)	(2,183)	(1,844)	(318)	(3,749)	(8,094)

[a]Degree recipients: "Do you think the degree will help . . . ?"; nonrecipients: "Do you think a degree would have helped . . . ?"

[b]This table excludes those who were NA in each student/degree category and those sent on special-group programs at a university (N = 1,846).

111

But a degree was so generally seen as exerting a favorable influence upon careers that closer analysis failed to reveal other significant variations among trainees. We believe that if the large number of participants not trained at universities had also been asked these questions, they would have been no less positive in their evaluations than, for example, special students who did not earn a degree. The reasons given by university trainees for their judgments were of essentially the same character, whether they had earned a degree or not. (Those who had not were slightly less voluble or more dubious.) Of all the career contributions a degree was seen as making, three stood out in particular: The resulting gain in personal capacity (knowledge, ability, self-confidence), or in social or professional prestige, or in the heightened chances for gaining a better job.

One inference from these data is that greater trainee satisfaction can be achieved by offering more participants the prospect of earning a degree at the end of their training. But an increased emphasis upon training programs which lead to a degree can be dysfunctional for the development projects and schemes which participant training is meant to serve. The great virtue of a degree program to a participant is its chief defect in the eyes of the development planner: It tends to enhance measurably the returned participant's potential for occupational mobility.

The lasting value of such a program accrues to the person who earns the degree, whatever the original intention of his sponsors. And unless his post-training job placement is appropriate in the trainee's eyes, or his mobility is rigidly controlled, for example by some contractual obligation to serve in a specific job for a defined period of time, the resulting temptation to seek out other opportunities which a foreign degree makes possible may be too great to resist. In recognition of this possibility, a requirement is now written into each selectee's training agreement that he obligate himself to serve

for a certain period after his return; how many participants actually honor or keep this obligation is
unknown.   It is in this connection that we point out
that the net balance of consequences of degree programs can be negative for the production or use of
high-level skills needed for national development.[16]

    We will analyze data on occupational mobility,
its relation to earned degrees, and the consequences
of both facts in succeeding chapters.   Foreign study
and the earning of a degree have functions other
than occupational mobility.   They represent one link
in a chain of geographic mobility whose net effects
have been described as the "nonreturning foreign
student" problem and the problem of the "brain drain."
The magnetic attraction exerted upon foreign students by a sojourn in an advanced industrial society
and the limited opportunities to make progress in
their careers or to exercise their talents and skills
in their own countries lead increasing numbers to
prolong their stays abroad and to seek permanent
residence.   There is a remigration (internal and
external) problem too; the sense of futility arising
from poor placement after training or impatience at
the slow pace of acceptance of their modernizing
initiatives are two reactions which can lead a returned trainee to give up or lower the felt priority
of the societal goals for which training was undertaken and to replace them with the pursuit of his
personal interests.[17]

    Many points of contrast among the various types
of training programs are reflected in or intrinsically related to differences in their over-all length.
The duration of a program is a crucial determinant
of the impacts that training can have, not only on
skills and knowledge but also on a participant's
beliefs and values.   The focus of the surveys of
returned participants was upon the former class of
effects; but it is worth noting that a trainee's
sense of commitment to an occupation or development
task or his determination or motivation to persist
in efforts to use his skills are necessary prerequisites for the effective utilization of his training.

And in this attitudinal realm, the duration of the sojourn plays an important role, because it sets limits upon the chances that such effects will occur.

Our final dimension is the duration of training programs. A few substantive propositions can be developed about the relationships that can exist between the duration of training programs and re-socialization--the shaping of attitudes or values. University training, for example, being invariably much longer, is also less forced in pace; personal contacts between the visitor and citizens of his training country (mainly the United States) are likely to be freer and thus ultimately more influential in forming attitudes toward the United States and friendly or productive personal ties.[18] By comparison, an observation tour runs a greater risk of superficiality in the treatment of subject matter and may also engender in its participants a somewhat corrosive set of irritations resulting from having to cope with the problems associated with a great deal of travel in a brief time span.

And even if immediately exhilarating, the net effect of tours may not be long lasting. Personal contacts of a social or professional character are more likely to be rather formal or even ritualistic; time pressures and the status of touring trainees as "visiting firemen" are factors that provide for fewer and less mutually productive encounters.[19] We will review some data to test these propositions shortly; they are used here primarily to illustrate a few potentially significant implications of a program's duration, the most important of which is the greater leverage for changes in attitudes that longer programs seem to afford.

The measure of a program's duration was derived from answers to questions about the total time each trainee spent abroad. Thus, it includes the time he spent in orientation sessions or other special features of his program experience in addition to its substantive part. But the structural type of the program was the controlling element in its over-all

length, and all of the previously analyzed correlates of the major program types are, therefore,
related to the duration of training. Participants
were about equally divided into three groups: Those
sent on programs which lasted less than six months
(33%), between six and twelve months (32%), and
those whose programs took one year or longer to complete (34%). At one extreme, only 3 per cent were
in training longer than two years, while at the
other, 9 per cent spent less than two months abroad
as participants. The sharpest contrast, as expected,
is between those who went solely on an observation
or group tour and those sent for other types of
training, especially university studies. The median
program duration for the former was one third as
long as the median length of nine months for the
entire group of participants.

NOTES

1. The periodization of the history of U.S.
educational-assistance programs has been done in a
variety of ways. See, for example, Charles A.
Thomson and Walter H. C. Laves, Cultural Relations
and U.S. Foreign Policy (Bloomington: Indiana University Press, 1963), Part I; also see John P.
Powelson, "Educational Assistance, Economic Development and United States Foreign Policy," in Don C.
Piper and Taylor Cole, eds., Post-Primary Education
and Political and Economic Development (Durham:
Duke University Press, 1964), pp. 136-44; and
Francis J. Colligan, Twenty Years After: Two Dec-
ades of Government-Sponsored Cultural Relations,
Department of State Publication 6689 (Washington,
D.C.: U.S. Government Printing Office, 1958).

2. While three quarters of the participants
had been interviewed by the end of 1961 (and all had
returned by then), only 1 per cent actually departed
in that year. (The cut-off date initially aimed for
in the survey was the end of FY 1960.)

3.   One limiting factor in the use of these
survey materials for historical purposes is that
they exclude data on participants from European
countries, who comprise 20 per cent of all former
participants as of 1968, and on participants from
a few Latin American countries. Among those for
whom we have data, the number of countries represented in the earliest time period affects the gen-
erality of statements about trends. Participants
from only five countries are included in the period
up to 1950:   Brazil, Chile, Ecuador, Greece, and
Turkey. Data on participants from twenty countries
are combined in the 1951-54 period, and on participants from all twenty-three in the two subsequent
periods.

4.   The field of public safety, a euphemism for
police and internal security forces, has blossomed
in recent years, and statistics are now kept on it
separately. The total number trained in it is about
one third of all those in public administration
among U.S. arrivals since 1943. See AID's Horizons
Unlimited: A Statistical Report on Participant
Training: 10th Annual Edition (Washington, D.C.:
Statistical Control Branch, Agency for International
Development, November, 1968), p. 11.

5.   See Harley O. Preston, Operations of the
Participant Training Program of the Agency for Inter-
national Development (Washington, D.C.: Office of
International Training, AID, November, 1966), pp.
30-34. On the general scarcity and variable quality
of manpower surveys of developing countries, see
Frederick Harbison and Charles A. Myers, Education,
Manpower and Economic Growth: Strategies of Human
Resource Development (New York: McGraw-Hill Book
Company, 1964), pp. 24-26.

6.   In AID parlance, the host country is the
"first," the United States is the "second," and any
other place is the "third country" for training.

7.   More recently, partly as a result of the
furor over the brain-drain issue, AID's policy

statements stress the fact that U.S. training is used only where local or third-country facilities are not available or adequate; see its annual report, Horizons Unlimited, op. cit., pp. xi-xii.

8.   The distinction between primary (or sole) and secondary training sites requires further comment. A large majority of participants go on programs that take place solely in one country; in this survey, seven out of eight spent all their time in one country. An additional 8 per cent went to one country primarily but also spent a lesser period of time in another. Only 5 per cent visited three or more countries, for successively briefer periods. Sojourns in only one country usually lasted longer than two months, while stays in additional countries were usually for less than two months. Therefore, even for those trained in more than one country, our classification of their training site was made on the basis of the primary country.

9.   Participant interview schedule (Form A): question #55. Participants' programs have been so diverse that even this carefully worded statement failed to preclude ambiguity or misunderstandings in their responses, particularly among trainees who went on brief programs or as members of a group. Time lags and the perils of translation of this statement into many languages also created additional problems in assessing their replies.

10.   This last category is ambiguous and residual in character: It laid primary stress upon what training was not, rather than what it was. Much confusion between it and observation tours or group programs was discovered; as a result, we dropped it as an analytical category.

11.   This similarity was strongly confirmed in a set of interviews with staff and administrators at some of the universities and training facilities in the United States on the operation of the program. See Robert D. Dugan et al., A Pilot Study of Participant Training in the United States (Washington, D.C.: Institute for International Services, 1963).

12. The studies of this "problem" are quite
numerous. In the 1950s, the Social Science Research
Council supported a set of seven studies, the last
of which tried to synthesize the disparate findings
and points of view in the series. It also added new
findings to the swelling body of research on this
captive (and fortunately compliant) population. See
Claire Selltiz et al., Attitudes and Social Relations
of Foreign Students in the United States (Minneapolis:
University of Minnesota Press, 1963). Ithiel de Sola
Pool has reviewed these and other studies, looking
with little success for empirical generalizations;
see his "Effects of Cross-National Contact on National and International Images," in Herbert C. Kelman,
ed., International Behavior (New York: Holt, Rinehart and Winston, 1965), pp. 106-29. More recently,
Barbara J. Walton has done a critical survey of this
genre of studies that is broad in coverage and informed by a close association with this area for
many years; see her Foreign Student Exchange in Perspective: Research on Foreign Students in the
United States, Department of State, Publication 8373
(Washington, D.C.: U.S. Government Printing Office,
September, 1967). All three works cited here contain large bibliographies; other references are
given in the one appended to this book.

13. A useful compendium of papers and reports
on this complex of issues was published as part of
the legislative thrust for the still-unfunded International Education Act. See U.S. Congress, House,
Committee on Education and Labor, International Education: Past, Present, Problems and Prospects, 89th
Congress, 2nd Session, House Document No. 527 (Washington, D.C.: U.S. Government Printing Office,
1966); other pertinent references appear in Notes
to Chapter I and Chapter II of this book.

14. These data are reported in a paper written
for a conference of social scientists on the participant training program; see Forrest G. Moore, The
Collegiate Environment: The Experience and Reactions
of Foreign Students, Government-Sponsored and Self-
Sponsored, Background Paper for a Conference on

Non-Technical Aspects of Participant Training (Minneapolis, Minn.: Office of the Foreign Student
Advisor, University of Minnesota, October 11, 1965),
pp. 81-84.

15. Unfortunately and inexplicably, those who
did not attend a university as part of their training program were not asked this set of questions.
The opinions on a degree's career impact of this
strategic group of participants are, therefore, not
available for comparative purposes.

16. The injunction that the consequences of an
item are multiple and that their net balance must be
assessed before inputing its positive or negative
contributions to a social system is a tenet of Robert
K. Merton's functional paradigm; see his Social
Theory and Social Structure (rev. and enlarged ed.;
Glencoe: The Free Press, 1957), p. 51. Philip J.
Foster has made essentially the same point in an
essay on education and manpower development: "It
must be recognized that wherever technical education
is given largely in institutions which are part of
the formal educational structure, the expectations
of the students may pervert the intentions of the
planners." See his "The Vocational School Fallacy
in Development Planning," in C. Arnold Anderson and
Mary Jean Bowman, eds., Education and Economic Development (Chicago: Aldine Publishing Co., 1965), pp.
142-66.

17. In addition to earlier citations on the
brain-drain issue, see Herbert G. Grubel, "The Brain
Drain: A U.S. Dilemma," Science, Vol. XLIV, No.
3755 (December 16, 1966), pp. 1420-24; American
Council on Education, "International Migration of
Intellectual Talent," Bulletin on International Education, Vol. IV, No. 10 (November 17, 1966), pp. 1-8;
and two articles that are a reply to Grubel's econo-
mistic, optimistic position: John C. Shearer, "In
Defense of Traditional Views of the 'Brain Drain'
Problem," and Paul Ritterband, "Toward an Assessment
of the Costs and Benefits of Study Abroad," both in
International Educational and Cultural Exchange

(Fall, 1966), pp. 17-25, 26-35. For a work which
places the brain drain in the context of general
migration, see Edward P. Hutchison, ed., "The New
Immigration," Annals of the American Academy of
Political and Social Science, Vol. CCCLXVII (September, 1966). A valuable methodological discussion
can be found in Robert G. Myers, "Brain Drains and
Brain Gains," International Development Review, Vol.
IX, No. 4 (December, 1967), pp. 4-9.

18. This seems to be a general finding of the
research on foreign students. See Richard T. Morris,
The Two-Way Mirror: National Status in Foreign Students' Adjustment (Minneapolis: University of Minnesota Press, 1960); Selltiz et al., op. cit. The
difficulties of fitting outsiders into settled
social systems, even if they stay for a relatively
long time and have roles that are institutionally
well defined, are illustrated by the case of the
visiting foreign scholar; see Renate Mayntz, "The
Visiting Fellow: An Analysis of an Academic Role,"
American Sociological Review, Vol. XXV, No. 5 (October, 1960), pp. 735-41.

19. This point was stressed repeatedly by people at stop-over locations for AID observation tours.
See Jane Bristol and Robert D. Dugan, A Pilot Study
of Participant Training in the United States--Execu-
tive Report (Washington, D.C.: Institute for International Services, June, 1963), p. 27 passim. Also
on this point see Department of State, Agency for
International Development, Training for Leadership
and Service, Proceedings of the National Conference
on the International Training Programs of AID, June
25-26, 1962, pp. 49-64.

CHAPTER **5** EVALUATIONS OF
TRAINING: THREE
PERSPECTIVES

    The program objectives that have emerged in the
evolution of participant training are usually classified into two sets, termed "technical" and "nontechnical." The former has to do with how effectively
the process of equipping individuals with skills
needed for national development has been carried out.
Data in the survey related to this goal deal with a
number of specific aspects of a program--its type,
level, language needs, and duration--that bear most
directly on the issue of its quality. The second
set of objectives, by comparison, are more diffuse;
they include the modification of attitudes and motivations, as well as effecting a satisfactory cross-
cultural adjustment. Much of this falls under the
concept discussed earlier, the resocialization of
trainees.

    The survey produced a good deal of materials
related to the program's technical objectives, but
very little with a direct bearing on the nontechnical ones, and nothing at all on attitudinal side
effects. The agency's primary interest in gathering
data on the quality of training and its uses, and
its concern not to trip over politically sensitive
issues,[1] led to the inclusion of questions that dealt
only with those nontechnical aspects most closely
related to substantive issues of training programs.
The evaluative judgments of participants, both specific and general in nature, on aspects of their
training, form a sort of "consumer's perspective" on
their experiences; some of these have already been
described. As a second, independent source of data,
the former trainees' work supervisors (whenever it

proved feasible) were asked for evaluations of the
training their subordinates took. A third perspective is provided by the views elicited from a smaller number of AID program officers and technicians in
a position to assess the quality and outcome of the
training of individual participants. Evaluations
made by all three of these groups form the basis for
this chapter. They provide insights into the operations and impacts of the program and set the stage
for our analysis of its consequences.

TRAINING AS SEEN BY PARTICIPANTS

Technical Aspects

Participants' views on the technical aspects of
their programs were tapped directly and indirectly
in the interview. They were asked if they had been
"required to do or see too many different things."
Behind this question about what might be called the
variety of training was a concern over the focus and
pace of the various program types, especially the
observation or group tour. Had too much or too little variety been introduced into the programing of
training? Just over one half (51%) were satisfied,
30 per cent would have preferred still more activities, while 19 per cent felt they had seen and done
too much.

This ratio of approximately 5:3:2 varied little
among subgroups of participants, with one understand-
able exception: Those sent on observation or group
tours complained more often of an excess of activities. But, while the variety of their programs was
second only to the duration of training in evoking
trainees' disapproval, little of any consequence
seemed to flow from this fact. Those who disapproved
in either direction were only marginally less satisfied with the general value of training and made only
slightly less extensive use of it upon their return
than the group who felt their program's variety was
satisfactory.

The <u>level</u> of the training taken by foreign students and trainees has often been a source of personal difficulty and institutional concern. In part, difficulties encountered by them arise from faulty selection and placement or the poor quality of their prior education and preparation for training. But a more basic issue is involved in a claim that is sometimes made, that specialized or technical training in economically developed countries is <u>inevitably</u> conducted at too advanced a level, that it is overly complex or ill suited to the conditions with which students must ultimately contend, leaving them "fit in an unfit fitness."[2] In this sense, the level of training must be judged as appropriate both in terms of its suitability for the work context of the returned student and its relation to his prior education and experience.

Participants were asked about the level of their program; four in five felt it had been "about right," 14 per cent thought training had been conducted at "too simple" a level, and 6 per cent felt it had been "too advanced" for them. Differences among trainee groups are relatively minor but instructive. For example, those trained at most third-country sites (whose programs were shorter) were appreciably more often critical of the level of their training, claiming it was too simple, than were those trained in the United States or Lebanon. Conversely, almost all those in training for three or more years were satisfied with the level at which training was conducted. One can infer from these findings that judgments about a program's level were affected by its specific locale (i.e., at a university) and consequences (i.e., gaining a degree) as well as by its quality.

Of all the dimensions of training programs whose quality participants were asked to evaluate, the <u>duration</u> of their training was the one most often criticized. Less than one half (47%) thought it had been "about right" in length; of the rest, almost all thought it had been "too short." More refined analysis showed this to have been a very general

reaction among trainees; with the sole exception of
a small number who had spent three or more years in
training, between 50 and 57 per cent were dissatisfied with the length of their training program,
whether it had actually lasted two months, twelve
months, or two years.

When the preferences of these dissatisfied
trainees are examined in the light of the length of
their own training programs, the resulting pattern
can be fairly succinctly expressed: The more they
got, the more they wanted. Closer analysis leads
one to infer that the better prospect it offered for
earning a degree was the main although not the sole
underlying cause of uniform preference for a longer
program. Comparisons of groups with successively
longer programs show that they expressed desires for
correspondingly longer periods of training, amounts
of time that would have put the earning of a degree
well within reach (Table 5.1). In a few cases, the
desire to gain practical work experience was at the
root of their dissatisfaction. But because the demand for longer training was especially strongly
voiced by shorter-term university trainees, those in
the setting and type of program where the hope of
earning a degree is most easily acquired by participants (or fanned higher, if they already had the
hope), it seems fair to infer that a good deal of
dissatisfaction arose from disappointment over foregone chances of earning a degree. One can note,
parenthetically, that the small group (4.3%) who
felt training was too long were of course expressing
another, perhaps more damning form of criticism.

The "language problem," a recurring theme in
discussions of cross-cultural education or exchange,
is also an issue in participant training. Painful
difficulties arise for students or trainees sent on
programs that require facility in the use of English.
These problems can be handled administratively by a
choice among several available strategies. First,
and ideally, one can select only those candidates
who are able to demonstrate, by tests or otherwise,
that their command of English is adequate to their

TABLE 5.1

Desired Length of Training Program and
Actual Duration of Dissatisfied Participants
(In Percentages)

Desired Length of Training	Actual Duration of Training (in Months)				
	Less Than 2	2 to 4	4 to 6	6 to 12	More Than 12
Less than 2 months	24	5	2	1	[a]
2 to 4 months	56	16	8	3	1
4 to 6 months	6	18	6	2	[a]
6 to 12 months	10	45	43	13	4
More than 12 months	4	16	41	81[b]	94[c]
Total Per Cent[d]	100	100	100	100	100
(N)	(811)	(1,565)	(888)	(3,210)	(3,329)

[a] Less than .5 per cent.

[b] Seventy-one per cent wanted one more year of training; the rest wanted more than one year.

[c] Eighty-one per cent wanted one year more than they received: If one, they wanted a second, and if two, they wanted a third, and so forth.

[d] This table excludes those who were NA on desired length and those who were satisfied with the length of their programs (N = 9,222).

program's demands. Or, one can sponsor students for
study in their own countries or in a third country;
difficulties can be minimized by making use of more
familiar linguistic and cultural contexts. Finally,
one can tutor the prospective trainee or run a special program of language instruction for larger
groups.

These are interrelated options or contingencies
for participant training. For more extensive or
technical programs (e.g., in atomic energy), a prospective trainee's language skills must become a
more rigid qualification for selection. Greater
flexibility is possible in other fields. Interpreters can be used to accompany groups or individuals;
short trips to the United States can be tacked on to
lengthier programs in third countries; special-
training programs can be adapted to trainees' existing skill levels, and so on. Thus, facility in
English is an important but not absolute criterion,
and in the presence of other compelling reasons,
some slippage in its rigorous application can be
expected.

Since 1956, attempts have been made to employ
systematic tests as a means of assessing facility in
the use of English of potential selectees, and selection standards have been stiffened to include the
attainment of adequately high test scores. A minimum required score, initially set at 50, has been
raised to 65; prospective university trainees must
achieve a score of 80 (out of 100). Test scores are
available for only 12 per cent of the surveyed participants; these data can be used to evaluate the
relative worth of the strategies outlined above.

Test scores recorded in the Mission's files on
participants were based on several versions or revi-
sions of oral and written tests and can only be used
for comparative purposes, and even then with caution. Only 7 per cent of the participants' scores
on the oral tests and 14 per cent on the written
tests were below the minimum required score of 50.
A correlational analysis indicated that the tests

are measuring two interdependent but distinct dimensions of linguistic skills and cannot be used inter-
changeably in assessing English language facility.
As we will show, however, they can be used inter-
changeably as predictors of future language difficulties.[3]

If the tests are valid measures of achieved-
skill levels, scores on them ought to correlate with
the difficulty that trainees experience in using
English during training. Those whose programs required a knowledge of English were asked, "If you
had any difficulty at all with your English during
the program, was this mainly in making yourself
understood, in understanding others, or both?"

Fifty-six per cent of the participants claimed
they had no difficulty; the rest were about equally
distributed among the other categories. When these
groups' test scores were compared, the predictive
value of the tests became obvious. The higher the
score on either test, the more likely was it that
"no difficulty" was reported. Scores were made
prior to training (and kept in the Mission's files),
while participants' judgments about linguistic difficulties were gathered in interviews conducted several years after training was over; their retrospective judgments, therefore, cannot have been confounded
by knowledge of the test results. Thus, scores are
predictive of later events, or at least expressed
judgments about them, assessed subsequently and inde-
pendently. These data strongly support the value of
pursuing a testing approach and then taking the test
results seriously in making selections if one wishes
to forestall later difficulties (Table 5.2).

Another set of findings raises questions as to
the value of special, intensive training in English
offered prior to departure. Those whose programs
required a knowledge of English were asked about
their need for such training, and whether they received any or not. An index of claimed proficiency
was developed from their answers and correlated with
their reports of difficulty with English during

TABLE 5.2

Absence of Language Difficulty
During Training by Scores on
Oral and Written English Tests

| Test Score | Per Cent "Had No Difficulty"[a] | |
	Oral Test	Written Test
90-99	73 (99)	60 (96)
80-89	54 (239)	44 (305)
70-79	37 (357)	40 (308)
60-69	27 (270)	31 (221)
50-59	14 (144)	24 (123)
01-49	18 (91)	20 (167)

[a]Percentages in each cell based on unweighted number (N) of participants on program requiring English with test scores. (The same people are classified twice in this table; almost all took both tests.)

training. The results affirm the conventional wisdom that the language problem is best avoided by selecting people who have already acquired an adequate command of English. Briefer courses of instruction, even if relatively intensive, have little value in overcoming past shortcomings or preventing future difficulties, especially in the case of older foreign nationals such as these. Eight out of nine rated "high" in proficiency said they had no difficulty, while only two out of nine classified as "low" (who took special training) reported the absence of problems associated with English during their sojourn (Table 5.3).

An index of satisfaction with the major technical aspects of their programs--their duration, level and variety--was constructed and correlated with various attributes of participants and programs. A number of these factors seemed closely related with levels of satisfaction. One was occupational status: The higher the status of the selectee, the more often was the technical side of training evaluated in approving terms. Another set of correlates of satisfaction had to do with actions in the preparatory phase of the program. The more comprehensive the orientation received, or the more active the involvement of trainees in program planning, the more favorable were their judgments.

Interestingly, no clear relation existed between the specific types of programs that participants entered and their level of satisfaction. But the longer a program lasted, the more often it led to a degree, and both of these were correlated with participants' appraisals of technical aspects of training. As might be expected, degree recipients viewed all three elements of training in a more favorable light than anybody else, while, among university participants, the most relatively deprived group--those who received neither a degree nor a certificate-- were the most dissatisfied of all participant groups, including those who never went to a university.[4]

TABLE 5.3

Difficulty with English During Training
by an Index of English Language
Proficiency (In Percentages)

Difficulty with English During Training Program	Index of Proficiency[a]				
	High	Mod. High	Mod. Low	Low	Total
Had no difficulty	89	55	31	23	56
Had some difficulty	11	45	69	77	44
Total per cent[b]	100	100	100	100	100
(N)	(6,867)	(1,301)	(2,973)	(4,609)	(15,750)

[a]The index categories were defined by participants' answers to two questions: "Did you get some English language instruction in preparation for your program? Would some (more) have been helpful?" "High" = no, no; "Moderately high" = yes, no; "Moderately low" = no, yes; "Low" = yes, yes.

[b]This table excludes those whose programs didn't require English and those who were NA (N = 3,275).

The very diversity of technical-training programs makes attempts at further generalization on
this issue hazardous. While substantial numbers of
participants expressed reservations about various
details, the main common grounds for criticism appear to have been gaps in preparations for training
and shortcomings in training that flowed most directly from the time available to participants relative
to the time spans they felt were necessary or desirable.

Nontechnical Aspects

Participants were also questioned about various
topics more closely related to the nontechnical aspects of training: money made available to them,
free time left for pursuing their own interests,
social activities that had been arranged for them,
and so on. Judgments on these topics are our only
available indicators of a trainee's personal or social adjustment. Any serious problems or difficulties such as loneliness or unfulfilled expectations
encountered during the sojourn would be reflected
in their judgments about one or more of these aspects.

At the outset, it can be assumed that each participant's judgments on such matters would be shaped
by objective circumstances as well as personal status and associated expectations as to what constituted appropriate treatment. Judgments can also be
expected to vary with the demands of the technical
side of a participant's training, because the latter
sets limits on the time or opportunities for such
activities. Money did not pose any problems for a
majority of participants: Seven out of ten rated
their allotted funds as sufficient.

Judgments on two other, interrelated aspects
of programs revealed somewhat more disgruntlement
among participants. While 59 per cent were satisfied with the time they had free to pursue their
personal interests, 39 per cent felt they had too

little time; only 2 per cent found free time to be
in excess of their desires. It was not so much the
brevity of programs as their heavily scheduled pace
which gave rise to this complaint. But as was true
of money, criticisms of this aspect were not correlated with trainees' summary appraisals or subsequent uses of training, with one exception. The
small group who felt they had too much time on their
hands made appreciably less extensive use of their
training.

Finally, in most of the training countries,
especially when in the United States, program managers try to arrange for participants to take part in
social and cultural events, professional meetings,
and personal encounters of various sorts. The response to these arranged social activities, usually
quite favorable, was, in this case, also one of approval. Seventy-one per cent of the participants
felt they had done enough, and most of the rest (all
but 3 per cent) wished for still more of these kinds
of activities on their schedules. There was no con-
sensus among the critics as to desirable activities,
nor was there any clear-cut basis for distinguishing
those who were satisfied from critics, nor any consequences of their dissatisfaction.

The three items reviewed above were used to con-
struct an index of satisfaction with the nontechnical side of training which was then correlated with
various attributes of programs and participants in a
parallel fashion to our analysis of technical aspects. The status attributes of the participants
were even more closely related to their judgments on
these topics than on the technical aspects of their
programs. And at times they operated at cross purposes in the two cases. For example, the lower the
status of participants, the higher was the degree of
satisfaction with these nontechnical features. This
finding is the obverse of the one dealing with the
relation of occupational status to satisfaction with
the technical component of training. Age and years
of experience were inversely related to satisfaction,
as was education. Women were more often pleased

than men, and single participants more often than
married ones.   All of these findings can be compressed into one empirical generalization: The more
<u>socially integrated</u> (in status and experience) or
cosmopolitan in outlook the participants were, the
more critical they were in judging the nontechnical
aspects of their programs.

A number of program attributes were also closely associated with expressions of trainee discontent:
the country of training and its duration.   Mainland
U.S. training programs, except for those taken in
Asia, were given the lowest ratings on this index.
This was the case despite the much greater official
attention paid to the care and cultivation of U.S.-
trained participants' good opinions and despite the
fact that U.S. programs tended to be longer on the
average than those taken elsewhere.

The reasons for these site-related differences
are complex.   The higher living costs of a sojourn
in the United States played a role; it is also possible that many who went to the United States on
briefer stays may have found it more difficult to
adjust their aspirations to the available time and
facilities than did those sent elsewhere.   The often-
proclaimed advantages of third-country training appear to be supported by this finding: Complaints
about nontechnical aspects, reflecting social-adjust-
ment problems, are reduced among those not sent to
the United States.   But such relative contentment is
purchased at a price--the poorer quality of technical training at non-U.S. sites.   Trainees' ratings
on the index measuring the latter component of their
programs showed an almost inverse rank ordering of
these sites.   This is one more example of the variability in participants' judgments of the two compo-
nents, the technical and the nontechnical.

The relationship between participants' satisfaction with nontechnical aspects of their programs and
their duration is clear-cut: The longer they were, the
greater the satisfaction.   Indeed, on almost every
empirical measure of satisfaction with training we

used--with technical and nontechnical aspects, career impact, general value, and so on--the longer the duration, the higher the proportion of satisfied trainees. It is one of the very few correlates of participants' evaluations of training which produced so consistent a pattern of findings.

One activity in international educational and cultural exchange programs that has found near-universal favor is the home visit or, in its more prolonged version, the homestay. Personal contacts in the informal atmosphere of private homes are said to be an effective way of altering or clarifying stereotyped views and also of creating social bonds that can both help the visitor to orient himself and lead to social and professional relationships that will endure after the visitor goes home.[5] One can question the view that these cross-national encounters have self-evident value in affecting deeper sentiments; long-established predispositions tend to be more potent shapers of attitudes or conduct than the warm glow generated by a pleasant evening or two. But as a leavening element in an otherwise tightly scheduled or demanding program, home visits can serve as a pleasant interlude, and almost all of the participants who were offered such opportunities valued them highly.

People associated with international exchange programs have on occasion proposed that a period of time should be routinely set aside at the end of the sojourn, to help the foreign visitor sort out his impressions and to gain a broader perspective on the tasks awaiting him as a key actor in the development process. A period devoted explicitly to problems of introducing innovations can help the participant to reenter his own society and maintain the momentum that his training may have built up. Technical training rarely prepares students directly to confront the problems of inducing social change, nor does it prepare them to meet the "reentry problem" of reverse cultural shock that they can experience in the process of reintegration into their own society.[6]

Beginning in a small way in 1958, and in increasing numbers since then, participants trained in the United States have attended a specialized seminar on problems of communicating and using their new skills and knowledge upon their return home.   Among the surveyed participants who had gone to one of these seminars, almost all praised them highly.   Most also said they had made some use of what they learned and cited some way in which they found the seminar lessons to have been valuable.

One can question how effective such training has been, apart from these "testimonials."   For example, attendance at the seminar is not correlated with more extensive use of training upon their return as measured empirically by how much they used and transmitted their technical training.[7]   Nor is it associated with favorable evaluations of the worth of the entire training experience.   Those who attended did not differ from those who had not on these criterion measures of the program's end products. Nor were those who had attended evaluated differently by their work supervisors as to how well participants had conveyed their training to others.   By these indirect, long-range criterion measures, the seminar had no discernible occupational impact that would tend to corroborate the trainees' own favorable judgments.

To summarize, available evidence indicates that the social status of trainees and the country of training are the primary sources of variation in their opinions about specific, nontechnical aspects of their programs.   Smaller proportions seemed concerned with these aspects, compared to the technical component of training, and few consequences flowed from such discontent.   The personal problems that may have arisen from the dislocations which the program imposed upon their lives, or from having to cope with the role of "stranger" in a society often vastly different from their own,[8] do not seem to have been numerous or to have had long-lasting effects in the judgments of most participants.

In addition to evaluating specific aspects of
their programs, participants were asked to give a
few summary judgments at the end of the interview.
One question was phrased as follows: "From an over-
all viewpoint, how satisfactory was that training
program? Was it very . . . moderately . . . not too
. . . or not satisfactory at all?" In response to
this direct query, few participants expressed themselves in a negative vein. Almost one half (48%)
said they were very satisfied, and 44 per cent said
they were moderately satisfied. Another 7 per cent
said they were not too satisfied, and only 1 per
cent were not satisfied at all. This last proportion seems to be a bedrock figure for total rejection of the training experience; an approximately
equal proportion gave such an unqualifiedly negative
response to almost every major evaluative item in
the survey.

Another question presented a set of deliberately exaggerated alternatives. "Some participants,
after they return, think their program was one of
the most important things they ever did, some think
it was a waste of time, and others rate it somewhere
in between. How would you rate your program? Why
do you feel that way?"

A large majority continued to express their
approval of training: Two thirds agreed that it
proved to be one of the most important things they
had ever done, while only 1 per cent considered it
a waste of time. The reasons offered in support of
the former judgment show clearly that often the
personal gains derived from training are paramount
to a trainee, relative to the occupational purposes
it was manifestly intended to serve. For, while the
occupational usefulness of the program to national
development was the one class of reasons cited most
often, the personal impacts of the training experi-
ence--heightened self-perception that contributed to
greater understanding, to a greater sense of human
relatedness, or to such clear advantages as a better
job--figured as strongly in their statements.

The perception that training can enhance one's personal status or bestow other career advantages is potentially strategic: It can foster the achievement of technical and nontechnical objectives alike. Most individuals do not have a strong sense of "calling"; incentives or inducements are required to sustain their commitment during schooling and to encourage trainees to use the skills they have acquired. The fusing of public goals of national development to private goals of self-improvement or gains in status can have a powerful effect: It can help to provide trainees with new ideas and the learning of techniques that will improve their performances on critical occupational tasks.

Statements of the objectives of training--the official ideology of this program--eschew any appeals to the self-interest of the participants.[9]   But the history of programs of planned social change, and of technical assistance in particular, is a graveyard of well-intended initiatives from on high which failed to take adequate account of the calculated self-interests of those who were to have been helped. As John Kenneth Galbraith has succinctly stated, "It is difficult to understand why an Andean or Middle Eastern peasant should seek to enhance his income by irrigation, improved seed, or acceptable livestock when he knows that anything in excess of subsistence will be appropriated by the landlord, tax collector, money lender, or merchant."[10]   As with the peasant and his seeds, so too with these more favored, highly placed individuals and their skills.   The rhetoric of national service that they employ may bear little relation to the level and direction of their efforts. Some data showing how personal advantages gained through training were related to later role performance and their implications for the transfer process will be presented in Chapter 8.

SUPERVISORS' VIEWS ON TRAINING

The design of this study called for two sets of questions to be addressed to the current work

supervisor of each participant: Judgments on the
training of individual subordinates and assessments
of participant training as a programatic whole.
(The former set can be compared with the views of
their subordinates directly and can thus serve to
some extent as a means of corroborating their assertions.[11]

Supervisors' answers to questions about their
subordinates' training indicated a generally high
degree of approval. Two questions had to do with
the organizational value of training. First, supervisors were asked: "Do you think that this training
program /of participant X7 was worth the cost and
difficulty it caused your organization, or . . . not?"
Five out of six trainees' programs (84%) were judged
to have been worthwhile, while only 4 per cent were
flatly adjudged not to have been. A more direct
indicator of the organizational value of their subordinates' training was the supervisors' replies to
a question on "how suitable" training had been for
a participant's "usefulness to your organization."
As before, five out of six (84%) trainee programs
were judged as suitable, while only 7 per cent were
rated as unsuitable.

A final question was asked on the importance of
training for the subordinate's current work: "As a
qualification for his present job, how important was
/participant X's7 training program--essential, very
important, helpful but not very important, not useful, or would he have been better off without it?"
From this standpoint, one third of the subordinates'
programs were judged "essential," and an additional
42 per cent were rated as "very important." Only 3
per cent were rated "not useful" or "harmful." One
program attribute stood out as central in all these
supervisors' evaluations: The longer the duration
of training, the more often was great importance ascribed to it (Table 5.4).

One factor that appeared to be related to the
supervisors' responses to these questions was their
own early involvement in planning and programing

TABLE 5.4

Supervisors' Evaluations of Importance of
Participants' Training Programs by Duration
(In Percentages)

Importance of Training for Participant's Job	Duration of Training Program (in Months)				
	Up to 2	2 to 6	6 to 24	24 and Over	Total
Supervisor rates it as:					
Essential or very important	63	71	79	89	77
Helpful, not very important	30	25	18	10	20
Not useful, harmful	7	4	3	1	3
Total per cent[a]	100	100	100	100	100
(N)	(273)	(1,111)	(3,797)	(173)	(5,354)

[a]This table excludes "don't know" and NA answers by supervisors on either item (N = 246) and participants with no supervisors' ratings (N = 4,068).

139

their subordinates' training. The greater or more active the involvement, the more highly was a program's importance judged to be later on. Both of these variables are linked to another significant aspect of a trainee's work context: His rate of interaction with his supervisor after returning home. Trainees whose programs were adjudged more important, and in whose preparations the supervisors took a more active part, reported substantially higher rates of subsequent discussion with their supervisors about the uses to which training could be put.

Evidence from both sources indicates that the work supervisor is a key figure in the transfer process. He has been shown to be the primary source of information and orientation and to play a dominant role in selection. By virtue of his formal status as a "gatekeeper" of organizational rewards and facilities, he mediates the relationship between his subordinate's innovative strivings and his organization's response.[12] We know little, from the survey, about the supervisors' attributes. What has been shown so far is the reciprocal relationship between the supervisors' degree of involvement in training subordinates and the importance attached to it in attitude and in action. At a later point, we will analyze the consequences of supervisory actions for the transfer process.

TRAINING AS SEEN BY U.S. TECHNICIANS

Systematic interviews with knowledgeable AID technicians in each of the surveyed countries provide a third body of data, one reflecting a perspective quite different from the concerns of host-country respondents. Two sets of questions were also posed relating to specific trainees whose training and current work they could evaluate and to the conduct of the program as a whole. The aim of the former was to provide an independent check on the judgments of both participants and supervisors.

This part of the study design was not successfully realized. No technicians were interviewed in
four countries; in the remainder, often none could
be found who knew participants well enough to supply
information on their training or current activities.[13]
This was invariably the case for participants who had
returned home four or more years prior to the time
of the survey. The practice of short-term hiring or
rotation in assignments of U.S. technical advisors
together with their normally very limited numbers
were the principal causes of this difficulty. Findings based on data obtained from U.S. technicians
must, therefore, be considered mainly as suggestive
and will be treated only briefly.

Technicians were asked to assess the contributions of training programs to the work of participants, and almost two thirds stated that the contribution had been major. If ambiguous answers are
excluded, the proportion climbs to almost three
quarters. And, in clear agreement with both participants and supervisors, the longer the duration
of training, the greater the proportion of technicians who felt that such programs had made a major
contribution (Table 5.5).

The unanimity of the three groups on the importance of this dimension of training and on the over-
all value of the program, despite differences in the
phrasing of questions, is impressive. It is also
supported by many other parallels that emerged in
more detailed analysis. For example, programs that
consisted solely of an observation tour were uniformly viewed more critically by all three groups. The
training of those highest and lowest in occupational
status was seen by all three as less significant or
important than that of the middle-status groups of professionals, technicians, and supervisors. One conclusion is that brief programs, and especially
observation tours, cannot be justified primarily in
terms of their value in achieving the occupational
objectives of training; the empirical data all point
in the opposite direction.[14]

TABLE 5.5

Technicians' Evaluations of Contribution of
Participants' Programs by Duration
(In Percentages)

Contribution to Present Work	Duration of Training Program (in Months)				
	Up to 2	2 to 6	6 to 24	24 and Over	Total
Technician rates it as:					
Major contribution	54	64	75	85	71
Minor contribution	36	29	20	11	23
No contribution, or reduced usefulness	10	7	5	4	6
Total per cent[a]	100	100	100	100	100
(N)	(216)	(580)	(1,523)	(75)	(2,394)

[a]This table excludes "don't know" or NA answers by technicians on either item (N = 251) and participants with no technicians' ratings (N = 7,023); figures are unweighted.

Technicians also rated certain personal qualities of the participants, but little room for improvement could be discerned. Five out of six
trainees, or more, were evaluated as having adequate
amounts of intelligence and prior education and good
attitudes toward training and their present job.
Nor did they seem critical of the suitability of the
training that participants received: Six substantive dimensions (e.g., level, locus, subject) of the
training received by the individuals they rated were
evaluated as satisfactory in over nine out of ten
cases.

The technicians' criticisms of programs centered around three topics--selection, practical
training, and subsequent placement. In assessing
what the Mission was doing to facilitate the use of
training, its ineffectiveness in securing the adequate placement of trainees was the one shortcoming
that was cited most often. The over-all impression
from reviewing all the data provided by these U.S.
technicians is that the most critical issue is neither the quality of participants nor training programs but the placement of trainees. They see the
primary source of difficulties in the effective
transfer of skills and techniques as residing in
the post-training environment of returned participants, and it is to this last phase of the program
cycle that we now turn.

NOTES

1. Sensitivity is inevitable in foreign-area
research, and especially with cooperating countries
who see a study (such as this) as having direct implications for the continuation of U.S. foreign aid.
But out of an initial total of fifty-eight countries
(European nations were deliberately excluded), by
1968 the survey had been completed in thirty-two.
Waivers for political reasons were rarely sought and
were withdrawn at a later date in a few instances.

The main problem lay in staffing the survey in many
countries, not in its potentially sensitive character. Had the survey gone into political or social
questions, the fall-off might well have been greater.

The nontechnical objectives of the program,
especially in the realm of ideological effects, have
only recently assumed some importance. For an exam-
ination of these issues in the light of social-
science research findings, see the report by the
Bureau of Social Science Research, Social Science
Perspectives on Training for Development, Report and
Recommendations of a Workshop and Conference on Non-
Technical Aspects of the AID Participant Training
Program (Washington, D.C.: Bureau of Social Science
Research, November, 1966).

2. The phrase was originally coined by Kenneth
Burke; Robert K. Merton has placed it in a more general theoretical context: The trained incapacity of
individuals to respond appropriately to changed conditions; see Merton, Social Theory and Social Structure (rev. and enlarged ed.; Glencoe: The Free
Press, 1957), p. 198.

3. The notion of interchangeability of indices,
developed in a series of methodological papers by
Paul F. Lazarsfeld, has been described as "one of
the foundations of empirical social research." See
Lazarsfeld, "Problems in Methodology," in Robert K.
Merton et al., eds., Sociology Today: Problems and
Prospects (New York: Basic Books, 1959), pp. 39-78.
For an earlier formulation by him (coauthored pseu-
donymously), see Hortense Horwitz and Elias Smith,
"The Interchangeability of Socio-Economic Indices,"
in Paul F. Lazarsfeld and Morris Rosenberg, eds.,
The Language of Social Research (Glencoe: The Free
Press, 1955), pp. 73-77.

4. Only brief reference can be made here to
the concept of "relative deprivation." For a stimu-
lating theoretical exegesis of the concept, see
Merton, op. cit., pp. 227-80.

5.   The results of a recent large-scale survey
of returned exchangees provide a good deal of evidence on the diverse and long-term effects of their
personal and professional encounters, including home
visits, while in the United States. See U.S. Advisory Commission on International Educational and
Cultural Affairs, A Beacon of Hope--The Exchange-of-
Persons Program, A Report from the Commission (April,
1963), pp. 12-30. Herbert C. Kelman has argued that
the programing of social contacts for visitors should
be keyed closely to their professional identities
rather than to their status as foreign visitors in
order to increase the chances for meaningful social
encounters and attitude change. See Kelman, "The
Reactions of Participants in a Foreign Specialists
Seminar to Their American Experience," Journal of
Social Issues, Vol. XIX, No. 3 (July, 1963), pp. 61-
114; and his "Changing Attitudes Through International Activities," Journal of Social Issues, Vol. XVIII,
No. 1 (1962), pp. 68-87.

6.   For a discussion of the re-entry problems
that were confronted by the first groups of returned
Peace Corps Volunteers, see Ernest Fox et al., Citizen in A Time of Change: The Returned Peace Corps
Volunteer, A Report of a Conference, March 5-7, 1965
(Washington, D.C.:   The Peace Corps, 1965). Lengthen-
ing the adjustment cycle of foreign visitors to take
account of their reentry has led to a modification
of the concept that adjustment follows a "U-curve"
pattern. Now it is claimed that a "W" is the more
appropriate figure. See John T. Gullahorn and
Jeanne E. Gullahorn, "An Extension of the U-Curve
Hypothesis," Journal of Social Issues, Vol. XIX,
No. 3 (July, 1963), pp. 33-47.

7.   The index of utilization of training is
described in Chapter 7.

8.   See Erling O. Schild, "The Foreign Student,
as Stranger, Learning the Norms of the Host-Culture,"
Journal of Social Issues, Vol. XVIII, No. 1 (1962),
pp. 41-54. The classic treatment of the stranger in
the sociological literature is that of Simmel; see

Kurt H. Wolff, trans. and ed., The Sociology of
Georg Simmel (Glencoe: The Free Press, 1950), pp.
402-8.

9. "The Participant Training Program is designed for the improvement of a country and not for
the personal advancement or the intellectual satisfaction of individuals." See Harley O. Preston,
Operations of the Participant Training Program of
the Agency for International Development (Washington,
D.C.: Office of International Training, AID, November, 1966), p. 32.

10. John Kenneth Galbraith, Economic Development (Cambridge: Harvard University Press, 1964),
p. 17. For graphic illustrations of failures that
have occurred even when the role of social and motivational factors were anticipated and, to some degree, taken into account, see Kusum Nair, Blossoms
in the Dust: The Human Factor in Indian Development
(New York: Frederick A. Praeger, 1961). The mes-
sage in her book was the basis for the ironic comment once made by a symposiast: "How do you get
people to feel their felt needs?" A variety of
other case illustrations of failures or partial suc-
cesses in innovative programs is contained in Edward
H. Spicer, ed., Human Problems in Technological
Change (New York: Russell Sage, 1952). For a knowledgeable anthropological treatment of motivations
for change, see George M. Foster, Traditional Cultures: And the Impact of Technological Change (New
York: Harper and Row, 1962), pp. 145-62.

11. An earlier study of returned ICA participants, in many respects a pilot study for this world-
wide effort, discovered that there were sizable
discrepancies in the views of participants and their
supervisors. See Lawrence E. Schlesinger and Hollis
W. Peter, Using U.S. Training in the Philippines,
Vol. I, p. 84.
The twenty-three countries whose data are combined here varied widely in the successful execution
of this phase of the study design. And within each
country, supervisors of certain types of trainees

were underrepresented in the aggregate. For these
reasons, we have not weighted the replies of the
supervisors as we did those of participants. In all,
3,909 supervisors gave their own views on training
and rated 5,871 participants; this latter total was
reduced in later data processing to 5,600 participants for whom supervisors' opinions were available.

12. The gatekeeper aspect of a supervisor's
role in facilitating social change was adapted from
Kurt Lewin's discussion; see his "Group Decision and
Social Change," in Guy E. Swanson, Theodore M. New-
comb and Eugene L. Hartley, eds., Readings in Social
Psychology (New York: Henry Holt, 1952), pp. 459-73.

13. Interviews with 511 U.S. technicians from
19 countries yielded ratings on 30 per cent of the
returned participants. As a result of further processing of the data, this figure was reduced to
2,645, or 27 per cent of the 9,668 former trainees
who were interviewed in our set of countries. Often
only a fraction of them could answer certain questions about early phases of the program.

14. The brief tour is the vehicle par excellence
for providing political and cultural exposure, and
in other exchange programs has, until recently, always been viewed as such. Perhaps under the spur of
the development-assistance ideology that has pervaded
exchange programs, claims are increasingly being
heard that even brief sojourns have occupational or
developmental significance. See U.S. Advisory Commission on International Educational and Cultural
Affairs, A Beacon of Hope, op. cit., pp. 21-24.

PART THREE

THE CONSEQUENCES OF TRAINING

CHAPTER **6** THE AFTERMATH
OF TRAINING:
CAREER PATTERNS

We have traced the stages of the program to the
point of the participants' return home, and we now
turn to events in the aftermath of training. Our
main focus of attention will be on consequences
which occurred in the wake of training and those
which came about as a result of training. We will
be especially concerned with the issues of occupational placement and mobility and with the relationship of training to the career patterns of the participants. Their current work contexts will be a
subsidiary topic, as the survey contained only a few
items dealing with this area.

PLACEMENT AND CAREER PATTERNS

Available data on the participants' careers
refer to jobs at three points established relative
to the training period--at selection, immediately
upon return home, and currently (at interview). The
link between the first two is central to an analysis
of the issue of <u>placement</u>: The fit between training
and the occupational roles that participants were
called upon to perform. The links between the first
and third and between the second and third are useful measures of longer-term career consequences of
training.

Patterns of occupational mobility have to be
discussed with reference to a time dimension that is
uniform for all participants. One serious problem
in analyzing their careers is that the questions
refer to periods defined with respect to the training

sojourn, rather than to specific time periods. The
dates of participants' selection or return from the
twenty-three countries were spotted across a period
of more than twenty years, and the dates of interviewing spanned a period of approximately thirty-six
months (1960-63). The only means by which participants can be uniformly classified, for analytical
purposes, is the length of time each had been back
from training (whenever concluded) at the time of
interview (whenever conducted). By this means, one
can create cohorts of trainees who had completed
training and been at home for equivalent lengths of
time, although the precise dates that define these
periods are not identical. This variable will be
used in the analysis that follows to show analogous
changes over time in the participants' career patterns, use of training, and other variables related
to the post-training period.[1] In a later chapter,
its use will help to clarify the question of the
status of training as an economic commodity: Is it
a "wasting asset" whose value is realized relatively
quickly, or is it an asset whose value is realized
only with the passage of time?

Occupational Status and Mobility

Descriptive data were gathered in the survey on
the occupational status of each participant, at
selection and interview, and were coded into identical categories. The distributions at both points
in time were presented in Chapter 2; those gross
proportions conceal the turnover--net gains and
losses--in each of the status categories between the
two points in time. Some participants retired in
the interim, while others (e.g., students) entered
the world of work; a few dropped a rung or two,
while many more apparently climbed; some moved from
professional positions into administration, while
others moved in the opposite direction.

Interpretations of changes in status by participants within each country are unambiguous; when the
national contingents are combined, however, we

confront the problem of structural comparability of
these occupational categories.   But, if we assume at
least a moderate equivalence across countries in the
meaning of these categories, the survey data can be
employed to make a rough assessment of one type of
occupational mobility.   From this perspective, <u>status
mobility</u> was experienced by about one quarter of the
participants.   Each move was classified as represent-
ing a gain, a loss, or equivalent status; we then
found that more moved laterally than gained or lost.
And, even given this imprecise mode of assessment,
the extent of status mobility varied sharply with
the participants' status at selection: The lower
the status, the greater the proportion who moved,
usually upward (Table 6.1).

The main dividing line, as one could expect,
fell between those in professional or administrative
jobs and those of lower status.   Mobility among the
former was primarily within the upper ranks, mainly
into middle-management positions or to other professional assignments.   Among those selected from lower
ranks, mobility was into the higher-level positions,
primarily into administrative or professional jobs.
If for this numerically small group there was no
place to go but upward, a gain in status that may
have been facilitated by this foreign training, for
those initially more favored there was little likelihood of their falling far or at all.   These objective data do not permit one to assess the role of
foreign study in these mobility patterns.   But the
over-all finding alerts us to the fact that one type
of career consequence of training--a gain or loss in
occupational status--cannot have been widespread,
however dramatic the gains made by a few.   The status groups that are most heavily represented among
former participants do not show much movement in the
aggregate.

This finding can tell us something about the
topic of career patterns among professional and administrative elites in underdeveloped countries,
because these people hold positions ranging from the
middle to near the apex of the pyramid in the public

TABLE 6.1

Patterns of Mobility in Occupational Status, from Selection to Interview

Occupational Status at Selection	Mobility: Status at Interview (In Percentages)[a]			Same Status	Inactive	Total[b] Number (=100%)
	Mobile in Status					
	Higher	Lower	Equivalent			
1, 2. Top and secondary policy makers, executives	--	9	3	83	5	(1,447)
3. Administrative officials, managers	8	2	6	82	2	(5,450)
4. Engineers	3	2	23	71	1	(2,044)
5. Professionals: scientists, teachers	4	3	14	78	1	(6,608)
6. Subprofessionals, technicians	27	2	2	67	2	(1,704)
7. Supervisors, foremen	30	3	4	62	1	(546)
8. Artisans, craftsmen	34	4	--	59	3	(288)
9. Workers, others	40	--	--	56	4	(349)
All Participants	9	3	10	76	2	(18,436)

[a]Definitions of mobility categories:

For Category:	Higher	Lower	Equiv.		For Category:	Higher	Lower	Equiv.
1,2.	--	3-9	1,2		6.	1-5	8,9	7
3.	1,2	6-9	4,5		7.	1-5	8,9	6
4.	1,2	6-9	3,5		8.	1-7	9	--
5.	1,2	6-9	3,4		9.	1-8	--	--

[b]This table excludes those who were "students" and NA at selection or interview (N = 589).

154

bureaucracies in their own countries. By and large,
as many have asserted, jobs at the next levels above
those held by these participants are heavily political; recruitment and succession are based primarily
on such ascriptive criteria as class or caste affil-
iation, kinship, community, or ethnic status. This
fact sharply limits opportunities for upward movement.[2] A more subtle consideration also serves to
retard mobility among professionals and others engaged primarily in development work.

> There is . . . a tendency to look down
> upon, and therefore avoid, work in pri-
> vate or public development enterprise.
> . . . A related problem is the compara-
> tively low social and administrative
> status of scientists, engineers and
> others whose professions are based in
> the physical sciences . . .[3]

Whatever its multiple reasons, the limited
amount of status mobility shown in these aggregate
data confirms to some degree the image of a restricted opportunity structure even for these strategic professional elites and middle-management
groups. This interpretation is made only tenta-
tively, because comparative data are lacking on
occupational-mobility patterns in these countries,
particularly in the public bureaucracies in which
most participants are employed. We are also dealing with a select group rather than a representative
one--those sponsored for U.S. training who returned
home and were found by this survey. An accurate
attribution of status gains and losses can only be
made in full knowledge of the institutional contexts
in which job changes have occurred and in the light
of shared beliefs about their significance.[4] Because we lack systematic data on these matters, we
can only document an apparently low degree of mobility and suggest some implications, using additional
data from the surveys to amplify this finding in
several ways.

Economic Sectors Then and Now

The participants' occupations at selection and interview were also classified into economic sectors or "areas of activity," using standard ICA categories; the distribution of jobs at the two points in time was quite similar. Education, governmental administration, and agriculture were the three largest sectors; they included more than one half of the participants both before and after training. These aggregate figures mask a small amount of <u>sector mobility</u>, movement by participants across the boundaries of these major work sectors. Just over 15 per cent were in a different sector at the time of interview than at selection; a few of the sectors showed appreciably lower proportions of stable participants. By comparing the sectors on gains and losses together with the net balance of mobility reflected in the job histories of participants, we can formulate some hypotheses about the relative "attractiveness" of each work sector for this strategic group. To do so, we assume only that the empirical patterns of stability and change which are found in these data reflect some exercise of personal choice by the participants and that they are not wholly the result of such impersonal market forces as economic stagnation or of tight constraints on job mobility exercised by a central authority.

The attractiveness of a sector is defined both by its holding power and its relative gains. To measure the holding power of each of the sectors, we simply compared the proportions that were in the same sector at interview as at selection. To measure relative gain, we constructed an index whose values reflected each sector's net turnover--the number who moved into it divided by the total number who moved into and out of it between the two time periods.[5] On each of the measures of attractiveness, a few clear differences among sectors can be observed: Some are more stable than others, and some have gained more than their "share" of those who have moved (Table 6.2).

TABLE 6.2

Classification of Economic Sectors by
Two Measures of Participants' Job Mobility

Economic Sector	Per Cent in Same Sector[a]	Index of Relative Gain[b]
Education	88.3	55
Transportation and communications	87.9	54
Medical services	86.7	47
Manufacturing and mining	85.5	54
Government administration	84.4	56
Agriculture, forest, and fisheries	83.3	40
Utilities	81.9	40
Commerce and banking	81.4	61
Engineering and construction	79.1	47
Labor	68.2	22
Community development	61.3	43
Total[c]	84.7	50

[a]Proportion of those in each sector at selection who were still in it at interview.

[b]The index score for each sector may be defined as the proportion of gains over the total of its gains and losses. If the score is above 50, the sector has gained (and if below 50, lost) relative to others, in its net turnover.

[c]This table includes only participants in these eleven economic sectors; it excludes those in other (unnamed) sectors and those who were inactive or NA at selection (N = 1,367).

The two modes of classification yield rankings of these eleven sectors that are moderately inter-correlated (r_s = 0.49). If we classify each sector by its location above and below the mean on both measures jointly, a few of them seem to have been differentially more (or less) attractive. Four sectors--education, transportation, manufacturing, and government administration--have kept a relatively higher proportion and gained relatively more adherents than others. Two others--labor and community development--have just as clearly lost more and gained fewer adherents; the other sectors fall into less congruent patterns.

The mobility patterns reflected in these findings do not reflect changes in employer but rather shifts in the locus of employment; at both points in time, the national government was the employer of the vast majority of participants. Sectoral shifts really indicate these participants' patterns of movements between governmental ministries or bureaus. These findings have some interesting implications for national development. If the "attractiveness" of economic sectors (as reflected in the occupational choices of such high-level manpower as these) does not correspond with their importance, as indicated by priorities established in national plans, then one may be faced with a choice between two contrasting strategies of manpower allocation. One is coercive: Institute rigid controls over mobility and direct trained manpower into sectors with the highest priority claims. The other is persuasive: Offer special inducements that symbolize greater prestige or visibly improve the chances for long-term career improvement in certain sectors, in order to overcome the disparity between personal preference and national need.

Placement After Training

One of the main issues in the AID study was placement: Had participants returned to the positions for which they were trained? In principle, a

need for training must be documented with respect to
a particular job for the prospective trainee before
a program is approved. Ideally then, the placement
of participants after training will have been a
settled matter before they depart and will thus ensure the fulfillment of one necessary condition for
technological transfer. What have the realities
been?

Most trainees are selected for training relevant
to their then-current jobs rather than for advanced
or specialized study prior to assuming a new one.
Therefore, most participants were not asked directly
if they came back to a job they expected to hold;
mobility upon return was apparently not expected to
be a frequent occurrence. Questions on this topic
were posed in the following order: "The first job
you had after you returned . . . . Was it the same
as the job you had before you left for training, or
was it different? /If different7 Was it the job you
had expected to get on your return? /If not7 In
what respects was it different?" Because the latter
two questions were asked only of those who had different jobs, it is impossible to classify people
among all logically possible patterns (e.g., those
who expected a different job but nonetheless returned
to their old one), nor can we give a clear answer to
the question of whether they had been placed as
planned.

Over three quarters (77%) returned to the same
job, 14 per cent took a different but expected one,
and 8 per cent experienced an unexpected change in
jobs upon their return. If we assume that the first
two categories represent trainees who were placed as
planned, then more than nine in ten returned to the
jobs for which they were trained,[6] a proportion that
has varied little (± 5%) over the years covered by
the survey. Younger participants or those lowest in
occupational status were placed in unexpected jobs
somewhat more often than were other groups of participants. A few differences appeared when participants
were classified by their countries: The proportions
assumed to have been placed appropriately ranged from

Ethiopia's low of 72 per cent to Surinam's high of
95 per cent, with the remainder bunched closely together on this measure of placement. Thus, variations both in time and space and with respect to
participant attributes are relatively minor.

One further point can be made about those who
returned to be placed in an unexpectedly different
job. Considered from the perspective of the person,
or of the fit between training and job assignment,
the new job could have been seen as better, worse, or
merely different. After recombining their coded
responses to highlight this distinction, it was
found that 35 per cent said it was a better job
(i.e., more important, a regular job, or in their
field of training), 29 per cent said it was worse
(i.e., lower status, not as promised, not in field
of training), and the remainder gave answers that
were not readily definable in these terms (e.g.,
switched to a different office, to another sector).
From these evaluations, we can infer that an unexpected job change immediately upon return home was
at least as often _favorable_ to a trainee's career
or to better utilization of training as it was harmful. In all, between 2 and 5 per cent of the participants were shunted off or shuttled around after
training, to their short-term disadvantage as well
as to the probable detriment of their training goals.

Another series of questions dealt with the linkages between the returned participant's first job
after training and his current position: Was it the
same or different, and if the latter, in what respects? After glancing at their answers, we will
combine them with the earlier set to form patterns
of occupational mobility based upon jobs at three
points in time--at selection, upon return, and currently (at time of interview). Just over one half
(51%) of the participants changed jobs since their
initial placement after training. Almost all of the
rest (47%) were still in their first job after training; the balance were inactive due to retirement or
unemployment. Even more often than in the previous
instance, job changes were characterized in favorable

terms (by 69%)--as promotions or shifts to training-
related work. Only a small fraction (3%) claimed to
have suffered a decline in status or to have fewer
opportunities to make use of training.

From these characterizations, we can conclude
that job mobility just after training, and especially
since that point, has tended to carry with it a gain
in responsibility or status. One rough correlate of
this is the declining proportion of participants who
had no subordinates, with a correlative increase in
the numbers being supervised: At selection, 30 per
cent had no subordinates, while 22 per cent had 50
or more; at interview, only 19 per cent had none,
while 33 per cent had 50 or more. With greater authority and growing responsibilities, and with larger
numbers of them performing supervisory roles, the
participants appear to have increased their chances
to diffuse the substance of their training more widely. Because of this, we have tended to equate the
answers of mobile trainees who referred to a better
job after training with those who spoke of work more
concordant with training, even though the former may
actually have led to fewer opportunities to make use
of training. The affinity between some personal or
career gain resulting from training and its ultimate
contribution to national development has been discussed previously and will arise in a later context
as well.

PATTERNS OF OCCUPATIONAL MOBILITY

Now that we have considered each of two links
in a chain of potential job switching, we can fuse
them into several patterns that define more clearly
the careers of these participants. The mobility
patterns are defined in Table 6.3; as can be seen,
only two contain sizable numbers of participants who
described their careers in these analogous terms.
It is also apparent that the extent of job mobility
has been greater than was reflected in the data on
status or sector mobility. And, whether participants
returned to the same job or a different one, an

TABLE 6.3

Patterns of Occupational Mobility

Patterns of Occupational Mobility		
From Selection to Return Home, Job Was--	From Return Home to Now, Job Is--	Per Cent of Participants
1. Same	Same	37.1
2. Same	Different	37.5
3. Different (expected)	Same	6.6
4. Different (expected)	Different	6.7
5. Different (unexpected)	Same	3.0
6. Different (unexpected)	Different	6.0
7. Currently inactive, unemployed, NA		3.0
Total per cent		99.9
(N)		(19,025)

almost equal proportion moved at a subsequent point
in their careers. Further, while a majority moved
at least once since being selected for training, the
two career patterns which reflect the least change
are clearly modal for participants: Three quarters
of all participants are either still in the same job
they held at selection or have shifted only after
having returned to it from training. (The full extent of mobility can have been greater than is cap-
tured in the latter pattern; some participants may
have changed jobs more than once in this period.)
As expected, the longer the time since the completion of training, the greater the occupational mobility. Among those back less than one year, 58 per
cent had never changed jobs, while 17 per cent had
already switched between placement and interview.
Among those back seven or more years, only 21 per
cent had never changed jobs, while 51 per cent
changed jobs after returning to the same one.

Other types of variables, such as rates of
economic growth, may also have affected the extent
of occupational mobility reflected in these proportions. In an expanding economy, especially in
development-related fields, the new positions that
are created will be filled at least some of the time
by those who have acquired the most relevant skills.
These data on individual participant's job mobility
are, however, too gross in nature to correlate with
existing unit data on the growth rates of these countries' economies in order to test this proposition.[7]

The survey findings on unemployment can be
quickly summarized. In theory, viewed from the
wholly rational standpoint of meeting national manpower needs, people with advanced training and special skills should not lack opportunities for full
employment. By the same logic, unemployment ought
to be rare among this foreign-trained group; overseas training should, in principle, have augmented
their considerable value as scarce, high-level manpower. In fact, these participants have been unemployed very infrequently at any point in their post-
training careers. Since their return home, only 4

per cent have had any periods of joblessness. A
minute fraction (.3%) has never worked, for reasons
rarely related to training; the rest typically were
without a job only once, for a median period of
seven months.[8] Foreign-training programs are also
alleged to be used at times as excuses for handling
personnel problems; unwanted people are sent on them,
and in their absence jobs are shut off and they are
rendered unemployable. There is little evidence of
this in the participants' assessments of why they
had been unemployed. Only one quarter of those ever
unemployed (1 per cent of all participants) drew an
explicit connection between their training and an
episode of joblessness.

Value of Training to Career

Participants were asked directly for a subjective appraisal of the consequences of training for
their careers: "Suppose that you had not gone on
this training program. Do you think that you would
now have about the same kind of position as you currently hold, a better position, or one not as good?"
Their answers constitute the least ambiguous evidence
available to us on the career consequences of training.

By this subjective criterion, training turns
out to have been unimportant or, on balance, more
often favorable than detrimental to the careers of
this strategic group. As foreshadowed in our analysis of status mobility, a clear majority (62%) said
they would be in about the same position if they had
not gone for training. But five times as many believed training had helped their careers as those
who felt that they were worse off because of their
training (26% vs. 5%); the remainder could not judge
the effects. (Those who were inactive or unemployed
were not asked this question.)

Judgments about the career value of training
were closely associated with a number of attributes
of participants and programs. The younger the

participant, the more often was training rated as
helpful (rather than irrelevant) to his career.   Age
is a fundamental input variable in participant training, as we have seen; on it, the type of program
(and its length) which was given to participants,
with all their correlates or by-products depend in
no small part.   Older participants, for example,
went on brief tours far more often; by contrast,
younger trainees were sent more often to universities or combined university work with some practical,
on-job training.   Not surprisingly, then, the career
impacts of the latter two types of programs were
assessed in more favorable terms than the former.
In a related vein, programs for people working in
more highly professionalized sectors such as health
or education (which also made greater use of university training) were more often rated as helpful to
the careers of their recipients.

    As these findings would lead one to expect, the
impact of a degree program on the subsequent careers
of participants was profound.   Almost one half (47%)
of those who earned a degree in training believed
that training had enhanced their careers (Table 6.4).
This finding supports our earlier argument that earning a degree abroad could facilitate later occupational mobility.   It remains to be shown, however,
whether earned degrees and subsequent mobility were
actually dysfunctional for the process of technological transfer.

    Finally, as expected, the perceived career value
of training was closely related to the patterns of
job changing that have characterized the participants' careers.   Those who had not changed jobs at
all could be expected to view training as largely
irrelevant; those who were "groomed" for a new job
could, by the same logic, be expected to view their
programs more often as distinct contributions to
their careers.   Lastly, those who confronted an unexpectedly new job and remained in it ought to have
viewed training in the most jaundiced terms of all
those who had been mobile.   These hypotheses are
strongly supported by the findings in Table 6.5.

TABLE 6.4

Career Value of Training by Site of
Program and Earned Degrees
(In Percentages)

| Career Value | Program Site | | | |
| | At a University | | | |
Without Training Job Now Would Be--	Earned a Degree	Received a Certificate	Received Nothing	Not at a Universit
Worse (training helped)	47	29	27	22
About the same	39	59	60	67
Better (training hurt)	5	5	6	4
Can't say, don't know	9	7	6	7
Total per cent[a]	100	100	100	100
(N)	(2,513)	(2,910)	(3,388)	(8,929

[a]This table excludes those who were inactive or NA on eith
item and those whose university training was taken as members o
a special group (N = 1,285).

TABLE 6.5

Career Value of Training by Participants'
Patterns of Occupational Mobility

Pattern of Occupational Mobility[a]	Career Value--Without Training Job Now Would Be: (In Percentages)				Total[b] Number (=100%)
	Worse	About the Same	Better	Can't Say	
1. No change since selection	12	81	4	4	(7,024)
2. Returned to same job, changed since	32	56	4	8	(7,096)
3. Returned to differ- ent (expected) job, still in it	49	38	5	8	(1,252)
4. Returned to differ- ent (expected) job, changed since	48	36	6	10	(1,274)
5. Returned to differ- ent (unexpected) job, still in it	26	48	14	12	(576)
6. Returned to differ- ent (unexpected) job, changed since	32	45	10	13	(1,146)

[a]The patterns are numbered in conformity with Table 6.3, which shows their derivation.

[b]This table excludes those who were inactive or who were NA on either item (N = 657).

The passage of time since their programs, which
affected the over-all extent of job mobility, is also
implicated in these findings. The longer they had
been back, the greater the proportion who assessed
training in favorable terms. (This relationship is,
however, mediated by whether or not job mobility had
actually occurred.) The small proportion who perceived the program as actually detrimental in its
effect on their careers varied little among trainee
subgroups, with one notable exception. Those who
initially had not been placed as planned were two to
three times more likely to have made a negative appraisal of the career impact of training. Almost
one third of this group had characterized that initial position as having been a worse job or one that
involved a loss in status. Thus, the very early
placement of participants had differential effects
in shaping their careers long afterward.

To summarize, for one subgroup of participants,
training supplied a strong momentum for career as-
cent; for another, it was of more marginal significance compared to the effects of seniority (i.e.,
the passage of time) or the use of other channels of
upward mobility. For a few, training led to a net
loss in career terms. For a majority of participants,
however, training was perceived as largely irrelevant
to their subsequent careers.

WORK CONTEXTS AND MISSION CONTACTS

The work place in which a returned participant
is situated can be viewed analytically as a mélange
of material, social, and cultural facts with which
he must contend in making use of his training. For
example, scarcity of material resources or other phys-
ical and environmental aspects of his organizational
setting place limits on the scope and direction of
his efforts. It is at the work place that cultural
values and social norms affecting the adoption of
modernizing ideas and practices find their most direct, concrete expression. And no participant, however well motivated or superbly equipped through

specialized training, can achieve much if he is confronted by apathetic or hostile work associates or
superiors or if he works in an organization whose
traditions and practices are inhospitable or resistant to change. These factors have been shown to
have a crucial bearing on the diffusion and adoption
of innovations; they apply with special force to attempts at planned change through technical assistance.[9]

Despite the mass of information that was collected on jobs held by participants, the survey
yields few items which can be used to delineate
their occupational settings as contexts for innovation. This was a by-product of the survey's focus
on the individual participant, rather than on his
sociocultural context. As a result, we are unable
to locate the participants in settings that can be
empirically assessed as differing in their potential
responsiveness to technological transfer. Only two
items in the survey can be directly translated into
measures of contextual attributes: Does the participant work in a setting in which others have been
trained abroad, and what is his supervisor's attitude toward his efforts to make use of his training?
Other items that pertain to the participants' associations with the U.S. Mission upon their return
also have some bearing on their post-training environments and will be discussed at the end of this
chapter.

The analytical significance of the distinction
between settings in which participants are the only
foreign-trained members of the staff and those in
which they are not unique in this respect can be
briefly stated. If foreign study induces new attitudes and creates stronger motivations to act as
innovators, then those in the same work setting who
have undergone this experience can make common cause;
by developing mutually supportive relationships
based on their shared experience, they can form a
"community of innovators" who work together to find
ways of translating new skills and ideas into practice and to effect organizational change. From this

perspective, an individual located in such a setting is more likely to find support from others for his innovative efforts than one who is in a setting where he alone has had foreign training.[10] Moreover, a participant in the latter situation might find himself estranged from his colleagues, either because he has changed or because such an experience is at least marginally prestige-conferring (especially if a degree were acquired), and others at his work place might become resentful or jealous. In either case, the returned participant would have a more difficult task, because he would be isolated from those on whom his effectiveness ultimately depended.

This argument applies with equal or greater force to the work supervisor and to his own past foreign study or training, because he occupies a position of pivotal importance in the participant's organizational setting. If he were trained abroad and became more development-minded, the supervisor would be more likely to encourage his subordinates in their attempts to effect technological changes, or the participant at least would perceive him as helpful in such efforts. Thus, anything (such as foreign training) that affects a supervisor's innovative attitudes or actions can have implications for establishing the organizational climate in which participants operate.

The survey item did not refer only to AID-sponsored training or even to study in the United States. Participants were asked simply if there were "anyone with whom you work who has been trained abroad." Their answers, therefore, reflected long-standing traditions in former colonies (or in countries like Thailand) of sending people abroad for advanced study or training. Just over two thirds of the participants worked in a setting which included others with foreign training. They were also asked specifically about their supervisor: More than two fifths had a supervisor with foreign training or education.[11] The proportions in each type of context vary considerably among the countries that entered the survey (Table 6.6).

TABLE 6.6

Organizational Setting of Participants
Trained Abroad, by Country of Origin

Country of Origin	Organizational Setting of Participant[a] (In Percentages)		No One Else Trained Abroad
	Someone Else Trained Abroad		
	Supervisor	Other Co-Worker(s)	
Thailand	81	11	8
Nicaragua	76	16	8
Jamaica	67	20	13
British Guiana	59	21	20
Jordan	67	10	23
Philippines	54	22	24
Turkey	43	32	25
Vietnam	55	16	29
Egypt	35	35	30
Korea	45	24	31
Pakistan	52	16	32
Taiwan	37	31	32
Surinam	41	26	33
India	42	25	33
Greece	28	35	37
Costa Rica	47	15	38
Ethiopia	24	34	42
British Honduras	41	16	43
Chile	21	36	43
Brazil	19	36	44
Ecuador	11	39	50
Morocco	29	18	53
Israel	17	25	58
All Participants	43	25	32

[a]This table excludes those with no supervisors, those not trained in their occupational specialty (who weren't asked this question), and those who were NA on this item. Each row adds to 100 per cent.

The relationship of this contextual attribute
to the participants' utilization of training will be
shown in Chapter 8. Its link with the other aspect
of organizational settings on which we have some
data is noteworthy and tends to support our view of
the supervisor as an organizational gatekeeper. Participants were asked about their current supervisor:
"Does he help you in utilizing /your7 training?
Would you say he was very helpful, somewhat helpful,
or not helpful?" Supervisors who were trained abroad
were perceived as helpful more often than those who
were not. And supervisors in settings where they or
others had been trained abroad were seen as helpful
more often than those in settings where the participant
were unique in their foreign training (Table 6.7).

This and related findings further underscore
the strategic role played by the supervisor in the
process of technological transfer. Those who said
they were more deeply involved at the early stages
of training were perceived as helpful by participants
more often than those who were not. The participants'
perceptions also were congruent with their supervisors' claims of how closely they worked together to
make use of training in its aftermath.

The U.S. Mission: Follow-Up and Assistance

Another potential source of assistance to returned participants is the U.S. Mission, the original sponsor of their programs of technical training.
Through its programs and technical advisors, USOM
can provide direct moral and material support to
participants. Through its policies and long-term
projects, it can indirectly influence their environment to facilitate their modernizing efforts. The
importance of reaching out to "follow up" on its
assistance programs has been increasingly recognized
within AID, especially in the case of participant
training, not only to assess the results of development work but also to demonstrate a continuing interest in those sent for special training, to identify

TABLE 6.7

Supervisors' Helpfulness in Using Foreign
Training, As Seen by Participants
(In Percentages)

Supervisor's Help in Using Training	Supervisor Trained Abroad			
	Yes	No (Co-worker[s] Trained Abroad)	No (No One Trained Abroad)	Total
Very helpful	54	44	34	47
Somewhat helpful	27	26	26	26
Indifferent	9	13	17	12
Not helpful	10	17	23	15
Total per cent[a]	100	100	100	100
(N)	(7,661)	(3,576)	(3,883)	(15,120)

[a]This table excludes those with no supervisor, those not asked the question, and those who were NA (N = 3,905).

173

the conditions affecting the successful transfer of
skills and knowledge which they acquired, and to
give further assistance whenever possible. Follow-
up activities can take many forms;[12] personal contacts are usually judged to be the most effective.
As was recognized at their inception, these surveys
represented a form of follow-up, especially in the
case of participants who had long been lost to view
by the Missions.

In Chapter 3, we reviewed data on participants'
work contacts with the USOM prior to training and
found a majority to have had none. Their subsequent
patterns of association are quite congruent with
their earlier ones. For example, while over one
half (57%) had some contacts with USOM since their
return, the numbers who had and the character of
their contacts (i.e., work-related or not) varied
with their pretraining association with the Mission.
Those who had previously worked for or with the USOM
tended to have worked with it subsequently; those
with more casual contacts tended to have continued
to do so; a majority of those who had no contacts
remained in an isolated status.

At both pre- and postprogram stages, those in
professional, technical, and middle-level administrative positions were linked with the Mission in
work relationships more often than others. These
contacts presumably occurred in their capacity as
employees or counterparts or as development-project
personnel. Those at the highest status levels also
showed more frequent contacts than others but not
as often in a work-related context. Those in the
public sector, agriculture, community development,
health and education, had more contacts with USOM,
and reflected the greater technical manpower which
the United States devoted to these areas.[13]

There remains a substantial segment (43%) of
returned participants who were not involved further
with U.S.-aid efforts after completing training.
In fact, one third of all participants said they
had no contacts with the Mission either prior to

their training or subsequently.   Among those over-
represented in this category were trainees from the
private sector or labor (who usually were selected
through other channels, as noted earlier), those at
the lowest levels of occupational status (e.g., fore-
men, artisans, workers), and those who said no U.S.
technician was available to them.   This last finding
is the crux of the matter: The factor most closely
associated with subsequent Mission contacts is the
availability of a U.S. technician (Table 6.8).

   The principal determinant of their availability
is of course the scope of U.S. programs in certain
fields in the host countries.   But even if they are
present, other factors hinder contacts.   The U.S.
technicians who were interviewed were asked what
might have interfered with their follow-up contacts
with specific, returned participants; in over one
half of the cases, they indicated that nothing interfered.   The main reason they cited for lack of contacts was the location of the participant's job;
this was particularly apparent in the case of participants who lived in provincial centers rather
than in the national capital or in rural areas.
Another reason cited by a sizable number of technicians was their own work load, the numbers of participants for whom they were responsible: Those
working in economic areas in the private sector
cited this factor more often than others.   A scatter-
ing of other reasons also was offered--the language
barrier, a participant's lack of initiative or personality, or some political or organizational problem.   Another cross tabulation revealed that the
more important a participant's job was held to be
for economic development, the more likely was a
technician to say that "nothing" interfered.[14]
Given a need to choose whom to work with intensively,
they seemed to focus their efforts upon those they
defined as more strategic for development.   Other
data on how often they said they were in contact
with these participants show parallel results:
Those in provincial city areas or whose jobs are
viewed as less central to economic development tend
to be seen less frequently, if at all.

TABLE 6.8

Postprogram Contacts with USOM by Availability
of a U.S. Technician to Participant
and Frequency of Contact

| Availability of a U.S. Technician (And Contact) | Postprogram Contacts with USOM (In Percentages) | | | Total[a] Number (=100%) |
	Worked for/with USOM	Had Any USOM Contacts	Had No USOM Contacts	
U.S. Technician Available				
Frequent contact	57	32	11	(3,449)
Occasional contact	33	45	22	(3,124)
Never met him	10	33	57	(512)
No U.S. Technician Available	11	31	58	(11,808)
All Participants	23	34	43	(18,893)

[a]This table excludes those who were NA on either item
(N = 137).

In general, the outreach of the Mission depends
upon the sheer availability of U.S. technical advisors. An inadequate supply of these specialists on
the local scene has two consequences. One is simply
that more participants will be lost to view, and the
application of their training may suffer for lack of
reinforcement. Further, because the support given
to a participant's efforts by his supervisor is variable both in quality and consistency, the lack of a
U.S. advisor as an alternative source of support can
affect his later actions in ways that are dysfunctional for the transfer process. Other forms of
follow-up cannot compensate for the limited numbers
of U.S. advisors with whom returned trainees can
consult.

As a final measure of their post-training relationship with the Mission, participants were asked
whether they had requested help and what the Mission's response to their requests had been. Again,
the data show a relatively small number of transac-
tions between them: Seven out of nine participants
never asked for any form of assistance from the USOM.
The minority who had requested help were asked to
describe their requests and to state how much of the
hoped-for assistance they actually received. Their
answers only reinforce the image of lost opportunities on both sides; 65 per cent of all requests which
were made were fully satisfied by USOM, and another
15 per cent were at least partially met. The substance of the requests varied, but in the main they
were for equipment or materials, advice, money, or
publications.

By field of training and by current occupational
status, the proportions who requested help (and received it) follow the familiar pattern for contacts
with the USOM in general. Those in higher-level
jobs, or in the fields of agriculture, health, education, or community development were more likely to
have called upon the Mission for help. A small irony
is that the few low-status participants who did seek
assistance were less likely to have gotten it in full
measure than their more highly placed colleagues.

Thus, occupational status is directly associated
with requests for help from and receipt of assistance by the USOM: The higher the status of the participant, the more of either he receives. This was
presumably due in part to U.S. advisors' estimation
of their jobs as being, on the whole, more important
for national economic development.

     The patterns of association between USOM and
the returned participants reflected in these data
indicate that the Mission's role as a potential
source of support is hardly being discharged to good
effect. Follow-up is relatively infrequent, advice
or assistance is rarely available or requested, and
work- or project-related contacts are not as widespread as one would expect, given the focus of this
program upon project needs as a basis for providing
foreign training. Many participants "disappear"
from view and are thus unaware of the kinds of help
they can get from the Mission or are unable to find
a way to do so. Contacts are more frequent and
fruitful with higher-status or professional participants. If the activities of the Mission were
viewed as a form of institutional "follow-through"
on its heavy investments of the past, rather than
"follow-up" of individuals on a spasmodic, hit-or-
miss basis, the full weight of the Mission's presence and influence could be brought into play in the
transfer process. The central problem that has to
be resolved is the limited manpower for such tasks:
Contacts with the Mission and calls upon it for
assistance are a function of the perceived availability of a U.S. advisor. Without this personal
link, many returned participants might be loath to
approach the Mission directly on their own. The
fact that most requests were met in whole or in part
by the Mission indicates that much potential help is
being foregone by returned participants.

NOTES

1. The cross-sectional design of the surveys
and the variability in the time referents of this
variable preclude the possibility of studying changes
over time more rigorously. The methodologically adequate designs for handling changes over time are
longitudinal--panel surveys or quasi-experimental
studies that permit comparisons within and among
groups. See Donald T. Campbell and Julian C. Stanley, "Experimental and Quasi-Experimental Designs
for Research on Teaching," in N. L. Gage, ed., Handbook of Research on Teaching (Chicago: Rand McNally,
1963), pp. 171-246.

2. Case studies and analyses of comparative
public administration, or its offshoot--development
administration--provide documentation on the operation of ascriptive criteria and non-Western (i.e.,
"nonrational") procedures in the administrative institutions of underdeveloped countries. See William
J. Siffin, ed., Toward the Comparative Study of Public Administration (Bloomington: Indiana University
Press, 1959); Joseph LaPalombara, ed., Bureaucracy
and Political Development (Princeton: Princeton
University Press, 1963); Martin Kriesberg, ed., Public Administration in Developing Countries (Washington, D.C.: The Brookings Institution, 1965); Fred
W. Riggs, Administration in Developing Countries
(Boston: Houghton Mifflin, 1964); and Howard Wrig-
gins, "Foreign Assistance and Political Development,"
Development of the Emerging Countries, An Agenda for
Research (Washington, D.C.: The Brookings Institution, 1962), pp. 181-208.

3. Jay B. Westcott, "Governmental Organization
and Methods in Developing Countries," in Irving
Swerdlow, ed., Development Administration (Syracuse:
Syracuse University Press, 1963), pp. 44-67. Also
see Harley O. Preston, Operations of the Participant
Training Program of the Agency for International
Development (Washington, D.C.: Office of Interna-
tional Training, AID, November, 1966).

4. On the problems of studying these topics and issues, see Robert E. Mitchell, <u>Occupations, Organizations and National Development</u>, A Conference Paper (Berkeley: Survey Research Center, University of California, October, 1965); Wilbert E. Moore and Arnold S. Feldman, eds., <u>Labor Commitment and Social Change in Developing Areas</u> (New York: Social Science Research Council, 1960); Bert F. Hoselitz and Wilbert E. Moore, eds., <u>Industrialization and Society</u> (Paris: UNESCO, 1963); Seymour Martin Lipset, "Research Problems in the Comparative Analysis of Mobility and Development," <u>International Social Science Journal</u>, Vol. XVI, No. 1 (1964), pp. 35-48; see also Neil J. Smelser and Seymour Martin Lipset, eds., <u>Social Structure and Mobility in Economic Development</u> (Chicago: Aldine, 1966).

5. We are using data derived from participants' occupational histories to characterize attributes of these sectors. This approach was adapted from the logic of panel analysis; the concepts are analogous to what have been called "preserving" and "generating" effects. Other methods of computing net turn-over yielded essentially the same relative ordering of these sectors. See Hans Zeisel, <u>Say It With Figures</u> (4th rev. ed.; New York: Harper and Row, 1957), pp. 215-54. See also James A. Davis, <u>Panel Analysis: Techniques and Concepts in the Interpretation of Repeated Measurements</u> (Chicago: National Opinion Research Center, University of Chicago, November, 1963).

6. Two earlier attempts to assess the consequences of foreign training for job placement and performance dealt with a relative handful of students from India and Mexico. Both studies showed them to have been rather poorly placed for using training in subsequent work. See John Useem and Ruth Hill Useem, <u>The Western-Educated Man in India</u> (New York: The Dryden Press, 1955), and Ralph Beals and Norman Humphrey, <u>No Frontier to Learning: The Mexican Student in the United States</u> (Minneapolis: University of Minnesota Press, 1956). One small study found that between 66 and 100 per cent of Israeli-trained

foreign students (depending upon the field) are employed in their field of training; see Ya'acov Yannay,
"Technical Cooperation Between Israel and the Developing World," International Development Review, Vol.
VI, No. 3 (September, 1964), pp. 10-15. The difference presumably lay in the unsponsored character of
the Indians' and Mexicans' sojourns, compared to the
government-to-government agreements that existed in
the case of those trained in Israel and in this U.S.
program.

7. The field of cross-national research has
depended heavily upon correlational analysis of indicators of system processes; in this tradition of
analysis, the rate of economic growth has been a
prime variable. The methodological adequacy of the
data which define this variable has been frequently
called into question. See Goran Ohlin, "Aggregate
Comparisons: Problems and Prospects of Quantitative
Analysis Based on National Accounts," in Stein Rokkan, ed., Comparative Research Across Cultures and
Nations (Paris and The Hague: Mouton, 1968), pp.
163-70. For a more thorough critique, see Oskar
Morgenstern, On the Accuracy of Economic Observations (Princeton: Princeton University Press, 1963),
especially pp. 297-301.

8. Lacking data on unemployment rates among nonfor-
eign trained compatriots of these participants, those at
comparable levels and with comparable backgrounds, we cannot say whether this figure is low or high relative to others.

9. See Everett M. Rogers, Diffusion of Innovations (New York: Free Press of Glencoe, 1962), especially Chapters III and IX; Elihu Katz, Martin L.
Levin, and Herbert Hamilton, "Traditions of Research
on the Diffusion of Innovation," American Sociological Review, Vol. XXVIII, No. 2 (April, 1963), pp.
237-52; and Bernard J. Siegel, "Some Recent Developments in Studies of Social and Cultural Change,"
Annals of the American Academy of Political and
Social Science, Vol. CCCLXIII (January, 1966), pp.
137-53. Also see Homer G. Barnett, Innovation: The
Basis of Cultural Change (New York: McGraw-Hill

Book Company, 1953) for an earlier theoretical syn-
thesis, and Margaret Mead, ed., Cultural Patterns
and Technical Change (New York: New American Library,
1955).

10. It was partially because of this imputed
"group effect" on the transfer process that teams of
participants were chosen, especially in the early
years of the program, in order to maximize the
chances for the application of training upon their
return to a common setting.

11. Data from the supervisors indicated that
one third had been AID participants.

12. The official policies governing this phase
of Mission activities refer to it as "an essential
and integral part of participant training." Eight
types of activities are specified, ranging from paying for correspondence courses to founding alumni
associations, to regular meetings of AID training
officers with former participants, and so forth.
These activities are not often pursued consistently,
the principal reason being a lack of staff at the
Mission to perform these not highly esteemed functions. See Preston, op. cit., pp. 57-66.

13. In the period 1959-61, these four areas
included 63 per cent of some 1,545 U.S. technical
advisors to these 23 countries.

14. Such a pattern of preferences is also
likely to be influenced by the U.S. technicians'
professional role conceptions. Hired primarily for
their professional skills, they tend to focus their
activities on the projects which are their main responsibilities, rather than engage in activities
that have been broadly defined as institution building; the cultivation of former trainees would fall
into the latter class. Such a narrow role orientation has been the object of both approval and criticism. See F. J. Tickner, Technical Cooperation
(London: Hutchison, Ltd., 1965), pp. 149-64;
George M. Guthrie and Richard E. Spencer, American

Professions and Overseas Technical Assistance (University Park: Pennsylvania State University Press, 1965), pp. 42-82; Francis C. Byrnes, "Role Shock: An Occupational Hazard of American Technical Assistants Abroad," Annals of the American Academy of Political and Social Science, Vol. CCCLXVIII (November, 1966), pp. 95-108; Conrad M. Arensberg and Arthur H. Niehoff, Introducing Social Change: A Manual for Americans Overseas (Chicago: Aldine, 1964); Angus Maddison, Foreign Skills and Technical Assistance in Economic Development (Paris: Development Centre of the Organisation for Economic Cooperation and Development, 1965), pp. 13, 67-73; Rogers, op. cit., pp. 254-84; George M. Foster, Traditional Cultures: And the Impact of Technological Change (New York: Harper and Row, 1962), pp. 177-94.

CHAPTER **7** TRAINING INTO
PRACTICE

This chapter will be concerned with the uses of
training--the manifest goal of this program of technical assistance. In earlier chapters, we traced
the paths taken by participants through training.
Underlying our account of who they were, what they
encountered, and how they responded was an analytical issue: What are the connections between these
personal and program attributes and the outcome of
the transfer process? The main objectives of this
assistance program and the goals of educational strategies for human-resources development are not simply the diffusion of knowledge but its purposive
transfer for later application. Charles J. Wolf
remarked: "Technical assistance, viewed as services
only, may change production possibilities in the sta-
tic sense of what is known without providing the
means to change what is done."[1] To move from knowledge to application, using individuals in their
occupational roles as the efficient agents of change,
is the essence of the process of technological transfer envisaged in this program's strategy.[2] The linking of training to broader development projects (for
which capital and other forms of assistance are provided) is the institutional counterpart to the transfer of skills to individuals: Together they constitute the means for developmental change.

THE CONCEPT OF PROGRAM EFFECTIVENESS

Building on the concepts and findings discussed
previously, we can extract ten indicators or partial
definitions of the effectiveness of a training program from the survey data. As defined by these

criteria, effectiveness is a multidimensional concept: It embraces facets of a program's administration, consequences of training directly related to
its objectives, and program outcomes whose relation
to objectives are more ambiguous. Thus, norms governing the program's operation, individual behavior
and attitudes, and the training and work settings
through which participants have moved are viewed as
potential determinants of effectiveness. The first
six of these defining criteria have been discussed
already and will be recalled only briefly in this
context.

   The effectiveness of a trainee's program can be
assessed by whether he: (1) completes his program
(96% do so); (2) returns home to be placed in an
appropriate job (91% appear to have been); and (3)
has remained continuously employed since training
(96% have been).

   These are formal <u>preconditions</u> for effectiveness: The first attests to the fact that a participant's program was at least minimally in accord with
the original intent of his selectors rather than
having been truncated or indeterminate in scope.
The second and third criteria represent necessary
but not sufficient conditions for establishing a
meaningful link between the substance of training
and its concrete occupational relevance. A better
indicator of the occupational relevance of training
would be whether the trainee is currently or ever
was located in a job for which his training was a
prerequisite. Data from supervisors indicate this
to have been the case for most trainees. But for
some reason no direct question was asked of the
participants, either about their appropriate placement or the specific pertinence of training to their
current jobs--these conditions were assumed, rather
than explored.

   Two attitudinal indicators of a program's effectiveness are whether a participant: (4) judges
his program as having been satisfactory (92% rated
it as "very" or "moderately" so); (5) judges it as

having been important to him (66% rated it as "one
of the most important things" they had ever done,
and 1% termed it a "waste of time"; the rest were
in between).

As current appraisals of the over-all worth of
training, they are not unrelated to or independent
of what has happened to participants in the interim
or even of the dynamics of the interview situation.
Nevertheless, it is reasonable to expect that an
effective program should, on balance, induce positive sentiments of this kind as long-term by-products.
These indicators are crude and not very reliable
measures; other items that tap the domain of attitudinal effects could have served as alternative
indicators, such as expressed criticisms of programs
or suggestions for changes made by participants or
other respondent groups. All of these indicators
are methodologically defective as measures of attitudinal effects of training, for reasons noted elsewhere in our discussion: The problem of courtesy
bias, of comparability in meaning across language
and sociocultural boundaries, of halo effects, and
so on. Without better measures of attitudes and
values, we present these findings in this context
as suggestive rather than as firm indicators of one
important class of program effects.

A negative indicator of a program's effectiveness is whether the participant: (6) found training
to have been dysfunctional for his later career
rather than having it prove to have been neutral or
beneficial (5% felt that their job was worse because
they went on a training program, 26% felt it had a
beneficial effect, and the rest adjudged it irrelevant to their careers).

Being promoted or moving to a better job as a
result of training is in most cases an unintended
bonus or by-product. Yet, if in boomerang fashion,
a program has actually led to a loss in status or
in some other way has harmed those it sought to
serve, it can hardly be seen as effectively fostering technological transfer by adding to the stock

or quality of high-level manpower in an underdeveloped country. The extent to which such an unintended and undesirable consequence of training occurs is, therefore, a useful inverse indicator of program effectiveness.[3]

The six criteria described thus far are less important than those more directly related to the issue of the transferability of training. Among such indicators of a program's effectiveness for which we have data are whether a participant: (7) has made use of his training at work; (8) can specify the kind of use made of it in some innovative action he has taken since his return; (9) has plans for using training in the future; (10) has conveyed aspects of his training to others. Data on each of these four measures of effectiveness will be reviewed separately.

The Uses of Training

At this point, we are confronted with the "criterion problem," the issue which has bedeviled all research on action programs and especially those whose means and ends are located in the educational realm. The problem has two facets--conceptual and methodological. The conceptual problem arises from the multiplicity of objectives toward which action programs are oriented and the imprecise manner in which objectives are usually formulated. International programs are peculiarly prone to this, especially those which are governmentally sponsored. The policy maker must simultaneously attend to several reference groups in stating a program's objectives: His administrative superiors, the U.S. Congress, the intended beneficiaries, the host country's government, and those institutions (e.g., universities, private agencies) which will be called upon to implement the program. Because he hopes to secure not merely consent but active, reliable support for the program, the policy maker typically solves his dilemma by adopting a posture of studied ambiguity in stating its objectives.

This often-noted attribute of action programs
creates the second facet of the criterion problem.
In confronting the complex reality of a program and
its diffusely formulated objectives, the researcher
must find and define standards against which results
can be measured and at the same time develop a design and instruments for the study which permit him
to perform these comparisons in an "objective, systematic, and comprehensive" manner.[4] Additional
problems are created by the fact that research must
be conducted in a field setting rather than a laboratory; this in turn limits the researcher's choice
of designs and his ability to manipulate or control
the variables and effects that are of greatest interest.

Most research studies on the effects of action
programs resolve the criterion problem by defining
several levels of effects, by settling upon a variety
of indicators for each, and by gathering data on them
from several sources.[5] This was the pattern followed
in the present study: The uses of training were explored through a variety of questions directed to
the participants, and verification of their answers
was sought whenever possible in parallel interviews
conducted with their work supervisors and U.S. technical advisors.[6] Near the conclusion of the interview, a series of direct questions was addressed to
participants who were currently employed; as a methodological precaution, these questions were prefaced
by a lengthy statement.

> Thinking now of the skills, techniques or
> knowledge that participants learn during
> their training programs--a good many par-
> ticipants tell us they are not actually
> using much of what they learned in their
> usual work. How about you personally?
> In your current job, have you ever been
> able to use any of the skills or knowl-
> edge that you learned on the program we
> have been discussing? /If Yes/ Would
> you say you have used practically none,
> only a little, some, quite a bit or al-
> most everything?

Leading into the topic with these reassuring, low-pressure phrases, it was hoped, would signal a participant that if he had not used his training he was not alone, nor would he shock or disappoint anyone in admitting it. By establishing this point in advance, it was hoped that any hesitation on the part of "beneficiaries" of training to report failure to their "benefactors" might be overcome, that frankness would be encouraged by stating explicitly that such a negative outcome was expected and accepted. Responses to these two questions indicate that just over one half made substantial use, and another one quarter made at least some use, of their training; the rest admitted they had done little or nothing with it (Table 7.1).

TABLE 7.1

Extent of Participants' Use of
Training in Current Jobs

Extent of Use in Work	Per Cent
Almost everything, everything	20.2
Quite a bit	31.6
Some	23.2
Only a little	8.8
Practically none, none	12.9
Inactive or unemployed; NA	3.3[a]
Total per cent	100.0
(N)	(19,025)

[a] Currently inactive participants were 2.6 per cent of this group.

As with all findings based on testimonials,
this quasi-ordering of the participants' claimed
amounts of use is difficult to interpret. It is at
best a measure of relative achievement whose meanings can be very diverse in character. The kinds
of use to which a complex commodity such as education and training lends itself vary with the precise
nature of the work and opportunities available to
the participants in their organizational settings.
Because this measure was used as one component of an
index constructed to explore these issues, it need
not be analyzed further at this point.

Types of Use at Work

A clearer idea of the uses made by participants
can be gotten from responses to other questions in
the series devoted to this topic. The participants
were asked to describe "one or two interesting or
outstanding things" they had done since returning
from their program. Then, only after they had done
so, they were probed as to the role (if any) their
training had played in these activities. This had
a twofold purpose: It gave each Mission an efficient
means of collecting "success stories," testimonials
on the actual benefits derived from training, and
the question forced the participants to illustrate
in concrete terms the uses they had made of training
rather than letting their initial claims of use re-
main unverified. Thus, another criterion of a program's effectiveness is that a participant was able
to specify to an inquirer some accomplishment in
which his training had figured prominently.

Over two thirds (71%) of the participants described some significant activity of this type; just
over one third (36%) in fact mentioned two, and
training was asserted to have been directly implicated in all but a handful of them. Among the categories of activities into which their multiple answers were coded, six were mentioned with some frequency:

some change in organizations, procedures,
laws or curricula (49%)

training of others by lectures, demonstra-
tions (27%)

institution of a new service or organization (14%)

improved performance of regular occupation
(13%)

conduct of research or survey (10%)

publication of books, articles, or manuals
(8%)

This set of activities and the half-dozen others
which were described by lesser numbers of participants provide a more concrete basis for suggesting
where the value of training lies: Not often in fostering radical departures or large-scale (and presumably imitative) innovation but in producing
incremental gains, adjustments in prevailing practices, the grafting of newer ways onto the stock of
accepted organizational or institutional patterns.
These data are in rough accord with other research
on the spread of modernizing items, which suggests
that sharp breaks with the past are rarely found in
the responses to innovation of traditional social
systems.[7]

Barriers to Use

The paths taken by individuals who are cast in
the role of innovators in their societies are beset
by many common problems and difficulties. Some
reside in themselves and are primarily motivational
in character. Those who go for foreign training
vary greatly at the start in their desires to put
it into practice. Some will make efforts and persist in them for only limited periods, depending on
the results they see themselves achieving, their

"need for achievement," and so on. The dimension of motivation was not explored in these surveys; one possible indicator is whether the participants still had plans to use their training. Although this is not a measure of motivation, it is related to an expectation with motivational implications. A second dimension of personality is the skill or ingenuity with which participants approach the problem of use; this attribute is linked with both intelligence and motivation. (The communications seminar discussed in a previous chapter is designed to sharpen this skill by deliberately training participants in the role of change agents.) The survey provides no clues to the operation of personality variables such as these in the utilization of training by participants; thus, one can only refer to this class of potential influences.

A second range of problems is represented by the features of the environment in which the returned trainee is located. These include the hurdles, barriers, social and cultural factors, and so forth which have been gloomily or analytically reviewed by writers on technological-change processes.[8] The participants were asked what were the major difficulties they had encountered in using the skills they had learned. The coded responses are rather prosaic, but the distribution of replies is instructive; it should be noted that just over one quarter (27%) asserted that they had encountered none (Table 7.2).

The most pressing difficulties are those which intrinsically define a country as underdeveloped-- scarcity of resources, traditional social structures, and people's resistance to innovative change. The first of these, concretely illustrated by a lack of material and capital resources, accounts for almost two fifths of the problems that were cited. Problems with people in their organizational setting, especially with those in positions of authority, form another substantial set of obstacles to technological transfer.[9] Relatively few difficulties were cited that related to job placement or to the fitness of

TABLE 7.2

Major Difficulties in Using Training

Type of Difficulty		Per Cent
Resources or general conditions		76
Lack of equipment, material, transport	35	
Lack of money	25	
General conditions (government, society) not amenable	16	
Organizational factors		39
Top leadership uncooperative, resist new ideas	10	
Lack of trained staff	9	
Colleagues, others resist new ideas	8	
Clients, colleagues lack educational preparation	8	
Supervisor unhelpful, unsympathetic	4	
Job or work		18
Current job does not permit use; lack opportunity	6	
Current job not related to field of training	5	
Lack authority to use training	4	
Lack time to use training	3	
Training program		10
Substance too different, too advanced for local use	9	
Did not learn anything useful	1	
All other responses		9
Total per cent[a]		152
(N)		(13,694)

[a]This table excludes those who encountered no difficulty (N = 5,106) and those who were NA (N = 225). Multiple answers were coded.

training for their occupational role. These data
suggest that most of the problems arise not from the
quality of training or its administrative implementation but rather from the fundamental character of
the social and cultural environment to which the participants return.[10]

Plans for Future Use

As part of the series of questions on their use
of training, participants were asked: "Do you have
any plans for using that training which you have not
as yet been able to carry out?" An affirmative
answer was taken to be one hallmark of a program's
effectiveness, under two assumptions. First, if a
participant had not yet made any use of his training
but had plans, then some future application was more
probable; when not even an intent to use what he had
learned was signaled by a participant, then little
more was likely to be done with it. Second, whether
he had already made some use or not, if he could
document some plans for future use one could infer a
stronger motivation on his part to play an innovative role. A plan represents an expectation or commitment to future action; if no claim were made that
one exists, then motivation could be assumed to be
lower and use consequently less likely. Thus, without any other measures of motivation or interest, we
chose this item as a probable indicator of the participants' personal commitment.[11]

Fifty-four per cent said they had such plans,
and 43 per cent said they had none; the rest were
not ascertained. Those who had were asked to supply
further details, and a great majority (73%) were
coded as having described some _definite_ plan. The
main categories of activities to which they referred
were: to effect some reorganization or a change in
procedures (29%); to teach others (14%); to institute a new organization or service (12%); to conduct
research or surveys (9%). These are the same activities described earlier as the main types of use
that participants had already made. The other

participants who claimed they had plans for using
their training made their realization <u>conditional</u> on
something, e.g., if equipment or money became available or if the consent of higher officials were
given; the barriers to use noted previously are
echoed in these comments. Both sets of answers are
congruent with those made in response to other questions and reinforce the interpretations made earlier.

Two interrelated factors are concomitants of
the existence of plans for future use--the length of
time participants had been back from their training
and the past use of training. In the preceding
chapter, we asked whether technical training is a
wasting asset or one whose value is realized only
over a period of time. Plans for future use and the
motivations underlying them are equally susceptible
to the erosions of time. They are also likely to be
affected by past use in either of two ways. Use can
stimulate further plans which in turn can lead to
greater use, or once he has used his training, a
participant may find he has exhausted its potential-
ity and thus foregoes intentions of use in the future.

The passage of time is clearly associated with
the existence (or persistence) of plans: The proportion who report such plans is highest within the
first year after return and declines steadily among
those back from training for successively longer
periods. This finding suggests that the holding of
plans is a functional substitute for actual use among
newly returned participants. Moreover, if some use
has already been made, plans for some future use are
more likely to persist than if no substantial use of
training has occurred (Table 7.3).

Both of these findings suggest that if training
is a wasting asset it is one mainly among those who
have done nothing with it so far and not even for a
large majority of them. Further, those who have
made some use <u>conserve</u> their intentions or plans to
a greater extent than those who have not. Among the
latter group, plans for use are held by proportions

TABLE 7.3

Plans for Future Use of Training
by Time Since Program Completion
and by Use of Training

Item	Per Cent "Has Plans"	Total[a] Number
Time back from program		
Up to 1 year	68	(729)
1 to 2 years	66	(3,036)
2 to 4 years	60	(5,940)
4 to 5 years	56	(2,124)
5 to 7 years	50	(3,702)
7 years and over	41	(2,825)
Total sample	56	(18,356)
Extent of use		
Any use	58	(15,548)
None, practically none	42	(2,730)
Total	56	(18,278)

[a]This table excludes those who were NA on either item; those who are currently inactive or unemployed are excluded from "Extent of use."

that decline steadily with the passage of time; among the former, however, over one half of those back seven years or longer still held some plans for use. Thus, although the data are far from firm on this point, it would seem that an initial commitment (i.e., motivation or expectation) to make use of training is reinforced by successful application and extinguished by failures or by inaction.

Training Others: The Role of Communicator

As we have seen, one of the uses of training involves a participant's assumption of a teaching role in which he diffuses his acquired knowledge and techniques to others. This activity is as important a medium for effective transfer as the occupational role for which the participants are trained. It can serve two purposes: By instructing others formally and informally, by exhortation, and by example, a returned trainee can effectively multiply the productive potential of his overseas experience. The other function is a more tenuous one; it is possible that by acting as a trainer, he can alter the outlook of other members of his work group and make them more receptive to the innovations he seeks to introduce.

The former purpose has been called, appropriately enough, the "multiplier effect" of training; borrowed from monetary theory, the concept is also serviceable as a metaphorical description of the circulation of ideas.[12] The latter, more properly termed a latent function of this activity, is plausible but, to our knowledge, untested by research in international education.[13]

The participants' communications behavior was ascertained by a direct question which, however, was again slanted away from the expectation that all participants must have found it possible to play this role.

> Now I would like to ask about whether or
> not you have conveyed to other people the
> things you learned on that program. Have
> you ever been able to convey any of what
> you learned in the program to other peo-
> ple? /If Yes/ About how much of that
> training have you been able to transmit
> to other people--practically none, only
> a little, some, quite a bit, or almost
> everything?

As with the previously cited question on the
extent of use at work, this question's referents are
not easy to specify. (As an illustration, what is
meant by a participant trained in animal husbandry
who says he has conveyed "quite a bit" of his training to others? What has he conveyed, to how many
others, and with what results?) Answers can be considered as only rough indicators of the participants'
levels of activity rather than of the scope of whatever they conveyed. Over one half claimed to have
engaged in a substantial amount of this activity;
less than one in five said they had done little or
nothing about communicating the lessons of their
training to others (Table 7.4).

To specify this "two-step flow" of technical
assistance still further,[14] those who said they had
were asked how they went about conveying their training to others. Multiple channels were mentioned by
over two thirds; the major channels were informal
discussions (75%), formal lectures or training programs (65%), articles or other published works (35%),
and on-the-job training of others (20%). Interestingly, those at higher-status levels laid greater
stress on their formal training roles, while engineers or lower-level supervisory personnel mentioned
informal discussions or practical training of others
more often.

Comparative data on this mode of use are available from the work supervisors of almost one half of
the participants, and they largely corroborate this
finding. The empirical correspondence between the

TABLE 7.4

Extent to Which Participants
Conveyed Training to Others

Extent Conveyed to Others	Per Cent
Almost everything, everything	16.3
Quite a bit	35.9
Some	29.7
Only a little	9.8
None, practically none	8.1
NA	.3
Total per cent	100.1
(N)	(19,025)

two sources on the fact of conveying is quite high:
Almost seven out of eight (86%) participants' claims
were in accord with observations made by their supervisors about whether or not they conveyed information acquired in training to others. Moreover, the
supervisors emphasized the same four channels of communication.

A few policy implications of these findings can
be noted. They suggest that the "multiplier effect"
of participant training would be enhanced by providing additional formally structured opportunities for
participants to act as trainers, helping them (perhaps literally) to find platforms for such instructional efforts. The U.S. Mission could develop
locally coordinated or sponsored training programs,
refresher courses, workshops, and so forth, in which
former participants held leadership roles in these
group sessions. By calling upon them to train others,
the Mission might also stimulate participants to re-
newed efforts in their own work settings.

Ultimately it may prove feasible or preferable
to shift most of the task of providing training for
later development workers to the returned participants, as their numbers grow large enough to sustain
this alternative policy. The thrust of U.S. assistance could be redirected toward building up the
indigenous facilities and educational institutions
they would need to carry out an enlarged and formal-
ized training role. This is one way in which a deliberately phased strategy of educational assistance
can contribute to the process whereby human-resources
development becomes self-sustaining at the local
level. If the "multiplier" concept is sound, as the
data seem to indicate, then providing greater institutional support for the spread of modern skills,
ideas, and practices would seem to be a logical way
of consolidating the gains now being realized in a
more inconsistent manner.

To summarize, in answers to a variety of types
of questioning, the participants represent themselves as having made considerable use of the skills,

techniques, and knowledge they acquired through training. Their concrete illustrations of past use and their plans for future use involve the same types of activity and in the same order of relative frequency. Moreover, the difficulties they have en- countered and the conditions they attach to future use are similar in nature; among these, the primary barrier is the scarcity of resources available to them--in the form of capital and equipment--but a strong secondary problem is the lack of support for their efforts from those in authority. All of these dampening influences, as we have noted, are condi- tions or problems integral to the settings to which they return from training.

A CRITERION MEASURE OF USE

The final task of analysis is to show how the variables discussed in preceding chapters are re- lated to the uses of training and to explore their status as potential sources of variation in the out- comes of the transfer process. A criterion measure of the extent of use is needed for such an analysis, one that will locate all participants along a scale of greater or lesser use. As we have seen, each of the four indicators reviewed in this chapter is di- rected at a different facet of use; the proportions of participants who report that they have used their training vary with the target and wording of the question. A more general indicator of this class of consequences is needed, one that is more adequate as a measure of the multidimensional character of the concept of use.

Index of Utilization

To meet this need, an index was formed out of answers to the questions dealing with the two main activities through which the value of training is realized: Directly by its application at work and indirectly by the transmission of its substance to others. Two sets of answers given by the participants

were cross-classified and first yielded an attribute
space, and ultimately an index whose categories have
several useful properties. They provide a more stable basis for defining each participant's extent of
use than would either of his answers considered separately. And in their dualities, the categories of
the index relate to a more comprehensive concept of
"utilization," one that embraces both of the indicated types of activities.[15] Table 7.5 shows how
the categories of the index were initially defined.

TABLE 7.5

Construction of an Index of Utilization
with Definition of Categories and
Proportion of Participants in Each

Extent Conveyed to Others	Extent of Use of Training at Work (In Percentages)		
	Almost Everything; Quite a Bit	Some	Only a Little; Practically None; None
Almost every-thing; quite a bit	1. 37.7	3. 7.1	6. 7.4
Some	2. 10.3	5. 12.8	8. 6.6
Only a little; practically none; none	4. 3.8	7. 3.3	9. 11.0

The nine answer combinations were reduced still
further to facilitate the presentation of findings;[16]
the "very high" category, however, conserves its
unitary, operationally defined meaning. The resulting distribution of participants into four categories

--levels of utilization--has no independent significance as a finding. A choice of different items or
cutting points would have produced a different set
of proportions. The prime value of the index is
that it is a measure of relative utilization, one
that blends the two main hoped-for outcomes of training (Table 7.6).

TABLE 7.6

Index of Utilization, Categories,
and Distribution of Participants

Index of Utilization	Original Categories	Per Cent
Very high	1.	37.7
High	2,3.	17.4
Moderate	4-6.	24.0
Low	7-9.	20.9
Total per cent		100.0
(N)		(19,025)

What evidence can be adduced that this measure,
however logical in its definition and construction,
has validity in terms of the concept it seeks to
objectify? Three sets of findings, based on the
three sources of information in the survey, can be
marshaled in support of such a claim. First, as
noted earlier, the participants were probed to describe some specific accomplishments in which their
training had a central role. Those who were able to
specify successively more such examples ought to

show correlatively higher proportions who have made
greater use of training. (This represents an internal comparison of evidence; the relationship among
indicators of use is a measure of the reliability of
the index.) Second, the supervisors of a majority
of the participants were asked about the importance
of their subordinate's training as a qualification
for his present job. Those whose training was judged
as a more important qualification ought to show higher proportions who have made greater use of their
training. Finally, U.S. technicians were asked to
judge the contributions of training to the job performance of individual participants. Again, those
whose training was rated as having made more of a
contribution ought to show higher proportions who
have made greater use of training. (Validity in
these last two comparisons consists in the probabil-
ity of agreement between a participant's dual claims
of use and the independent observations made by
others of his actions.) The tests of these three
propositions are shown in Table 7.7; only the two
polar categories of utilization are shown, to facilitate the presentation of findings.

     The findings on all three tests are consistent-
ly and clearly in the predicted direction and lend
empirical support to the claim that the index is a
reliable and valid measure of utilization. The participants' ability to specify some activities in
which training played a significant part was closely
associated with their extent of use. Put differently, this finding showed that 45 per cent of the
"very high" category described two such activities,
and 35 per cent described one; only 20 per cent were
unable to mention one. Conversely, only 17 per cent
of those classified as "low" by this index mentioned
two activities, and 28 per cent described one; the
rest (55%) failed to supply even one. In like manner, participants whose training was attested to as
having had greater value by their supervisors and
by U.S. technical advisors are classified as very
high users more often. The association between the
measures, although based only on subsamples of participants, was close in both of the latter cases.

TABLE 7.7

Cross-Validation of the Utilization
Index: Very High and Low Use Compared
on Items from Three Sources of Data

| Source and Validation Item | Index of Utilization[a] (In Percentages) | | Total Number (=100%) |
	Very High	Low	
1. Participant: Examples of training-related activity			
Mentions two	51.2	10.5	(6,348)
Mentions one	39.4	17.5	(6,269)
Mentions none	21.0	36.0	(5,984)
All participants	37.5	20.1	(18,601)[b]
2. Supervisor: Rates training's importance for work			
Essential	42.1	15.9	(1,843)
Very important	39.0	18.6	(2,352)
Not very, none	27.0	30.8	(1,231)
All rated participants	37.4	20.4	(5,426)[c]
3. U.S. technician: Rates contribution to job performance			
Major contribution	43.9	17.2	(1,707)
Minor contribution	38.0	22.6	(563)
None, harmful	28.0	34.8	(135)
All rated participants	41.5	21.8	(2,405)[d]

[a]Does not show "High" and "Moderate" categories of utilization; including them, each row adds to 100 per cent.

[b]Category 1 excludes those who are NA on validation item (N = 424).

[c]Category 2 is based on the unweighted number of participants who were rated by supervisors. It excludes those DK or NA on the validation item (N = 174), and those with no supervisor's rating (N = 4,068).

[d]Category 3 is based on the unweighted number of participants who were rated by U.S. technicians. It excludes those DK or NA on validation item (N = 240), and those with no rating (N = 7,023).

The index seems to be a good empirical indicator of
the general concept it purports to measure and will
be used as a criterion in exploring sources of variation in the use of training.

NOTES

1.   Charles J. Wolf, Foreign Aid: Theory and
Practice in Southern Asia (Princeton: Princeton
University Press, 1960), pp. 61-62.

2.   An AID deputy administrator once remarked,
"This program is the most concrete evidence I know
of our faith in the capacity of the individual to
change history."   Frank M. Coffin, "Thoughts on a
Development Leadership Program," Training For Leadership and Service, Proceedings of the National
Conference on the International Training Programs
of AID, June 25-26, 1962 (Washington, D.C.:   Agency
for International Development, 1962), pp. 19-28.

3.   For a thorough treatment of methodological
issues in studying unintended consequences of action
programs, see Herbert H. Hyman, Charles R. Wright,
and Terence K. Hopkins, Applications of Methods of
Evaluation (Berkeley and Los Angeles: University of
California Press, 1962), pp. 6-17.

4.   The quoted phrase is from Otto Klineberg,
"The Problem of Evaluation," International Social
Science Bulletin, Vol. VII, No. 3 (1955), p. 347.
He more recently surveyed the literature on exchange
programs, commenting on the lack of clarity of their
goals and the research dilemmas this creates.   See
his "Research in the Field of International Exchanges
in Education, Science and Culture," Social Science
Information, Vol. IV, No. 4 (December, 1965), pp.
97-138.

5.   The best methodological statements on the
application of systematic research techniques in

evaluating action programs are by Hyman, Wright, and
Hopkins, op. cit., especially Part I, pp. 3-86; and
Edward A. Suchman, Evaluative Research: Principles
and Practice in Public Service and Social Action
Programs (New York: Russell Sage Foundation, 1967).
Three other reviews which focus on international
assistance programs provide additional discussion
and bibliography. See Samuel P. Hayes, Jr., Measur-
ing the Results of Development Projects (Paris:
UNESCO, 1959); Hollis W. Peter and Edwin R. Henry,
"Measuring Successful Performance Overseas," International Development Review, Vol. III, No. 3 (October, 1961), pp. 8-12; Albert E. Gollin, Evaluating
Programs and Personnel Overseas (New York: Bureau
of Applied Social Research, Columbia University,
February, 1963).

   6. In theory, comparative data on the effects
of training were to be obtained from all three
sources. In fact, data are available for only 19
per cent of the participants from all three. One
third of the participants had no matching data from
either alternative source; 39 per cent had matching
data from supervisors only, and 9 per cent from U.S.
advisors only.

   7. One could with equal logic reverse this proposition and make of it a definition of a traditional
social system. The avoidance of tautology is perhaps
the most serious methodological problem in diffusion
research. See Everett M. Rogers, Diffusion of Innovations (New York: Free Press of Glencoe, 1962),
pp. 57-75, for illustrations of this problem.

   8. On the built-in pessimistic orientation of
many studies in the area of change induction, see
Margaret Mead, "Applied Anthropology, 1955," Some
Uses of Anthropology: Theoretical and Applied (Washington, D.C.: The Anthropological Society of Washington, 1956), pp. 94-108.

   9. Results of another large-scale survey show
much the same character. "Perhaps half the grantees
report problems and difficulties in putting their

new ideas into practice, chiefly in the less developed nations--'lack of facilities,' 'lack of funds'
or 'indifference of colleagues' /were cited most
often7." U.S. Advisory Commission on International
Educational and Cultural Affairs, A Beacon of Hope--
The Exchange-of-Persons Program, A Report from the
Commission (April, 1963), p. 26.

10. A recent survey of literature on foreign-
student exchanges makes the same point. "It is noteworthy that inappropriate U.S. training does not
bulk large as a factor determining usefulness"; see
Barbara J. Walton, Foreign Student Exchange in Perspective: Research on Foreign Students in the United
States, Department of State, Publication 8373 (Washington, D.C.: U.S. Government Printing Office, September, 1967), p. 11.

11. This is one of the perils or penalties of
a secondary analysis of data: Lacking the items one
would want, one is driven to use others in ways not
originally intended by the study design. The problem of inference is necessarily made greater when
one resorts to this stratagem.

12. Because economic concepts are the professional currency of high-level AID officials, it is
not surprising that this concept has also been applied to the agency's educational activities. As
one illustration of its pervasiveness, the title of
one of AID's internal publications, produced by its
communications media division, is The Multiplier in
International Development.

13. One approach would be to establish a sample for each returned participant on a sociometric
basis (e.g., "snowball sampling"), and inquire into
the effects, if any, that his activities have had
upon their attitudes toward change and on their occupational practices.

14. The "two-step flow of communications," a
notion devised originally in the study of mass media
and voting behavior, has value in describing the

process being discussed here. See Elihu Katz and Paul F. Lazarsfeld, _Personal Influence_ (Glencoe: Free Press, 1955); they define the role of an "opinion leader" who acts as a strategic intermediary between the mass media and various publics. This concept has figured prominently in diffusion research --an example itself of the diffusion of scientific ideas. See Rogers, _op. cit._, pp. 208-53.

15. The relation between their answers and this concept is necessarily probabilistic. One makes an initial assumption that those who are classified by the index as higher utilizers are likely to have made greater use than those classified as lower utilizers. This assumption must then be tested with other data. For an authoritative discussion of index construction and the relation between concepts and their empirical indicators, see Paul F. Lazarsfeld and Morris Rosenberg, eds., _The Language of Social Research_ (Glencoe: Free Press, 1955), Section I; Paul F. Lazarsfeld and Allen H. Barton, "Qualitative Measurement in the Social Sciences: Classification, Typologies, and Indices," in Daniel Lerner and Harold D. Lasswell, eds., _The Policy Sciences_ (Stanford: Stanford University Press, 1951), pp. 155-92.

16. This operation has been termed a "pragmatic reduction"; see Allen H. Barton, "The Concept of Property-Space in Social Research," in Lazarsfeld and Rosenberg, _op. cit._, pp. 40-53.

CHAPTER **8** PATTERNS IN THE
USE OF TRAINING

A select set of variables whose nature and in-
terrelationships were discussed in earlier chapters
was correlated with the index of utilization. These
measures were chosen on theoretical and empirical
grounds as potential sources of variation in the use
of training; their degree of association with our
criterion measure will be explored below. Each finding will be stated in brief; its implications for
propositions and findings discussed earlier will
then be considered.

USE AND ATTRIBUTES OF
PARTICIPANTS AND PROGRAMS

Age is related to subsequent use of training:
Those who were in the youngest (under 25) and oldest
(over 50) groups entering training are poorer utilizers;[1] among the rest, the older the participant,
the greater is the tendency for utilization to be
higher (Table 8.1). This finding suggests that
there are socially structured limits, a "floor-and-
ceiling effect" on the role of change agent in the
transfer process. For younger trainees, with less
education and fewer years of work experience, the
learning experience may have been built upon ill-
prepared foundations. This group was also subjected
to more initial job shifting, whose net effect can
have been to render training less pertinent to their
work. For the most senior group--officials embedded
in a job and the prevailing system and coming to the
end of their careers--the prospects for use may be
dimmed by limited incentives or inclination to assume the role of innovator. Among the rest, along

TABLE 8.1

Utilization of Training by
Participants' Age and
Prior Education at Selection

Attribute[a]	Index of Utilization (In Percentages)				Total Number (=100%)
	Very High	High	Moderate	Low	
1. Age (in years)					
Below 25	26.4	17.8	26.7	29.1	(1,510)
25-39	37.6	18.1	23.8	20.6	(11,584)
40-44	40.7	17.8	22.6	18.9	(2,774)
45-49	44.2	15.5	21.4	19.0	(1,777)
50-54	37.0	12.9	29.9	20.2	(838)
55 and over	34.9	11.8	31.9	21.4	(326)
2. Prior education					
University degree	40.5	17.3	23.0	19.3	(12,279)
University work	34.2	17.4	24.2	24.2	(1,668)
No university, special school	36.2	16.6	25.2	22.0	(2,878)
No university, no special school	27.2	19.0	27.4	26.2	(2,200)
All participants	37.7	17.4	24.0	20.9	(19,025)

[a]In this and succeeding tables on utilization, those who
are NA on any attribute are excluded.

211

with increasing age goes greater authority to get
things done or perhaps a stronger inclination to
identify career goals with one's modernizing work
tasks. Whatever the specific and multiple causes
for this finding, its implications for selection
seem reasonably clear: The likelihood of optimal
use of training is poorer among the youngest and
oldest. Being closely linked with other participant
and program attributes, age is implicated in other
findings to be presented as well.

   Prior education is related to subsequent utilization. University graduates have made greater use
of their training than others, while those with no
previous university work or vocational training of
any sort make substantially poorer use of their
training (Table 8.1). This attribute is related to
the previous one (the youngest group had the least
education) and to other attributes. The principal
significance of this finding, one can suggest, lies
in its implications for selection and programing
strategies. Training in advanced countries requires
a good deal of prior formal preparation if learning
obstacles are to be successfully overcome. The extent and type of educational qualifications needed
will vary with the precise nature of training. But
prior educational achievements are also (and ante-
cedently) linked with differences in the social status of trainees: The better educated form a substantial bloc among the elite in most societies,
particularly in skill-poor, underdeveloped countries.

   Thus, prior education must, from the perspective of later use, be considered not only as a programing challenge--to devise training suitable to
participants' backgrounds--but also as a predictor
of the chances that they will be so situated as to
be able to exert leverage on their systems in bringing about modernizing change, however close the fit
between their training and their educational backgrounds. In order to maximize use, those who are
(or are more likely to become) favorably placed (in
part, because of their prior education) would seem,

from this perspective, to offer more fruitful prospects as candidates for selection.

This argument receives strong empirical support
in the finding on the relationship of current occupational status to utilization. With one understand-
able exception, that of professionals--who are among
the highest in use--the higher the status, the greater the utilization (Table 8.2). In this table, the
effects of post-training occupational mobility have
been taken into account because it is the participants' current status that is being employed. But
the same positive association was observed when their
status at selection was related to utilization; the
size of the variations among those status groups was
somewhat smaller. Status at selection has been shown
to be closely related to many program-defining variables and to differential judgments on training
made by participants. As such, it is one of the
central input variables for the program.

In most of those earlier-reported findings,
people selected from the lower end of the status
structure differed sharply from their more favored
colleagues; now we see that those who have remained
at these lower levels have made markedly less use
of their training. It can be argued that there are
two principal bases for effectiveness in performing
the role of change agent: Personal expertise in
meeting a recognized need for one's services or the
prestige, authority, and command of resources inherent to one's office. Without much of either, as
those who have remained in lower-status jobs largely
do, one is unlikely to muster the authority needed
to facilitate innovative change.[2]

When we turn to variables that are closely related to the training period, we find that English-
language skill as a requisite for one's program and
a participant's difficulties with it are related to
the transferability of training. This variable is
intertwined with the site and character of training.
That programs not requiring English were associated
with lower levels of use is in large part a commentary

TABLE 8.2

Utilization of Training by
Current Occupational Status

Current Occupa-tional Status[a]	Index of Utilization (In Percentages)				Total Number (=100%)
	Very High	High	Moderate	Low	
Policy makers, executives	40.5	16.0	25.4	18.1	(2,090)
Administrators, managers	38.7	17.7	23.0	20.6	(6,307)
Scientists, teachers	41.8	17.8	22.0	18.3	(5,951)
Engineers	35.2	20.3	23.7	20.8	(1,782)
Technicians, sub-professions	33.1	18.2	25.4	23.2	(1,437)
Supervisors, foremen	30.3	14.9	31.8	23.1	(522)
Artisans, craftsmen	27.5	18.4	22.6	31.5	(196)
Workers	14.9	16.0	25.2	43.8	(276)
All participants	37.7	17.4	24.0	20.9	(19,025)

[a]See Table 2.4 for details on each of these categories; those who are currently inactive are excluded.

on the ultimate worth of third-country training compared to programs taken in the United States. But
those who encountered no difficulties made greater
use of training than others whose programs also required facility in the use of English (Table 8.3).
Our discussion in Chapter 5 of the failure of special-
language tutoring to prevent difficulties in training
should be recalled in this context. This finding
supports the view that language skill deserves more
rigorous application as a criterion of selection; to
do so would have a salutary effect both in the short
run (i.e., on adjustment and learning) and on the
transfer process at its terminal stage.

   Country of training, the site of one's program,
is related to utilization; on the whole, those
trained outside the United States, especially those
trained in Lebanon at The American University of
Beirut, were lower utilizers. Japan-trained participants were higher utilizers than others trained
solely at Far Eastern sites such as Taiwan or the
Philippines (Table 8.3). The seeming superiority of
U.S. training over that taken at almost any or all
third-country sites is a finding that needs to be
interpreted with considerable caution. As we have
seen, sites other than the United States differ considerably from it in the origins and types of participants they get and in the kinds and duration of
training programs they offer. The two main alternative categories of sites--United States and third
country--do not represent interchangeable training
options either in terms of people or programs. Only
controlled comparisons of matched groups sent to
each (using more sophisticated criteria of costs and
benefits and with better data on the actual substance
of training) could serve as a satisfactory design
for a test of their relative merits. For the present, although these data tend to support the conclusion that at least some third-country sites are
inferior to the United States in the net yield of
their programs, a Scotch verdict of "not proven"
would seem more appropriate.

TABLE 8.3

Utilization of Training by English-
Language Problems and by
Country (Site) of Training

Program Attribute	Index of Utilization (In Percentages)				Total Number (=100%)
	Very High	High	Moderate	Low	
1. English language in program					
Not required	29.5	17.5	27.9	25.1	(3,015)
Required; had some difficulty	37.3	17.6	22.7	22.4	(6,944)
Required; had no difficulty	40.9	17.2	23.7	18.3	(8,846)
2. Primary country (site)					
Japan	40.3	18.2	26.2	15.3	(431)
Mainland U.S.A.	39.3	17.4	23.5	19.7	(15,769)
Offshore U.S.A.	33.9	19.0	23.2	24.0	(500)
Taiwan or Philippines	26.3	16.7	26.8	30.1	(419)
Lebanon	18.3	19.8	28.3	33.5	(659)
All others	32.6	15.1	25.4	26.8	(1,214)
All participants	37.7	17.4	24.0	20.9	(19,025)

Various program types were differentially related to the use of training. All but one of the
program types involving study at universities were
associated with greater use (Table 8.4). Moreover,
people sent on programs under university sponsorship
(rather than being programed by AID) made substantially greater use of their training. Earlier we
noted that almost one half of the former group
earned degrees, compared to only one in nine of
those sponsored directly by AID. It is not surprising, then, to find that those who earned degrees in
training made more effective use than others, especially those who never went to a university (Table
8.4).

We have shown that degrees were highly prized
by participants and that they were linked with greater subsequent occupational mobility. This finding
suggests that apart from their career or prestige
value, earned degrees play a tangible role in technological transfer. Degree programs imposed higher
standards on the selection of participants and were
conducted mainly at the advanced professional level.
Professionalization seems also to have been a dimension underlying many of the participants' specific
judgments about training. Training that reflected
a less-than-professional quality, that did not lead
to degrees, or that was not lengthy (i.e., taken at
universities) was evaluated more critically by participants, especially those holding professional
positions. The implications of professionalization
as an interpretative concept will be elaborated by
other findings on the uses of training. This finding indicates that one of its central defining char-
acteristics--the earning of a foreign degree at an
advanced level--was functional for the transfer process.

The least productive types of training and the
ones that also evoked the greatest number of criticisms, as we have shown, were the observation tour
and the special-group program. Despite the hearty,
facile phrases often employed to justify them by
their proponents--"a breath of fresh air," "a chance

TABLE 8.4

Utilization of Training by Type of Program
and by University-Earned Degree

Program Attribute	Index of Utilization (In Percentages)				Total Number (=100%)
	Very High	High	Moderate	Low	
1. Typology of programs[a]					
University, OJT, and observation	43.9	16.4	21.8	18.0	(2,676)
OJT and observation	41.6	17.4	23.5	17.5	(2,616)
University only	41.3	18.2	22.9	17.5	(2,151)
University and observation	39.0	17.4	23.5	20.1	(4,000)
OJT only	36.1	17.3	22.6	23.9	(1,664)
University and OJT	34.0	17.9	23.1	25.0	(1,146)
Special group	31.4	15.9	23.6	29.1	(592)
Observation only	30.9	17.6	27.3	24.0	(4,180)
2. University and degree programs					
Earned a degree	43.7	19.5	21.3	15.5	(2,532)
Awarded certificate	37.1	16.2	23.2	23.4	(3,023)
Received nothing	41.9	17.8	22.9	17.4	(3,472)
Not at university	35.0	17.2	25.3	22.7	(9,953)
All participants	37.7	17.4	24.0	20.9	(19,025)

[a]See Table 4.3 for full description of types of programs.

218

to blow out the cobwebs," "a brief but intensive exposure"--these types of programs generated sentiments and results which were not comparable in favorability to those stimulated by more extensive training programs, for reasons noted at several places in earlier chapters.

The main reason for their unproductiveness, one can suggest, is their brevity. The duration of training is the one program variable that was linked most closely and consistently with almost every judgment that participants made about their program. It is strongly related to the use of training: The longer the program, the higher the utilization (Table 8.5). A partial exception to this finding is the lower use made by those trained for more than three years. (Over one half in this category were trained at The American University of Beirut, Lebanon; as we saw earlier, university studies taken there were far less productive than in the United States.) This finding provides powerful empirical support for the judgments of all three respondent groups as to the relatively greater merits of longer training. The issue of degree-earning is also implicated, since the longer the program, the more likely was it that a degree was gained in training.

Given the patterning of findings presented so far, we can expect that the fields of training will be variably associated with utilization, because each field reflects a certain configuration of the formal dimensions we have analyzed singly in this chapter. This finding can be viewed as a summary of the joint effects of such variables. A few fields such as health and education have demonstrated a higher degree of transfer on the part of those trained in them; a few others, notably labor and public administration, deviate from the rest in the poorer use made of training by those who took such programs (Table 8.5).

The contrasts in the degree of professionalization reflected in the two extreme sets of training fields lend added emphasis to our suggestion that

TABLE 8.5

Utilization of Training by Duration
and Field of Training

	Index of Utilization (In Percentages)				Total Number
Program Attribute	Very High	High	Moderate	Low	(=100%)
1. Duration of training					
Up to one month	27.7	14.1	23.6	34.5	(444)
One to two months	27.3	18.3	27.6	26.6	(1,058)
Two to four months	33.1	15.0	27.4	24.5	(3,052)
Four to six months	32.1	18.7	27.4	21.9	(1,733)
Six months to one year	38.9	17.6	23.1	20.3	(6,045)
One to two years	43.0	17.6	21.8	17.6	(5,942)
Two to three years	45.1	20.4	18.4	16.0	(409)
Over three years	33.6	18.0	29.7	18.6	(177)
2. Field of training					
Health and sanitation	46.4	18.4	21.2	14.0	(2,320)
Education	43.0	18.7	21.7	16.7	(2,692)
Agriculture	38.1	16.5	24.4	21.0	(5,043)
Atomic energy	36.5	14.7	18.9	29.9	(259)
Industry and mining	35.9	18.1	25.6	20.5	(2,811)
Transportation and communications	35.9	18.9	24.5	20.8	(1,847)
Community development	34.2	18.0	23.1	24.6	(432)
Public administration	29.8	16.2	22.6	31.4	(2,093)
Labor	28.6	13.5	34.1	23.8	(1,040)
Miscellaneous	37.5	19.5	22.4	20.9	(488)
All participants	37.7	17.4	24.0	20.9	(19,025)

this concept has a pervasive, explanatory significance. They differ systematically on all the criteria by which the concept can be defined: Education
and status of participants, locus and duration of
training, degrees gained in training, extent of spe-
cialization among subfields, and so on. The latter
two fields also seem particularly prone to the selection of trainees based on political grounds rather
than based on occupational needs, or to the problem
of institutional mismatching and to transferability
of the values, norms, and procedures involved in
work in these fields between the United States and
trainees' countries of origin. Other factors contribute to low utilization as well: Those trained
in labor took short-term tours, tended to be much
older, and so on. In fact, one half of them were
classified by the Missions as having taken training
whose content was actually peripheral to their occupational role. Moreover, training in both low-use
fields was seen by participants, supervisors, and
U.S. technicians as less consequential for their
jobs and less influential in their careers. Thus,
in terms both of subjective judgments and our criterion measure of occupational transfer, training
in these fields was less productive.

USE AND EVALUATIONS OF PROGRAM PROCESSES

The association of use with another set of
program-related variables was also explored. These
were the views and judgments expressed by participants and others on aspects of the program sequences
through which they moved. From a theoretical perspective, one can expect assessments of the adequacy
or quality of program elements that preceded or were
part of training to be associated with different outcomes. The interrelations among these variables
were analyzed in earlier chapters; we seek now to
show the consequences of the trainees' preparation,
the planning of training, and the implementation of
their programs for the transfer process. In so doing, the participants' judgments are not thought of
as determinants but rather as indicators of program

realities: The judgments are probable indicators of the ways in which these phases of training were carried out.

We traced the implications for use of three selection criteria judged to have been important by the participants. Those who asserted that the needs of their jobs were not significant criteria made far less use of their training (Table 8.6). The purposive character of training is officially stressed as a precondition in selection and programing. This finding underlines the wisdom of this: Training that was not seen as job-related was less functional for technological transfer. Language ability, as gauged by the participants, was also related to later use: Those who felt it had been insignificant in their selection made lesser use of their training (Table 8.6). In part, this finding reflects differences noted earlier between those trained in the United States (a great majority of whose programs required facility in English) and those trained elsewhere. But regardless of site, selection based on a participant's proved linguistic competence is likely to be functional for learning and social adjustment and thus improve prospects for later use.

Finally, the seemingly nonrational criterion of "personal contacts" is unrelated to the outcome of training (Table 8.6). One inference that can be drawn from this finding, in light of the discussion in Chapter 2, is that the selection of participants on this basis does not compromise the potential value to be derived from training, so long as it is not the sole or most significant reason for choice.

Another subset of findings provides empirical support for our hypotheses on the functions of various programing steps for the anticipatory socialization of trainees. Participants' satisfaction with their role in planning their programs was related to subsequent use (Table 8.6, Category 4). The greater the involvement, subjectively appraised, the higher the utilization. In part, this finding suggests that initial participation strengthens motivation for learning and casts the training experience in a more favorable light. It also may reflect a more general

TABLE 8.6

Utilization of Training by Views on
Three Selection Criteria and on
Participants' Roles in Program Planning

Evaluative Item	Index of Utilization (In Percentages)				Total Number (=100%)
	Very High	High	Moderate	Low	
1. "Job needs" as selection criterion					
Very important	39.5	17.5	23.7	19.3	(16,742)
Not very important	24.7	16.3	26.2	32.9	(1,836)
2. "Language ability" as selection criterion					
Very important	40.1	17.4	23.3	19.1	(12,257)
Not very important	32.9	17.6	25.0	24.5	(6,094)
3. "Personal contacts" as selection criterion					
Very important	39.6	16.2	24.2	20.1	(6,745)
Not very important	36.9	17.8	23.9	21.4	(11,136)
4. Participant's role in program planning					
Took sufficient part	45.9	18.1	21.7	14.3	(5,733)
Took insufficient part	36.4	17.7	27.9	18.1	(1,407)
Took no part at all	33.9	17.1	24.6	24.4	(11,832)
All participants	37.7	17.4	24.0	20.9	(19,025)

perspective taken on the program. A participant who took no part at all in planning training cannot ascribe the same value to it, viewed retrospectively, as one who had a hand in shaping its character. Thus, more intimate involvement at the outset can augment the value of the training experience in a participant's eyes and harness his motivation to occupational goals that have been mutually established. This finding is only one indicator of the visible consequences of a more carefully prepared program.

The fact of _information giving_ from authoritative sources, an indicator of how well instituted the program was, is related to utilization. Whether they received orientation from employers or the ministry which served as their sponsor, those who received some were higher utilizers (Table 8.7). One can suggest that the development objectives of training are taken more seriously when such actions are taken by an employer. When the sponsor or employer is more involved in the total programing process, it is more likely, therefore, that a participant's later efforts to use his training will be facilitated rather than met by indifference or resistance. It is not the _amount_ or scope of the advance information they receive that matters: Those expressing satisfaction with greater numbers of facets of their pretraining orientation did not make appreciably better use of their training. Instead, one suspects that it was the _identity_ of the purveyors; by doing so, they were signaling their convictions about the importance of this venture to those who embarked upon it.

The _satisfaction_ with which (as they remembered it) participants viewed their approaching period of training was related to utilization. Those who were "well satisfied" were higher utilizers than others (Table 8.7). This appraisal was shown in Chapter 3 to be linked with a participant's own involvement in programing and with his satisfaction as to the sources and types of information supplied to him in advance of training. It also can be interpreted as reflecting a somewhat better motivational state

TABLE 8.7

Utilization of Training by Sources of
Advance Information About Program and
by Satisfaction Prior to Training

	Index of Utilization (In Percentages)				Total Number
Evaluative Item	Very High	High	Moderate	Low	(=100%)
1. Advance information from employer					
Yes	41.3	18.0	23.2	17.4	(9,008)
No	34.6	16.8	24.5	24.1	(9,824)
2. Advance information from sponsoring ministry					
Yes (my employer)	41.2	19.6	24.3	14.9	(2,010)
Yes	40.0	18.5	23.8	17.6	(5,013)
No	36.3	16.7	23.7	23.4	(11,586)
3. Satisfaction felt prior to departure					
Well satisfied	41.3	17.7	23.4	17.5	(10,421)
Not well satisfied	34.7	15.5	25.2	24.5	(2,657)
Don't know, don't remember	32.9	17.7	24.2	25.3	(5,857)
All participants	37.7	17.4	24.0	20.9	(19,025)

induced in part by more careful preparation, a factor which yields cumulative benefits in the course of training and in its aftermath.[3]

Another element in careful programing is the early involvement of participants' work organizations in the program process. The scope of super-visory involvement in its advance stages, another sign of how well instituted a program was, is related to the use of training. The more active the supervisors were (i.e., recommending or helping to plan the training of participants), the greater the utilization by their subordinates (Table 8.8). The weighty role played by the work supervisor in the process of training has been a dominant theme in our analysis. His actions are even more decisive at the terminal stage in determining the program's effects, because he is in a commanding position to make resources available, to demonstrate approval of innovative work, and in general to facilitate or prevent organizational change. His assumption of a broader role in the initial formulation of a program is an indicator of a greater organizational investment in the training of its staff member(s), and can, therefore, signify an organizational setting more favorable to technological transfer.

Another finding provides further support for this line of reasoning. The existence of a plan for making use of a participant's training by his employing organization (as attested to by his supervisor) is strongly related to utilization (Table 8.8). This is another hallmark of good advance preparation, in this case, directed at the institutional conditions that can affect the transfer process. As was documented in Chapter 3, the supervisor's own program-related activities at this initial stage are related to such an advance commitment. The eliciting of such commitments in advance of training from employers and from participants represents ways of establishing at least two minimum conditions for later use.

TABLE 8.8

Utilization of Training by Supervisors'
Prior Involvement in Program and by
Prior Organizational Plans for Use

Early Organizational Involvement	Index of Utilization (In Percentages)				Total Number (=100%)
	Very High	High	Moderate	Low	
1. Supervisor's involvement					
Recommended participant and helped plan program	41.2	23.4	21.8	13.5	(1,265)
Did either	36.5	18.4	25.8	19.3	(928)
Did neither	33.5	17.6	26.6	22.4	(495)
All rated participants	38.2	20.6	24.0	17.2	(2,688)[a]
2. Existence of prior organizational plans					
Plans for use existed	40.5	20.9	23.0	15.5	(2,706)
No plans for use	28.7	14.0	31.0	26.3	(342)
All rated participants	39.2	20.2	23.9	16.7	(3,048)[b]

[a]Category 1 is based on the unweighted number of participants for whom supervisors' replies were available; it excludes those who were NA (N = 2,912) and those who had no data from supervisors (N = 4,068).

[b]Category 2 is based on the unweighted number of participants for whom supervisors' replies were available; it excludes those who were NA (N = 2,552) and those who had no data from supervisors (N = 4,068).

Plans for placing the trainee or making some specific use of his acquired skills are more likely to be made as by-products of a broader process of development planning and resource allocation. Where such planning has taken place, there is a greater likelihood that a climate more favorable to innovation (or even an "investment" in it) exists. The relationship between a prior organizational commitment to make use of a participant's training and his level of utilization provides a strong argument for our two-level conception of innovative transfer. It shows the necessity of insisting that technical-training programs be intrinsic to or part of larger development projects rather than being mounted on an ad hoc basis in the hope that some good may yet come out of them.

As might be expected, participants' judgments about specific qualities of their programs were related in diverse ways to utilization. For example, programs whose level of instruction was of "too simple" or "too advanced" a character (especially the latter) were associated with markedly lower use (Table 8.9). Both of these judgments reflect a program which lacked integration with a trainee's past achievements or present circumstances; not surprisingly, poorer use was one result. In lesser measure, programs which generated critical judgments as to their variety (pace or scope) were less productive. In particular, those who felt pressured, in the sense of being "required to do or see too many different things," made poorer use of their training (Table 8.9). As noted earlier, such judgments arose more often with respect to short-term tours. Thus, this finding can be interpreted as the "boomerang effect" of an excess of zeal in programing, an administrative disease that can infect the programs of all types of participants but especially those for whom only a brief time is available.

A program which evoked a desire for still more variety was only marginally less productive than one adjudged satisfactory in this respect. But the reverse flaw, that of under-programing, can be shown

TABLE 8.9

Utilization of Training by Participants'
Evaluations of Selected Program Aspects

Specific Program Aspect	Index of Utilization (In Percentages)				Total Number (=100%)
	Very High	High	Moderate	Low	
1. Level of training					
All right	39.1	17.7	24.1	19.2	(15,031)
Too simple	33.9	14.7	24.5	27.0	(2,741)
Too advanced	30.1	20.3	22.4	27.3	(1,047)
2. Variety (things to do or see)					
All right	39.3	18.6	23.1	19.1	(9,660)
Wanted still more	37.0	16.8	24.6	21.6	(5,590)
Too many things	34.9	15.4	25.3	24.4	(3,583)
3. Length of program					
All right	37.5	17.9	23.8	20.8	(8,980)
Too short	38.5	17.1	24.2	20.2	(9,177)
Too long	31.2	16.2	22.0	30.6	(826)
4. Time free for personal interests					
Too little	39.4	16.2	24.1	20.4	(7,483)
All right	36.8	18.4	24.0	20.8	(11,050)
Too much	31.4	14.3	22.3	32.0	(435)
All participants	37.7	17.4	24.0	20.9	(19,025)

to bear upon the later uses made of training. Those
who wanted an even longer program (like those who
wanted more in them) differed little in their levels
of later use from those who were satisfied. It was
among those few who felt their programs were too
long that utilization levels were sharply lower
(Table 8.9). This finding is related (in the same
table) to one showing that those who felt their program had left them with too much free time to pursue
their personal interests were much lower users of
training than others.

In both of these instances, the interpretative
image common to such judgments is that of participants who found no challenge in their program, for
whom time hung heavy. Such a situation is most congenial to boredom or withdrawal of interest and a
longing for the program to end. Poorer utilization
of such a devaluated commodity is quite understand-
able. In both cases, the survey findings supply
neat illustrations of the ultimate loss of transferability involved in programs that are not carefully
tailored to the trainees' backgrounds and expectations. Prior education, work experience, and occupational status all weighed heavily in the participants' judgments of these program aspects, as we
have shown in Chapter 5.

Measures that attempt to capture more summary
appraisals of the training are only slightly related
to utilization. An index which classified participants by the number of technical aspects they rated
approvingly was only moderately associated with
their levels of utilization (Table 8.10). In analyzing the index items separately, we saw that it was
not approval or disapproval per se but the type of
disapproval which distinguished among higher and
lower users. This summary measure tends to blur
such qualitative differences, but even in an imper-
fect manner, the finding suggests that it is not the
purely technical quality of a training program which
is crucial to its ultimate yield. A program of low
quality is more likely to prove unproductive, but
even the most satisfactorily realized instructional

TABLE 8.10

Utilization of Training by Indices of
Satisfaction with Technical and
Nontechnical Aspects of Training

Summary Index of Satisfaction	Index of Utilization (In Percentages)				Total Number (=100%)
	Very High	High	Moderate	Low	
1. With technical aspects					
High	39.5	18.8	23.8	17.9	(5,050)
Moderate	38.2	18.2	22.8	20.8	(6,303)
Low	36.2	15.8	25.0	23.0	(7,672)
2. With nontechnical aspects					
High	36.7	20.1	23.5	19.6	(6,433)
Moderate	38.7	15.7	24.4	21.2	(7,121)
Low	37.5	16.5	23.8	22.2	(5,471)
All participants	37.7	17.4	24.0	20.9	(19,025)

program is subject to other intrusive influences
which can measureably augment or attenuate its effectiveness.

Findings with respect to various <u>nontechnical</u>
aspects of a program are even more equivocal, or, in
some instances, nonexistent. For example, later use
of training is unrelated to whether or not participants attended a communications seminar at the end
of training, whether or not they were satisfied with
their money allotments, and so on. An index which
classified them by the number of nontechnical aspects rated with approval was uncorrelated with utilization (Table 8.10). By comparison with the findings shown so far, the two main aspects of training
programs, as measured by these indices seem to be
less fateful for the transfer process than one might
have reasonably expected. This is particularly the
case with respect to items linked with the social
adjustment of participants during training.

Earlier we expressed doubts about how crucial
such nontechnical features might be to the transfer
of training, or the assumption that one exerts efforts to make training a success as a <u>learning</u> experience. Based on this set of findings, the role of
nontechnical aspects in the utilization of training
appears to be not at all crucial. One can grant
that such activities contribute to a more pleasant
sojourn and may have social or political effects of
an order which the design and instruments of this
study do not capture. But they are of demonstrably
slight significance for the uses made by participants of their training upon their return.

Why this is so, in view of much conventional
wisdom pointing to an opposite conclusion, is an
issue on which the survey data are unenlightening.
Stimulated primarily by international, political
considerations, in past research dealing with foreign visitors, a good deal of stress was laid on
the implications of social adjustment and program
experiences for attitude formation and change, especially as related to U.S. policies. Long-term

consequences were infrequently explored, especially those relating to the uses of foreign study. Most of these studies were of much younger student groups, who were less settled into careers, and engaged in education and training of a less focused, occupation-related character than those we have studied.

Those who come as participants, it is suggested, are less susceptible to the shocks and dislocations that are potentially associated with a foreign sojourn. For one thing, increased international communications and interchanges have reduced the cultural isolation of the better-educated, technical-elite groups that form the pool of candidates for this program. Then, as a more mature group, one that is more socially integrated and with more sharply defined career or occupational goals, they can more readily discount or neutralize the effects of some personally inconvenient or distasteful aspect of their sojourn. Finally, as we have seen, they move through a rather well-structured programing sequence, a fact that serves to minimize the occurrence of the completely unexpected. All of these can make social adjustment and personal reactions less compelling factors affecting the uses of training than those program dimensions which define its professional or occupational relevance.

No data are available from these surveys on the effects of training on personality traits or social values, such as the need for achievement or a belief in the real possibility of economic and social development—two areas that are specified as objectives of concern to participant training. Further research of a different character would be needed to provide evidence on this class of outcomes. One can suggest, however, that such research is not likely to yield much evidence of changed attitudes or values among participants or of any links between attitudes and innovative-role behavior. The attitudinal effects such a program may seek must be filtered through the rather stable sets of values and beliefs held by such socially favored persons, who come from countries that vary widely in patterns of culture and

social structure. To expect that a training sojourn
can foster greater development-related efforts by
changing values or attitudes in a consistent direction would seem quite optimistic, given the diversity
and maturity of the people who enter this program.
The beliefs, values, and attitudes held by participants prior to training, and the conditions they confront after their return, are likely to be more
powerful determinants of their efforts to make use
of their training and the results achieved. We turn
finally to the latter set of factors, those implicated in the postprogram phase.

USE AND THE AFTERMATH OF TRAINING

The element of time must enter into any assessment of the consequences of training for technological change. Introducing new ideas or techniques or
effecting institutional change are innovative processes requiring long periods of time before the
outcome appears as certain. The speed of successful
innovation depends in part on the talents of the
change agent and the resources available to him.
But it is also likely to be strongly, perhaps deci-
sively, affected by the barriers represented by the
traditions, values, and organizational patterns that
confront him. Thus, we can expect some uses of
training to become possible and certifiable only
over a period of time.

The time since the completion of training is
directly associated with later use: The longer the
time back, the greater the utilization of training
(Table 8.11). This pattern, which peaks near the
fifth year and levels off, appears not only after
comparing various subgroups on this composite index
but also in parallel comparisons on each of its com-
ponents--use and transmission of training--considered
separately. It suggests that training is not a
"wasting asset" but has, instead, cumulative or
delayed-action effects upon innovative-role behavior
in its aftermath.

TABLE 8.11

Utilization of Training by Time Since
Completion of Program and by Index of
General Satisfaction with Training

Item	Index of Utilization (In Percentages)				Total Number (=100%)
	Very High	High	Moderate	Low	
Time back since training					
Up to one year	18.9	18.8	34.0	28.4	(758)
One to two years	28.2	18.6	28.2	25.0	(3,152)
Two to three years	34.5	17.4	25.1	22.9	(3,654)
Three to four years	36.8	18.9	23.5	20.7	(2,519)
Four to five years	44.0	18.2	21.2	16.7	(2,212)
Five years and over	44.4	15.9	21.3	18.4	(6,702)
Index of general satisfaction					
High	49.1	17.4	21.0	12.4	(7,250)
Moderate	32.6	18.4	25.8	23.1	(10,126)
Low	18.8	10.8	25.8	44.6	(1,649)
All participants	37.7	17.4	24.0	20.9	(19,025)

A few possible reasons for the lower initial use of training can be suggested.[4] First, a period of reorientation typically may be necessary before one sets about the task of innovation or change. It may take a sizable period of time to translate a concept or technique for application to one's own setting in an appropriate and fruitful fashion. A need to do some "lobbying" with others to promote acceptance of new ideas can slow the pace of modernizing transfer. And one can expect some ultimately successful plans to require a substantial amount of time before their success is <u>visibly</u> assured. A more ambiguous concomitant of the passage of time, as we saw earlier, is the increased likelihood of occupational mobility. This can mean moves to jobs unrelated to training or to retirement; it can also mean moves to positions where the desire to bring about change is now matched by the authority to effect them or to influence larger numbers of people in ways functional for innovative change. We will show the consequences of mobility for the use of training at a later point.

An index was formed from answers to the questions dealing with the participants' <u>over-all satisfaction</u> with training and their rating of its importance.[5] The finding showed satisfaction (more stably defined by this index than by either item alone) to be strongly related to utilization: The more satisfied their answers indicated them to be, the greater the utilization (Table 8.11). A different study design would be needed to go beyond this demonstration of a positive correlation between attitude and action, to sort out the time ordering of variables and establish their causal priority. One could argue that the more (or less) a trainee has been able to use his training, the higher (or lower) his estimation of its worth will become. With equal logic, one can assume that an initial judgment on the value of one's training is part of a more general motivational orientation linked to varying levels of effort and later success. Finally, and most probably, one can assume that the two go hand in hand, affecting each other in reciprocal fashion. These data do

not allow us to choose among the alternatives.
Nevertheless, the finding has value in part because
of its expected character: It would be a curious
finding that a poorly regarded program has been as
productive as a more highly esteemed one. And, because this index of satisfaction was closely related
to every measure of a program's worth in the survey
(derived from all three sources of data), some justification exists for considering this finding as
more than epiphenomenal in character.

The career value that training has had for participants is strongly related to their utilization
of training. Those who felt training to have had an
enhancing effect upon their careers were far greater
users than others, especially (and unsurprisingly)
those who felt they actually suffered as a result of
having been sent for training (Table 8.12). This
finding lends support to the assertion that it is
events in the aftermath of training which are decisive for the transfer process: A meaningful judgment as to whether or not one's program helped or
hurt one's career can only be made long after its
conclusion. It also provides substantial support
for assuming, as we have done at several points,
that the personal gains a participant can have derived from training are compatible with or contribute to the achievement of his program goals of
innovative work on development projects. The two
are mutually reinforcing; the chance of improving
one's position can provide powerful motivation for
a more positive approach to training and greater
productivity in work on a project of importance to
national development.

This finding is linked with many we have reviewed which bear upon the professional character
of training. Degree programs, so highly esteemed
by participants, were generally adjudged as more
career-enhancing, as was training taken at advanced
levels in more heavily professionalized fields such
as health and education. The identification of
self-interest with the fulfillment of social needs
is one essential element in the development of a

TABLE 8.12

Utilization of Training by Career Value of Training
and by Patterns of Occupational Mobility

| Career Item | Index of Utilization (In Percentages) | | | | Total Number (=100%) |
	Very High	High	Moderate	Low	
1. Career value: without training job would be[a]					
Worse (training helped)	51.9	18.5	19.3	10.4	(4,859)
About the same	33.7	17.6	25.1	23.6	(11,368)
Better (training hurt)	30.0	17.1	23.8	29.1	(899)
2. Patterns of occupational mobility[b]					
i. No change since selection	35.8	18.1	25.0	21.2	(7,060)
ii. Returned to same job, changed since	41.1	18.0	22.0	18.9	(7,141)
iii. Returned to (expected) new job, still in it	42.3	21.0	22.2	14.5	(1,255)
iv. Returned to (expected) new job, changed since	50.2	16.7	20.6	12.3	(1,280)
v. Returned to (unexpected) new job, still in it	27.2	17.0	22.5	33.4	(579)
vi. Returned to (unexpected) new job, changed since	32.9	15.1	25.3	26.6	(1,148)
All participants	37.7	17.4	24.0	20.9	(19,025)

[a]Excludes those who were NA or who are currently inactive
(N = 1,900).

[b]Patterns are numbered in conformity with Table 6.3, which
shows their derivation; excludes those currently inactive (N = 562).

238

professional self-image. A professional orientation
can fuse personal motives with national-development
priorities; foreign-training programs that emphasize
this dual role orientation and seek to develop it
further (instead of treating students as if they
were individual worshipers at the shrine of national
development) will, it is suggested, yield a higher
and more dependable return on its investment.

Another finding that suggests the positive functions of personal gains derived from training for
the transfer process is the empirical relationship
between occupational mobility and the uses of training. The two are related in complex ways (Table
8.12). In an earlier chapter, we showed that some
job mobility was a direct consequence of training
while some of it was related to normal career contingencies. Those who have never changed jobs since
the time of their selection can serve as a standard
against which every other group can be compared,
because training is usually not intended to be a
vehicle for occupational mobility.

The first finding is that all mobility was functional to some degree: Those who moved after returning home (to whatever type of job) made greater use
of training than those who remained in their initial
job. But the mobility pattern associated with the
greatest use of training is one where participants
returned to an expected new job, in particular the
one showing another movement after that. These are
examples of participants who were groomed for new
positions by their training: Both their greater use
and their subsequent shifts into better positions
can be attributed to participant training. The
groups that have made the poorest use of training
are those whose jobs were unexpectedly changed upon
their return, especially those who remained in that
job ever since then. This latter group had the highest unemployment rate and felt training had hurt
their careers most often of all mobility groups.
This finding suggests that in addition to being personally damaging to this group, or perhaps as a result of it, training proved to be economically or
socially unproductive as well.

As was true of the previous finding, this empirical relationship argues strongly for a view of utilization as being shaped primarily by events or circumstances linked with the postprogram period. It also documents the complex ways in which careers, training, and utilization are intertwined. The contours of a man's post-training career are, to an extent, shaped by training; they act in turn as an influence upon the opportunities he finds (and also perhaps upon his motivation) to apply the skills and ideas he has acquired. At every point, the reality of his personal situation intervenes: Career developments that were caused by training or occurred in its wake were powerful determinants of the effectiveness of training.

Data are available to test the relationship of only a few aspects of the participants' work settings to their use of training. We have already shown that prior organizational commitments and early involvement by supervisors in programing were associated with greater use. The supervisor's role in the aftermath is no less crucial: Participants who characterized their supervisors as "very helpful" in their efforts to apply their training made far greater use than those who rated their supervisors as less helpful, indifferent, or even hostile (Table 8.13). This finding is echoed by another, based on supervisors' responses. Training programs that supervisors judged as more important for the participants' current work were far more productive: The more importance ascribed to them, the greater the use. Judgments of a program's importance were closely associated both with rates of interaction between supervisors and returned participants and with the latter's appraisals of their supervisors' helpfulness in their attempts to make use of training. Thus, the findings on utilization build from this empirically determined set of associations between superiors and subordinates.

The vital contributions of supervisors' attitudes and actions, early and late in the program process, can be summarized in three propositions:

TABLE 8.13

Utilization of Training by Aspects
of the Organizational Setting

Organizational Setting	Index of Utilization (In Percentages)				Total Number (=100%)
	Very High	High	Moderate	Low	
1. Participant's rating of supervisor's role in using training[a]					
Very helpful	53.9	18.8	19.2	8.2	(7,065)
Somewhat helpful	31.8	22.1	27.2	18.9	(4,046)
Indifferent	24.8	15.7	24.8	34.8	(1,808)
Not helpful	21.3	12.3	24.6	41.8	(2,248)
2. Supervisor's view on importance of training for current job[b]					
Essential	42.1	19.2	22.8	15.9	(1,843)
Very important	39.0	19.9	22.4	18.6	(2,352)
Helpful, not very important	27.1	14.8	27.3	30.9	(1,063)
Not useful, harmful	26.2	11.3	32.7	29.8	(168)
3. Participant's setting, works with supervisor (others) trained abroad[a]					
Supervisor trained abroad	42.3	19.5	22.6	15.6	(7,775)
Co-worker(s) trained abroad	45.4	16.8	19.6	18.2	(4,526)
No one else trained abroad	27.9	15.3	27.5	29.4	(5,590)
All participants	38.5	17.5	23.5	20.7	(18,062)

[a]Excludes participants not trained in their occupational specialty who weren't asked these questions (N = 963).

[b]Based on the unweighted number of participants whose programs were rated by their supervisors; it excludes those NA or with no supervisor's rating (N = 4,242).

241

(1) The more active the supervisor's role in selecting trainees and in programing, the more helpful he
was seen to be by his subordinates in attempts to
make use of training, and the greater the utilization;
(2) The more active his role, the more likely was it
that a trainee's work organization had definite plans
for making use of his training, and the greater the
subsequent utilization; (3) The more active his role,
the more likely was he to rate his subordinates'
training as essential or very important to his current job and to interact with him frequently, and
the greater the utilization.

The involvement of indigenous work organizations and supervisory personnel in the training of
these participants plays a powerful role in the process of technical transfer. Involvement is no magic
key, especially if it is perfunctory or procedural
rather than active and oriented to substantive matters. But on all these indicators of institutional
commitment, the greater or more extensive the commitment, the greater the uses made of training by participants. These empirical findings support our
initial conception of the process of technological
transfer as operating at two levels: That of the
individuals who take training and return home and
that of the institutional settings within which they
are located. Foreign training can equip individuals
with new and needed skills, and it may alter their
role conceptions in ways that promote their innovative efforts. But without a corresponding concern
over their institutional settings and a willingness
to alter them in ways that will favor the acceptance
of innovations, the impetus to modernizing change
implicit in foreign study will be sharply curtailed.

Another attribute of the participants' work
settings is the presence or absence of others who
have been trained abroad. We argued that the introduction of innovations is facilitated by the presence of other foreign-trained co-workers in the
participant's immediate work setting, that they can
form a "community of innovators" and support each
other in bringing about organizational change. This

theoretical position has some empirical basis in studies made by others. Barbara J. Walton, for example, refers to three studies other than the present one which support her generalization that the "introduction of new ideas by the returnee is facilitated where . . . a substantial number of fellow-employees were also trained abroad."[6]

The findings of this study strongly support such a contention (Table 8.13). Those working in a setting with a supervisor or other co-workers who had also been trained abroad made greater use of their training than participants who were unique in their exposure to foreign training. Why this was so can only be speculated about with the data at hand. Earlier, we showed that supervisors who had foreign training were more often judged by participants as helpful and suggested that shared experience can be the basis for providing support to a trainee in his innovative efforts. One can also suggest that more highly professionalized settings are likely to contain a larger number of staff members who are foreign trained. Those holding jobs in the economic sectors of medical services, education, public utilities, and engineering--all of which are relatively highly professionalized--were far more likely than those in other sectors to be working with others who had been trained abroad. Thus, professionalization enters into this finding as well.

One final indicator of institutional support for innovation is the participants' relationships with the U.S. Mission. The pattern of contacts with the U.S. Mission is strongly related to utilization. These can have come about through work on U.S.-assisted development projects, or by consultative or advisory contacts with U.S. technicians, or by requesting help of some sort from the Mission after returning from training. However it came about, contact with the USOM was associated with greater use: The more extensive the contact, the greater the use of training made by participants (Table 8.14). Those who worked for the USOM, or on a cooperative

TABLE 8.14

Utilization of Training by Pattern
of USOM Contacts After Training

Pattern of USOM Contacts	Index of Utilization (In Percentages)				Total Number (=100%)
	Very High	High	Moderate	Low	
1. Postprogram work contacts with USOM Worked for/with					
USOM	47.4	18.6	21.3	12.7	(4,397)
Any contacts	39.7	18.8	22.7	18.7	(6,335)
No contacts at all	31.1	15.7	26.4	26.9	(8,203)
2. Frequency of contact with U.S. technician					
Frequent contact	50.9	18.0	19.6	11.5	(3,454)
Occasional contact	39.5	18.6	23.8	18.0	(3,143)
Never met him	26.7	14.9	30.7	27.8	(512)
None available at all	34.0	17.0	24.9	24.0	(11,857)
3. Help requested and received from USOM					
Request adequately met	55.6	16.7	18.3	9.5	(2,571)
Request partially met	50.5	20.5	17.4	11.4	(629)
Request not met	40.9	14.6	21.8	22.7	(844)
Never requested help	33.9	17.5	25.3	23.2	(14,850)
All participants	37.7	17.4	24.0	20.9	(19,025)

project, were higher utilizers; in a related vein, those who interacted more frequently with U.S. technicians available to them were also higher utilizers. (U.S. technicians were asked a parallel question on the frequency of their contacts with specific participants. The correlation between their depiction of how often they met and the designated participants' uses of training largely corroborated this response based on the participants' replies alone.) Finally, the successful granting of requests for further U.S. assistance made by returned participants was positively correlated with their levels of utilization.

These findings can be compressed into one generalization: The greater the Mission's support for returned participants, through personal contacts and assistance of various types, the greater the use they will make of skills and techniques they have acquired. The follow-through activities that the Mission engages in with returned participants represent a powerful catalyst for the transfer and application of their training. The Mission can work directly with participants prior to their training and, especially, after their return. It can strive indirectly to suggest and encourage changes in organizational settings in which participants will work, in ways favorable to innovative efforts. Thus, by its policies and practices, the Mission can affect the odds that the use of a strategy of investing in human capital will contribute to national development. The identification of acceptable modes of intervention and the limits on the alteration of institutional structures that can be encouraged by external agencies pose issues of great practical and theoretical interest.[7] They are two of the central issues that must be confronted in any cooperative-assistance program whose goals are to induce or facilitate technological change.

AN EPILOGUE ON THREE THEMES

This brief concluding section is devoted to a re-examination of three concepts that have been

introduced and elaborated on in the foregoing dis-
cussion--professionalization, institutionalization,
and human-resources development. All three concepts
have had a central place in recent works on change
and modernization in developing countries; it is not
surprising, therefore, that the findings of this
study could be recast and interpreted in relation to
them.

The operation of the first of these--the process
of professionalization--is reflected in many findings. Among personal attributes, the occupational
status of the trainees was closely associated with
many judgments about training, with many specific
features of their programs, and with the most significant consequences of the training experience.
Those who held professional status--engineers, scientists, teachers--usually stood somewhat (and in certain instances very much) apart from those in administrative positions or those holding lower-status
jobs. In general, the former were better prepared,
received training of a better quality or at least at
a higher level, and made more effective use of training in its aftermath.

As a characteristic of programs and fields of
activity, professionalization again plays a significant role. Programs that were more professional in
character (i.e., taken at universities, leading to
advanced degrees), typically met with greater favor
and proved to be more productive. Programs in
fields that are more professionalized (e.g., education, health, agriculture), "harder," more oriented
toward technological applications and the disciplined
growth of knowledge, were more productive than programs in fields that are "softer," defined more by
the predominance of social or political considerations (e.g., labor, community development, public
administration).

Closely linked with these two attributes were
the economic areas in which the participants' jobs
were situated. Again, the results show the imprint
of the professional factor. Education, health,

public utilities--all sectors of economic activity
in which professional roles are prominent and foreign
training of their occupants is more common--were
areas in which the extent of technological transfer
was greater. They were also among the areas with
the greatest "attractiveness" for job holders, kept
more of them over a period of time, and gained more
converts as well.

Other bits of evidence could be recalled in
this context; one suspects that the point has been
adequately made by these. What suggests itself as
the obvious reason for this pattern of findings is
the isomorphism of professional roles and activities
across widely varying social and cultural settings.
The professions, with their universally recognized
societal importance, are among the firmest bridges
linking modern societies with traditional ones. The
traffic in innovation moves most freely across them;
convergences in perspective, the common mastery of
advanced skills, and the high position accorded to
those in professional roles in both types of societies provide points of contact that facilitate the
ready transfer of skills and knowledge. And, as we
noted earlier, professional roles accommodate the
potentially conflicting elements of self-interest
and service to society more comfortably than do most
others.

Thus, a program that seeks to promote modernization by training people to perform critical occupational roles must give precedence to the training
and upgrading of those who perform professional
tasks and must also strive to introduce professional
orientations into the thinking of those, such as
administrators and managers, for whom universalistic
values and achievement-oriented standards do not as
commonly serve as guides for conduct or bases for
decision making. These people then may become the
"new element . . . carriers and interpreters of
world culture," who form the core of the modernizing
forces in what Richard Meier has termed "the developmental society."[8]

The second concept which has received considerable attention in our analysis is institutionalization. This is most clearly seen with respect to the
implementation of this cooperative-assistance effort.
The better instituted the programs were--in the
sense of selecting trainees carefully on the basis
of well-defined job needs, involving them in programing and providing orientation, gaining firm advance commitments on their later placement, coordinating training with significant authority-wielding
figures in the trainees' work settings, and supporting them in the aftermath of training with advice
and material assistance--the greater the value realized in the realm of technological transfer.

Other institutional factors have been referred
to, some on theoretical grounds and some on which we
have corroborative empirical data. Among these are
rates of economic growth, opportunities for occupational mobility, the presence of supportive supervisors or others with a receptivity to change, the
pace of change over time, and the availability of
outside assistance through the AID Mission. All of
these represent conditions for action that hinder or
facilitate an individual in his role as change agent.
The listing or analysis of various institutional
factors of significance for social and economic development has been a preoccupation of students of
the development process;[9] in documenting the specific
role of some variables of this type we have broken
no new ground, except that we have traced certain
implications at a micro-level of analysis. But our
secondary analysis of these survey data has brought
out the relatively greater importance of such institutional considerations, compared to various attributes of participants or their programs, in the
effective use of technical training. This was even
more pronounced in the case of indicators of institutional variables available to us that partially
defined the organizational context of the returned
trainee. Other students of the consequences of
foreign study for modernization have come to a similar conclusion. M. Brewster Smith remarks:

> Sufficient evidence /on the links between
> foreign education and development7 is at
> hand . . . to make it clear that obstacles
> to the utilization of knowledge and skill
> <u>after return</u> are the strategic factor that
> limits the effectiveness of much foreign
> study. /Italics added.7[10]

Finally, some comments may be made on the relevance of the human-resources development concept
that serves as a rationale for this program and
kindred educational-assistance efforts. This study
is one of a rather small number that has sought to
assess the long-term consequences of a strategy
which focuses on the cultivation of high-level manpower. In this case, the participants were located
in professional and administrative positions in the
public sector of their countries. Few would contest
the claim that these are posts of the greatest strategic importance for national development. What
have been the main outcomes of this strategy?

As we have noted, the uses of training usually
involved the adaptive, incremental, piecemeal introduction of new ideas or techniques that one would
expect in the predominantly bureaucratic milieus in
which the participants work. And the extent to
which they claimed the achievement of innovative
changes varied considerably, most notably in accord
with the institutional factors discussed earlier.
The barriers and bottlenecks that limit the absorptive capacity of underdeveloped countries for foreign assistance (which define them, in a sense, as
underdeveloped), play a powerful role in the extent
or rate of diffusion of technology, in particular,
in the form of ideas, skills, or new modes of organization.

We have also seen that foreign study, or education more generally, serves a variety of functions
only peripherally related (and sometimes opposed) to
the goals of national development. The enhancement
of prestige or mobility potential or the pursuit of
individual interests through migration can act in

such a way as to derail or subvert a job-training
strategy for human-resources development. This consideration leads one directly to the issue of motivation for study and for work. One shortcoming of
forced-draft schemes for meeting manpower needs, as
C. Arnold Anderson has noted, is that they "encourage the substitution of incentives for motives . . . .
/Ultimately/ reliance will be put on coercion and
labor assignment replaces labor commitment."[11] One
bias in an approach to human-resources development
through formal education is that it tends to place
undue stress on the supply side and is insufficient-
ly concerned with the demand side, including the
structure of incentives for the performance of the
high-priority tasks for which training was deemed
essential or useful. The provision of adequate incentives for career mobility must also accompany the
enhancement of the individual's skills through job
training; if not, as we have noted, foreign study
only encourages emigration or a concentration on
areas of activity that yield higher dividends.

Thus we are led, primarily on sociological
grounds, to call for a broadening of the concept of
human-resources development, to take account of its
noneconomic implications in a more explicit way. As
they stand, the metaphors of "human capital" and
"human resources" view people rather narrowly, as
units whose productive capacities can be raised by
added educational inputs.[12] Conflicts that arise
between development-related productive imperatives
and the goals of other sectors of the society (e.g.,
family, tribe, polity) are viewed merely as obstacles to the efficient combination of factors of production. Neil H. Jacoby's confident, iconoclastic
comment that "'the science' of foreign economic aid
consists in identifying the oncoming bottlenecks to
sustained rapid growth, as they appear, and removing
them one by one," reflects this perspective.[13]

Frustrating experiences in working with such a
conception, attempting to translate it into manpower
plans and national-educational strategies, do not
arise from flaws inherent in it alone. In many

cases, there never was a firm commitment to such a
rational approach on the part of the aid recipient,
merely a tolerant catering to the propensities of
the aid-giving agency to act with more dispatch or
confidence if such long-range plans were devised
(often by its own personnel), and to refuse to act
in their absence. But we find that the restricted,
occupational scope of concern embodied in the concept is also a source of its difficulty in the program whose operation and consequences we have examined. In addition to placing excessive faith in the
capacity of individuals, acting on their own in many
cases, to bring about needed organizational and institutional change, the strategy fails to recognize
that the reassertion, upon his return, of powerful
ties and obligations associated with a foreign trainee's other social identities often counteracts or
blunts his capacity to play such a role successfully.
The further delineation of the positive and negative
implications of such sociological factors for the
achievement of the economic-development objectives
of such educational strategies--including the discovery of the current linkages between educational
systems and the occupational structure of developing
countries--is one way in which the human-resources
concept can be made more empirically adequate and
more useful as a tool for national development.

NOTES

1. In our analysis of findings, we will employ
phrases such as "higher (lower) utilizers," or "use
more (less) of their training," or "make better
(poorer) use," simply as reportorial conveniences
in stating the degree or direction of association
between variables. These findings could be given
in a longer, more technically accurate form in which
group differences in percentages are specified. In
avoiding such formulations, we run the risk of mis-
leading the reader by overstating or distorting a
relationship. The data are shown in sufficient
detail to permit an independent appraisal.

Tests of significance have not been used on these findings. Their applicability to these data, aggregated in the manner employed in this study, is highly questionable. Given the size of the subgroups created in these cross-tabulations, percentage differences are invariably statistically significant; the problem of substantive significance remains. The issue of the relevance of these tests has been much debated in recent years. In this analysis we can, following Hanan Selvin's terminology, describe our procedure as involving both "fishing" and "hunting." See Selvin and Alan Stuart, "Data-Dredging Procedures in Survey Analysis," The American Statistician, Vol. XX, No. 3 (June, 1966), pp. 20-23. For another argument against the use of tests, one that concerns data from a multinational survey, see Gabriel Almond and Sidney Verba, The Civic Culture (Princeton: Princeton University Press, 1963), pp. 523-25.

2. This formulation is of course an adaptation of Max Weber's classical discussion of the bases of authority. See Weber, The Theory of Social and Economic Organization, A. M. Henderson and T. Parsons, trans. (New York: Oxford University Press, 1947), pp. 324-86.

3. Another interpretation is of course that of a retrospective "halo effect." Having made effective use of their training, some people may be overly generous in their remembrances of attitudes or judgments on earlier stages of training. Given the design of this study, it is impossible to sort out the time ordering of these variables.

4. In her summary of research on the uses made by foreign students of their training, Barbara J. Walton makes the general point that "those with a foreign education use their training eventually, but some have a long wait." See Walton, Foreign Student Exchange in Perspective: Research on Foreign Students in the United States, Department of State Publication 8373 (Washington, D.C.: U.S. Government Printing Office, September, 1967), p. 11.

5. For a discussion of these two items, see
Chapter 5; those classified as "high" said they were
"very satisfied" _and_ thought training to have been
"one of the most important things" they had done.
The "low" group termed training a "waste of time,"
_or_ "unsatisfactory" (usually both); the rest were
classified as "moderate" in their over-all satisfaction.

6. Walton, _op. cit._, p. 12.

7. Criticism has been levelled at certain
"interventionist" implications of this proposition,
one that has found a place in every study of the
fate of programs of planned social change. We take
it as a premise of cooperative international efforts
such as participant training that there is, at least
initially, not only a motivation to seek change but
also a will to reorient institutions where that appears necessary or useful. The determining of precisely what to change and at what pace can be a process of joint discovery; effecting such alterations
is the responsibility of the developing country.
The aid donor cannot or should not undertake this
task; it can assess the potential utility of further
aid in the absence of changes of a mutually agreed-
upon sort by the aid-receiving country. In this
sense, to seek and accept aid is to accept "intervention"; the issue for both parties is not whether
it _is_ intervention but at whose behest and for what
purposes. For a critique that stresses the power
differentials which warp such relationships, see
Luis Scherz-Garcia, "Some Dysfunctional Aspects of
International Assistance," _International Social
Science Journal_, Vol. XIX, No. 3 (1967), pp. 387-403.

8. See Richard L. Meier, _Science and Economic
Development: New Patterns of Living_ (2nd ed.; Cambridge, Mass.: The M.I.T. Press, 1966), pp. 205-35;
quoted on pp. 205-6. The distinctive countributions
that U.S. professional schools can make to international development, arising from this congruence of
perspectives, are discussed in a recent study by
Education and World Affairs, _The Professional School_

and World Affairs (Albuquerque: The University of
Mexico Press, 1967).

9.   Walton, for example, has identified nine
generalizations about the use of foreign training
in developing countries from a scrutiny of the research literature.   Among institutional variables,
she mentions an expanding economy, time lags, employment in fields unrelated to training, social
contacts, and family position.   See Walton, op. cit.,
pp. 11-13.   One admirably concise list of such prerequisites included: "a literate, adaptable, economically oriented population; administrative and technical talent; a framework of stable government; and
an adequate supply of capital."   See Neil H. Jacoby,
U.S. Aid to Taiwan: A Study of Foreign Aid, Self-
Help, and Development (New York: Frederick A.
Praeger, 1966), p. 241.

10.   M. Brewster Smith, "Foreign vs. Indigenous
Education," in Don C. Piper and Taylor Cole, eds.,
Post-Primary Education and Political and Economic
Development (Durham: Duke University Press, 1964),
p. 69.

11.   C. Arnold Anderson, "Economic Development
and Post-Primary Education," in Piper and Cole, op.
cit., p. 17.   Another writer has placed value conflicts of this type at the center of the field of
forces determining the transfer of technology.   It
cannot be viewed as an autonomous process that need
be considered only in terms of technical feasibility;
"it must also be appraised in the light of its social
acceptability."   See Neil W. Chamberlain, "Training
and Human Capital," in Daniel L. Spencer and Alexander Woroniak, eds., The Transfer of Technology to
Developing Countries (New York, Frederick A. Praeger,
1967), pp. 147-66.

12.   For an exception in economic analysis, see
the treatment of the concept in Frederick Harbison
and Charles A. Myers, Education Manpower and Economic
Growth: Strategies of Human Resource Development
(New York: McGraw-Hill Book Company, 1964).

13.   Jacoby, *op. cit.*

SELECTED BIBLIOGRAPHY

SELECTED BIBLIOGRAPHY

SOURCE MATERIALS: THE SURVEY OF
RETURNED PARTICIPANTS

The detailed guidelines, interview schedules, and other survey documents constituted a packaged kit for the conduct of social surveys. Because these materials are too voluminous to be incorporated in this work, we will briefly describe the major interview schedules used in the study and show the numbers of people with whom they were used.

"Participant (Form A)." For returned participants who were trained in their occupational specialty. Consists of 146 items, including contingent questions. Unweighted (N) = 9,192; weighted (N) = 18,062 participants.

"Participant (Form B)." For returned participants who were not trained in their occupational specialty. Consists of 151 items, including contingent questions. (All but 10 items are identical with those in Form A.) Unweighted (N) = 476; weighted (N) = 963 participants.

"Participant (Supplement)." For returned participants who went on more than one training program; deals with earlier program(s). Consists of 30 items, including contingent questions. Unweighted (N) = 251; weighted (N) = 508 participants.

"Supervisor--Part I." For a supervisor to rate individual participant(s) now working for him. Consists of 17 items on his actions and views relating to the training of each subordinate
259

being rated. Unweighted (N) = 5,600 participants rated by supervisors.

"Supervisor--Part II." For a supervisor to assess
participant training in general. Consists of
14 items; used for each supervisor only once.
Unweighted (N) = 3,909 supervisors.

"Technician--Part I." For a technician to rate
individual participant(s) known to him. Consists of 44 items on his actions and views
relating to the training of each former trainee.
Unweighted (N) = 2,645 participants rated by
U.S. technicians.

"Technician--Part II." For technicians to assess
participant training in general. Consists of
5 items; used for each technician only once.
Unweighted (N) = 511 technicians.

A complete listing of the documentation for
this world-wide survey, together with a review of
data-processing routines used to analyze the survey
data at several levels of aggregation, may be found
in the following technical report:

Gollin, Albert E., and Kert, John M., Jr. Evaluation
of Participant Training: Documentation and
Guide to the Study Materials. Washington, D.C.:
Bureau of Social Science Research, November,
1965.

BOOKS AND MONOGRAPHS

Adams, Walter, ed. The Brain Drain. New York: The
Macmillan Company, 1968.

Adler, John H. Absorptive Capacity: The Concept
and Its Determinants. Washington, D.C.: The
Brookings Institution, 1965.

Alexander-Frutschi, Marian Crites, ed. Human
Resources and Economic Growth. Menlo Park, Calif.:
Stanford Research Institute, 1963.

Almond, Gabriel, and Verba, Sidney. The Civic Cul-
     ture. Princeton: Princeton University Press,
     1963.

Anderson, C. Arnold. "The Impact of the Educational
     System on Technological Change and Moderniza-
     tion." Industrialization and Society. Edited
     by Bert F. Hoselitz and Wilbert E. Moore. The
     Hague: UNESCO and Mouton, 1963. Pp. 259-78.

_____. "Economic Development and Post-Primary
     Education." Post-Primary Education and Politi-
     cal and Economic Development. Edited by Don C.
     Piper and Taylor Cole. Durham: Duke Univer-
     sity Press, 1964. Pp. 1-26.

Arensberg, Conrad M., and Niehoff, Arthur H. Intro-
     ducing Social Change: A Manual for Americans
     Overseas. Chicago: Aldine, 1964.

Banks, Arthur S., and Textor, Robert B. A Cross-
     Polity Survey. Cambridge, Mass.: The M.I.T.
     Press, 1963.

Barnett, Homer G. Innovation: The Basis of Cultural
     Change. New York: McGraw-Hill Book Company,
     1953.

Barton, Allen H. "The Concept of Property-Space in
     Social Research." The Language of Social Re-
     search. Edited by Paul F. Lazarsfeld and Mor-
     ris Rosenberg. Glencoe: The Free Press, 1955.
     Pp. 40-53.

Beals, Ralph, and Humphrey, Norman. No Frontier to
     Learning: The Mexican Student in the United
     States. Minneapolis: University of Minnesota
     Press, 1956.

Beeby, C. E., ed. Fundamentals of Educational
     Planning. 6 booklets. Paris: UNESCO; Inter-
     national Institute for Educational Planning,
     1967.

Blau, Peter M. The Dynamics of Bureaucracy. Chi-
    cago: University of Chicago Press, 1955.

Blum, Robert, ed. Cultural Affairs and Foreign
    Relations. Englewood Cliffs, New Jersey:
    Prentice-Hall, Inc., 1963.

Butts, Freeman R. American Education and Interna-
    tional Development. New York: Harper and Row,
    1963.

Campbell, Donald T., and Stanley, Julian C. "Exper-
    imental and Quasi-Experimental Designs for Re-
    search on Teaching." Handbook of Research on
    Teaching. Edited by N. L. Gage. Chicago:
    Rand McNally, 1963. Pp. 171-246.

Cantril, Hadley. The Pattern of Human Concerns.
    New Brunswick, New Jersey: Rutgers University
    Press, 1965.

Chamberlain, Neil W. "Training and Human Capital."
    The Transfer of Technology to Developing Coun-
    tries. Edited by Daniel L. Spencer and Alexan-
    der Woroniak. New York: Frederick A. Praeger,
    1967. Pp. 147-66.

Coleman, James S., ed. Education and Political
    Development. Princeton: Princeton University
    Press, 1965.

Davis, James A. Panel Analysis: Techniques and
    Concepts in the Interpretation of Repeated
    Measurements. Chicago: National Opinion Re-
    search Center, University of Chicago, November,
    1963.

Education and World Affairs. The Foreign Student:
    Whom Shall We Welcome? New York: Education
    and World Affairs, 1964.

_____. The University Looks Abroad. New York:
    Walker, 1965.

_____. The Professional School and World Affairs.
    Albuquerque: The University of New Mexico
    Press, 1968.

Eidell, Terry L., and Kitchel, Joanne M., eds. Knowl-
    edge Production and Utilization in Educational
    Administration. Eugene, Oregon: University of
    Oregon Press, 1968.

Elder, Robert E. The Foreign Leader Program: Opera-
    tions in the United States. Washington, D.C.:
    The Brookings Institution, 1961.

Esman, Milton J., and Bruhns, Fred C. "Institution
    Building in National Development, An Approach
    to Induced Social Change in Transitional Socie-
    ties." Comparative Theories of Social Change.
    Edited by Hollis W. Peter. Ann Arbor, Michigan:
    Foundation for Research on Human Behavior, 1966.
    Pp. 318-42.

Foster, George M. Traditional Cultures: And the
    Impact of Technological Change. New York:
    Harper and Row, 1962.

Foster, Philip J. "The Vocational School Fallacy in
    Development Planning." Education and Economic
    Development. Edited by C. Arnold Anderson and
    Mary Jean Bowman. Chicago: Aldine Publishing
    Company, 1965. Pp. 142-66.

Galbraith, John Kenneth. Economic Development.
    Cambridge, Mass.: Harvard University Press,
    1964.

Gardner, John W. AID and the Universities. New
    York: Education and World Affairs, 1964.

Guthrie, George M., and Spencer, Richard E. Ameri-
    can Professions and Overseas Technical Assis-
    tance. University Park: The Pennsylvania
    State University, 1965.

Hagen, Everett E. On the Theory of Social Change. Homewood, Ill.: The Dorsey Press, 1962.

Halle, Louis J. The Society of Man. New York: Harper and Row, 1965.

Hansen, W. Lee. "Human Capital Requirements for Educational Expansion: Teacher Shortages and Teacher Supply." Education and Economic Development. Edited by C. Arnold Anderson and Mary Jean Bowman. Chicago: Aldine, 1965. Pp. 63-87.

Hapgood, David, and Bennett, Meridan. Agents of Change: A Close Look at the Peace Corps. Boston: Little, Brown and Company, 1968.

Harbison, Frederick, and Myers, Charles A. Education, Manpower and Economic Growth: Strategies of Human Resource Development. New York: McGraw-Hill Book Company, 1964.

Hayes, Samuel P., Jr. Measuring the Results of Development Projects. Paris: UNESCO, 1959.

Hirschman, Albert O. "Comments on 'A Framework for Analyzing Economic and Political Change.'" Development of the Emerging Countries: An Agenda for Research. Washington, D.C.: The Brookings Institution, 1962. Pp. 39-44.

_____. Development Projects Observed. Washington, D.C.: The Brookings Institution, 1967.

Horwitz, Hortense, and Smith, Elias /pseud.7. "The Interchangeability of Socio-Economic Indices." The Language of Social Research. Edited by Paul F. Lazarsfeld and Morris Rosenberg. Glencoe: The Free Press, 1955. Pp. 73-77.

Hoselitz, Bert F. "Investment in Education and Its Political Impact." Education and Political Development. Edited by James S. Coleman. Princeton: Princeton University Press, 1965. Pp. 541-65.

_____, and Moore, Wilbert E., eds. Industrializa-
    tion and Society. Paris: UNESCO and Mouton,
    1963.

_____, and Willner, Ann R. "Economic Development,
    Political Strategies, and American Aid." The
    Revolution in World Politics. Edited by Morton
    A. Kaplan. New York: John Wiley and Sons,
    1962.

Humphrey, Richard A., ed. Universities and Develop-
    ment Assistance Abroad. Washington, D.C.:
    American Council on Education, 1967.

Hyman, Herbert H. Survey Design and Analysis. Glen-
    coe: The Free Press, 1955.

_____, et al. Interviewing in Social Research.
    Chicago: University of Chicago Press, 1954.

_____, Wright, Charles R., and Hopkins, Terence
    K. Applications of Methods of Evaluation.
    Berkeley and Los Angeles: University of Cali-
    fornia Press, 1962.

Institute of International Education. Open Doors
    1968. Report on International Exchange. New
    York: Institute of International Education,
    July, 1968.

_____, Committee on Educational Interchange
    Policy. Military Assistance Training Programs
    of the U.S. Government. New York: Institute
    of International Education, July, 1964.

_____, Committee on Educational Interchange
    Policy. Twenty Years of United States Govern-
    ment Programs in Cultural Relations. New York:
    Institute of International Education, 1959.

Jacoby, Neil H. U.S. Aid to Taiwan: A Study of
    Foreign Aid, Self-Help, and Development. New
    York: Frederick A. Praeger, 1966.

Johnson, Walter, and Colligan, Francis J. The Ful-
    bright Program: A History. Chicago: Univer-
    sity of Chicago Press, 1965.

Katz, Elihu, and Lazarsfeld, Paul F. Personal In-
    fluence. Glencoe: The Free Press, 1955.

Kendall, Patricia L., and Lazarsfeld, Paul F. "Prob-
    lems of Survey Analysis." Continuities in
    Social Research: Studies in the Scope and
    Method of "The American Soldier." Edited by
    Robert K. Merton and Paul F. Lazarsfeld. Glen-
    coe: The Free Press, 1950.

Kerr, Clark, and Fisher, Lloyd H. "Plant Sociology:
    The Elite and the Aborigines." Common Frontiers
    of the Social Sciences. Edited by Mirra
    Komarovsky. Glencoe: The Free Press and
    Falcon's Wing Press, 1957.

Kriesberg, Martin, ed. Public Administration in
    Developing Countries. Washington, D.C.: The
    Brookings Institution, 1965.

LaPalombara, Joseph, ed. Bureaucracy and Political
    Development. Princeton: Princeton University
    Press, 1963.

Lazarsfeld, Paul F. "Problems in Methodology."
    Sociology Today: Problems and Prospects.
    Edited by Robert K. Merton, Leonard Broom, and
    Leonard S. Cottrell. New York: Basic Books,
    1959. Pp. 39-78.

_____, and Barton, Allen H. "Qualitative Measure-
    ment in the Social Sciences: Classification,
    Typologies and Indices." The Policy Sciences.
    Edited by Daniel Lerner and Harold D. Lasswell.
    Stanford: Stanford University Press, 1951.
    Pp. 155-92.

_____, and Rosenberg, Morris, eds. The Language
    of Social Research. Glencoe: The Free Press,
    1955.

Lesser, Simon, and Peter, Hollis W. "Training For-
    eign Nationals in the United States." Some
    Applications of Behavioural Research. Edited
    by Rensis Likert and Samuel P. Hayes, Jr.
    Paris: UNESCO, 1957.

Lewin, Kurt. "Group Decision and Social Change."
    Readings in Social Psychology. Edited by Guy
    E. Swanson, Theodore M. Newcomb, and Eugene W.
    Hartley. New York: Henry Holt, 1952. Pp.
    459-73.

McClelland, David C. The Achieving Society. Prince-
    ton, New Jersey: D. Van Nostrand, 1961.

Maddison, Angus. Foreign Skills and Technical Assis-
    tance in Economic Development. Paris: Devel-
    opment Centre of the Organisation for Economic
    Cooperation and Development, 1965.

Mason, Edward S. "Competitive Coexistence and Eco-
    nomic Development in Asia." International Sta-
    bility and Progress. Background Papers for the
    Eleventh American Assembly, Arden House, Colum-
    bia University, May 2-5, 1957. The American
    Assembly, Graduate School of Business, Columbia
    University, June, 1957. Pp. 59-97.

Mead, Margaret, ed. Cultural Patterns and Technical
    Change. New York: New American Library, 1955.

_____. "Applied Anthropology, 1955." Some Uses
    of Anthropology: Theoretical and Applied.
    Washington, D.C.: The Anthropological Society
    of Washington, 1956. Pp. 94-108.

Meier, Richard L. Science and Economic Development:
    New Patterns of Living. Cambridge, Mass.: The
    M.I.T. Press, 1966.

Merton, Robert K. Social Theory and Social Struc-
    ture. Revised and enlarged edition. Glencoe:
    The Free Press, 1957.

Moodie, Graeme C., ed. Government Organisation and
     Economic Development. Paris: Development Cen-
     tre of the Organisation for Economic Coopera-
     tion and Development, 1966.

Moore, Wilbert E., and Feldman, Arnold S., eds.
     Labor Commitment and Social Change in Develop-
     ing Areas. New York: Social Science Research
     Council, 1960.

Morgenstern, Oskar. On the Accuracy of Economic
     Observations. Princeton: Princeton University
     Press, 1963.

Morris, Richard T. The Two-Way Mirror: National
     Status in Foreign Students' Adjustment. Minne-
     apolis: University of Minnesota Press, 1960.

Nair, Kusum. Blossoms in the Dust: The Human Fac-
     tor in Indian Development. New York: Frederick
     A. Praeger, 1961.

OECD, Study Group on Education. Social Objectives
     in Educational Planning. Paris: Organisation
     for Economic Cooperation and Development, 1967.

Ohlin, Goran. "Aggregate Comparisons: Problems and
     Prospects of Quantitative Analysis Based on
     National Accounts." Comparative Research
     Across Cultures and Nations. Edited by Stein
     Rokkan. Paris and The Hague: Mouton, 1968.
     Pp. 163-70.

Platt, William J. "Conflicts in Educational Planning."
     Education and Political Development. Edited by
     James S. Coleman. Princeton: Princeton Univer-
     sity Press, 1965. Pp. 566-82.

Policy Conference on Economic Growth and Investment
     in Education. The Challenge of Aid to Newly
     Developing Countries. Paris: Organisation for
     Economic Cooperation and Development, 1962.

Pool, Ithiel de Sola. "Effects of Cross-National Contact on National and International Images." International Behavior. Edited by Herbert C. Kelman. New York: Holt, Rinehart and Winston, 1965.

Powelson, John P. "Educational Assistance, Economic Development and United States Foreign Policy." Post-Primary Education and Political and Economic Development. Edited by Don C. Piper and Taylor Cole. Durham: Duke University Press, 1964. Pp. 128-52.

Riggs, Fred W. Administration in Developing Countries. Boston: Houghton Mifflin, 1964.

Rogers, Everett M. Diffusion of Innovations. New York: The Free Press of Glencoe, 1962.

Rokkan, Stein, ed. Comparative Research Across Cultures and Nations. Paris and The Hague: Mouton, 1968.

Russett, Bruce M., et al. World Handbook of Political and Social Indicators. New Haven: Yale University Press, 1964.

Selltiz, Claire, et al. Attitudes and Social Relations of Foreign Students in the United States. Minneapolis: University of Minnesota Press, 1963.

Siffin, William J., ed. Toward the Comparative Study of Public Administration. Bloomington: Indiana University Press, 1959.

Sills, David L. The Volunteers. Glencoe: The Free Press, 1947.

Simmel, Georg. The Sociology of Georg Simmel. Translated and edited by Kurt H. Wolff. Glencoe: The Free Press, 1950.

Smelser, Neil J., and Lipset, Seymour Martin, eds. Social Structure and Mobility in Economic Development. Chicago: Aldine, 1966.

Smith, M. Brewster. "Foreign vs. Indigenous Education." Post-Primary Education and Political and Economic Development. Edited by Don C. Piper and Taylor Cole. Durham: Duke University Press, 1964.

Spencer, Daniel L., and Woroniak, Alexander, eds. The Transfer of Technology to Developing Countries. New York: Frederick A. Praeger, 1967.

Spicer, Edward H., ed. Human Problems in Technological Change. New York: Russell Sage Foundation, 1952.

Suchman, Edward A. Evaluative Research: Principles and Practice in Public Service and Social Action Programs. New York: Russell Sage Foundation, 1967.

Textor, Robert B., ed. Cultural Frontiers of the Peace Corps. Cambridge, Mass.: The M.I.T. Press, 1966.

Thomson, Charles A., and Laves, Walter H. C. Cultural Relations and U.S. Foreign Policy. Bloomington: Indiana University Press, 1963.

Tickner, F. J. Technical Cooperation. London: Hutchison, Ltd., 1965.

Useem, John, and Useem, Ruth Hill. The Western-Educated Man in India. New York: The Dryden Press, 1955.

Weber, Max. The Theory of Social and Economic Organization. Translated by A. M. Henderson and Talcott Parsons. New York: Oxford University Press, 1947.

Weidner, Edward W. The World Role of Universities. New York: McGraw-Hill Book Company, 1962.

Westcott, Jay B. "Governmental Organization and
     Methods in Developing Countries." Development
     Administration. Edited by Irving Swerdlow.
     Syracuse: Syracuse University Press, 1963.
     Pp. 44-67.

Wilson, Howard E. "Education, Foreign Policy, and
     International Relations." Cultural Affairs and
     Foreign Relations. Edited by Robert Blum.
     Englewood Cliffs, New Jersey: Prentice-Hall,
     Inc., 1963. Pp. 80-111.

Wolf, Charles J. Foreign Aid: Theory and Practice
     in Southern Asia. Princeton: Princeton Uni-
     versity Press, 1960.

Wriggins, Howard. "Foreign Assistance and Political
     Development." Development of the Emerging Coun-
     tries, An Agenda for Research. Washington, D.C.:
     The Brookings Institution, 1962. Pp. 181-208.

Zeisel, Hans. Say It with Figures. 4th rev. ed.
     New York: Harper and Row, 1957.

ARTICLES AND PERIODICALS

American Council on Education. "International Migra-
     tion of Intellectual Talent," Bulletin on Inter-
     national Education, IV, No. 10 (November 17,
     1966), 1-8.

Byrnes, Francis C. "Role-Shock: An Occupational
     Hazard of American Technical Assistants Abroad,"
     Annals of the American Academy of Political and
     Social Science, CCCLXVIII (November, 1966),
     95-108.

Carter, George E. "The Beginnings of Peace Corps
     Programming," Annals of the American Aca-
     demy of Political and Social Science, CCCLXV
     (May, 1966), 46-54.

Coch, Lester, and French, John R. P. "Overcoming Resistance to Change," Human Relations, I (1948), 512-32.

Coelho, George V., ed. "Impacts of Studying Abroad," Journal of Social Issues, XVIII, No. 1 (1962).

Dogan, Mattei, and Rokkan, Stein. "Quantitative Ecological Analysis: Contexts, Trends, Tasks," Social Science Information, VI, No. 6 (December, 1967), 35-48.

Furtado, Celso. "Intra-Country Discontinuities: Towards a Theory of Spatial Structures," Social Science Information, VI, No. 6 (December, 1967), 7-16.

Gable, Richard W., ed. "Partnership for Progress: International Technical Cooperation," Annals of the American Academy of Political and Social Science, CCCXXIII (May, 1959).

Galtung, Johan. "Some Aspects of Comparative Research," Polls, II, No. 3 (Spring, 1967), 1-19.

Grubel, Herbert G. "The Brain Drain: A U.S. Dilemma," Science, XLIV, No. 3755 (December 16, 1966), 1420-24.

Gullahorn, John T., and Gullahorn, Jeanne E. "An Extension of the U-Curve Hypothesis," Journal of Social Issues, XIX, No. 3 (July, 1963), 33-47.

Haas, Michael. "Aggregate Analysis," World Politics, XIX, No. 1 (October, 1966), 106-21.

Henderson, Gregory. "Foreign Students: Exchange or Immigration?" International Development Review, VI, No. 4 (December, 1964), 19-21.

Hoskins, Halford, ed. "Aiding Underdeveloped Areas Abroad," Annals of the American Academy of Political and Social Science, CCLXVIII (March, 1950).

Hutchison, Edward P., ed. "The New Immigration,"
    Annals of the American Academy of Political and
    Social Science, CCCLXVII (September, 1966).

Jacobson, Eugene, and Schachter, Stanley, eds. "Cross-
    National Research: A Case Study," Journal
    of Social Issues, X, No. 4 (1954).

Katz, Elihu, Levin, Martin L., and Hamilton, Herbert.
    "Traditions of Research on the Diffusion of
    Innovation," American Sociological Review,
    XXVIII, No. 2 (April, 1963), 237-52.

Kelman, Herbert C. "Changing Attitudes Through
    International Activities," Journal of Social
    Issues, XVIII, No. 1 (1962), 68-87.

_____. "The Reactions of Participants in a For-
    eign Specialists Seminar to Their American Ex-
    perience," Journal of Social Issues, XIX, No.
    3 (July, 1963), 61-114.

Klineberg, Otto. "The Problem of Evaluation," Inter-
    national Social Science Bulletin, VII, No. 3
    (1955), 346-50.

_____. "Research in the Field of International
    Exchanges in Education, Science and Culture,"
    Social Science Information, IV, No. 4 (December,
    1965), 97-138.

Lambert, Richard D., ed. "America Through Foreign
    Eyes," Annals of the American Academy of Politi-
    cal and Social Science, CCXCV (September, 1954).

Lepawsky, Albert, and Lepawsky, Rosalind. "Enskill-
    ing People," International Development Review,
    III, No. 3 (October, 1961), 16-22.

Lipset, Seymour Martin. "Research Problems in the
    Comparative Analysis of Mobility and Develop-
    ment," International Social Science Journal,
    XVI, No. 1 (1964), 35-48.

Lundstedt, Sven, ed. "Human Factors in Cross-
    Cultural Adjustment," Journal of Social Issues,
    XIX, No. 3 (July, 1963).

Maretzki, Thomas. "Transition Training: A Theoreti-
    cal Approach," Human Organization, XXIV, No. 2
    (Summer, 1965), 128-34.

Mayntz, Renate. "The Visiting Fellow: An Analysis
    of an Academic Role," American Sociological
    Review, XXV, No. 5 (October, 1960), 735-41.

Mitchell, Robert Edward. "Survey Materials Collected
    in the Developing Countries: Sampling, Measure-
    ment, and Interviewing Obstacles to Intra- and
    Inter-national Comparisons," International
    Social Science Journal, XVII, No. 4 (1965),
    665-85.

"Motivational Patterns for Modernization," Interna-
    tional Social Science Journal, XX, No. 3 (1968).

Myers, Robert G. "'Brain Drains' and 'Brain Gains,'"
    International Development Review, IX, No. 4
    (December, 1967), 4-9.

Perkins, James A. "Foreign Aid and the Brain Drain,"
    Foreign Affairs, XLIV, No. 4 (July, 1966),
    608-19.

Peter, Hollis W., and Henry, Edwin R. "Measuring
    Successful Performance Overseas," International
    Development Review, III, No. 3 (October, 1961),
    8-12.

Ritterband, Paul. "Toward an Assessment of the Costs
    and Benefits of Study Abroad," International
    Educational and Cultural Exchange. A Publica-
    tion of the U.S. Advisory Commission on Inter-
    national Educational and Cultural Affairs (Fall,
    1966), 26-35.

Rokkan, Stein. "Trends and Possibilities in Compara-
    tive Social Science: Report on an International

Conference," Social Science Information, IV,
No. 4 (December, 1965), 139-64.

Russett, Bruce M. "The World Handbook As a Tool in
Current Research," Social Science Information,
VI, No. 6 (December, 1967), 17-34.

Scherz-Garcia, Luis. "Some Dysfunctional Aspects of
International Assistance and the Role of the
University in Social Change in Latin America,"
International Social Science Journal, XIX, No.
3 (1967), 387-403.

Schild, Erling O. "The Foreign Student, as a
Stranger, Learning the Norms of the Host-
Culture," Journal of Social Issues, XVIII,
No. 1 (1962), 41-54.

Schultz, Theodore. "Investment in Human Capital,"
American Economic Review, LI, No. 1 (March,
1961), 1-17.

Selvin, Hanan, and Stuart, Alan. "Data-Dredging
Procedures in Survey Analysis," The American
Statistician, XX, No. 3 (June, 1966), 20-23.

Shearer, John C. "In Defense of Traditional Views
of the 'Brain Drain' Problem," International
Educational and Cultural Exchange. A Publication of the U.S. Advisory Commission on International Educational and Cultural Affairs (Fall,
1966), 17-25.

Siegel, Bernard J. "Some Recent Developments in
Studies of Social and Cultural Change," Annals
of the American Academy of Political and Social
Science, CCLXVIII (January, 1966), 137-53.

Smith, M. Brewster, ed. "Attitudes and Adjustment
in Cross-Cultural Contact," Journal of Social
Issues, XII, No. 1 (1956).

Yannay, Ya'acov. "Technical Cooperation Between
Israel and the Developing World," International

Development Review, VI, No. 3 (September, 1964), 10-15.

Young, Francis A. "The Conference Board of Associated Research Councils in the United States. A Brief Historical Account with Special Reference to National and International Manpower Problems," Social Science Information, IV, No. 2 (June, 1965), 111-27.

PUBLIC DOCUMENTS AND
OTHER PRINTED MATERIALS

Agency for International Development, Statistics and Reports Division. U.S. Foreign Assistance and Assistance from International Organizations, Obligations and Loan Authorizations. July 1, 1945-June 30, 1962. Washington, D.C.: Agency for International Development, April, 1963.

Bremseth, Cameron F. Followup Evaluation Study of Iranian Participants Who Received Training in the United States Under I.C.A. Sponsorship. Teheran, Iran: United States Operations Mission, 1956.

_____. An Evaluation of the Participant Training Program in Taiwan. Taipei, Taiwan: Mutual Security Mission to China, 1957.

Bristol, Jane F., and Dugan, Robert D. A Pilot Study of Participant Training in the United States-- Executive Report. Washington, D.C.: Institute for International Services, June, 1963.

Bureau of Social Science Research. Social Science Perspectives on Training for Development. Report and Recommendations of a Workshop and Conference on Non-Technical Aspects of the AID Participant Training Program. Washington, D.C.: Bureau of Social Science Research, November, 1966.

_____. Youth and Leadership in the Developing Nations. Summary Report on a Conference Sponsored by the International Education Subcommittee, Foreign Area Research Coordination Group. Washington, D.C.: Department of State, September, 1967.

Coffin, Frank M. "Thoughts on a Development Leadership Program." Training for Leadership and Service. Proceedings of the National Conference on the International Training Programs of AID, June 25-26, 1962. Washington, D.C.: Agency for International Development, 1962. Pp. 19-28.

Colligan, Francis J. Twenty Years After: Two Decades of Government-Sponsored Cultural Relations. Department of State Publication 6689. Washington, D.C.: U.S. Government Printing Office, 1958.

Dugan, Robert D., Bristol, Jane F., and Miller, Hope D. A Pilot Study of Participant Training in the United States--Technical Report. Washington, D.C.: Institute for International Services, 1963.

Fox, Ernest, et al. Citizen in a Time of Change: The Returned Peace Corps Volunteer. A Report of a Conference, March 5-7, 1965. Washington, D.C.: The Peace Corps, 1965.

Gollin, Albert E. Evaluating Programs and Personnel Overseas. New York: Bureau of Applied Social Research, Columbia University, February, 1963.

_____, ed. The International Migration of Talent and Skills: Proceedings of a Workshop and Conference. Washington, D.C.: Council on International Educational and Cultural Affairs, Department of State, October, 1966.

Instituto de Pesquisas de Opiniao e Mercado. An Evaluation of Selected Returned Participants

in the Point IV Labor Training Program, Brazil.
Report prepared for the United States Operations Mission. Rio de Janeiro, Brazil: Instituto de Pesquisas de Opiniao e Mercado, 1957.

International Cooperation Administration. Evaluation
of Participant Training Program. ICATO Circular
A 175, November 5, 1959. (Mimeographed.)

International Cooperation Administration, Office of
Participant Training. Participant Training
Operations: Statistical Report--June 30, 1960.
Washington, D.C.: International Cooperation
Administration, 1961.

International Research Associates. A Study of Reactions to the I.C.A. Exchange Program Among Returned Mexican Grantees. Vallarta, Mexico:
International Research Associates, 1959.

Mitchell, Robert E. Occupations, Organizations and
National Development. A Conference Paper.
Berkeley: Survey Research Center, University
of California, October, 1965.

Moore, Forrest G. The Collegiate Environment: The
Experience and Reactions of Foreign Students,
Government-Sponsored and Self-Sponsored. Back-
ground Paper for a Conference on Non-Technical
Aspects of Participant Training. Washington,
D.C.: October 11, 1965. (Mimeographed.)

National Science Foundation. Technology Transfer
and Innovation. Proceedings of a Conference,
May 15-17, 1966. Washington, D.C.: National
Science Foundation, NSF 67-5, 1967.

Oberg, Kalervo. "Culture Shock and the Problem of
Adjustment to New Cultural Environments."
(Unpublished paper.)

Preston, Harley O. Operations of the Participant
Training Program of the Agency for International
Development. Washington, D.C.: Office of
International Training, AID, November, 1966.

Schlesinger, Lawrence E., and Peter, Hollis W. _Us-
     ing U.S. Training in the Philippines: A Follow-
     up Survey of Participants_. 2 vols. Ann Arbor:
     Institute for Social Research, University of
     Michigan, 1959.

Spence, Ralph B. _Technical Training of Pakistanis
     in the United States: An Evaluation of the
     I.C.A. Program, 1951-55_. Karachi, Pakistan:
     United States Operations Mission, 1956.

Stabler, John B., and Mogannam, E. Theodore. _Follow-
     up and Evaluation Study of Returned I.C.A. Par-
     ticipants in Egypt_. Cairo, Egypt: United
     States Operations Mission, 1956

U.S. Advisory Commission on International Educational
     and Cultural Affairs. _A Beacon of Hope--The
     Exchange-of-Persons Program_. A Report from the
     Commission, April, 1963.

U.S. Congress, House, Committee on Government Opera-
     tions. _Government Programs in International
     Education: A Survey and Handbook_. 85th Cong.,
     2nd Sess., House Report 2712. Washington, D.C.:
     U.S. Government Printing Office, 1959.

_____, House, Subcommittee on International Organ-
     ization and Movements, Committee on Foreign
     Affairs. _Ideological Operations and Foreign
     Policy: Report No. 2_. 88th Cong., 2nd Sess.,
     House Report 1352. Washington, D.C.: U.S.
     Government Printing Office, 1964.

_____, House, Committee on Education and Labor.
     _International Education: Past, Present, Prob-
     lems and Prospects_. 89th Cong., 2nd Sess.,
     House Doc. No. 527. Washington, D.C.: U.S.
     Government Printing Office, 1966.

_____, Senate, Committee on Foreign Relations.
     _United States Foreign Policy--Compilation of
     Studies_. 87th Cong., 1st Sess., Doc. No. 24.
     Washington, D.C.: U.S. Government Printing
     Office, 1961.

U.S. Department of State, Agency for International
     Development. Training for Leadership and Ser-
     vice. Proceedings of the National Conference
     on the International Training Programs of AID,
     June 25-26, 1962.

_____, Bureau of Educational and Cultural Affairs.
     Changing Roles of Youth in Developing Nations.
     A Conference Report. Washington, D.C.: Policy
     Review and Research Staff, August, 1964.

U.S. Government. Science, Technology and Develop-
     ment. United States Papers Prepared for the
     United Nations Conference on the Application
     of Science and Technology for the Benefit of
     Less Developed Areas. 12 vols. Washington,
     D.C.: U.S. Government Printing Office, 1963.

United States Technical Cooperation Mission. Indo-
     American Participant Training Program: An Eval-
     uation Study. New Delhi, India: U.S. Tech-
     nical Cooperation Mission.

Walton, Barbara J. Foreign Student Exchange in Per-
     spective. Research on Foreign Students in the
     United States. Department of State Publication
     8373. Washington, D.C.: U.S. Government Print-
     ing Office, 1968.

ABOUT THE AUTHOR

Albert E. Gollin, Research Associate at the
Bureau of Social Science Research, Inc., Washington,
D.C., is a sociologist with extensive experience in
social science research and program evaluation in
the fields of foreign aid and educational and cultural exchange. Since 1962 he has conducted empirical research and organized research conferences for
the Agency for International Development, the State
Department, and the Peace Corps. He has served as
a consultant on research and training to the Peace
Corps since 1966.

Among his publications are papers and monographs
on the methodology and uses of program evaluation,
the role of social research in the policy process,
research problems in the study of international flows
of high-level manpower, and the role of foreign study
in modernization.

Dr. Gollin received his graduate training in
sociology and social psychology at Columbia University. Prior to assuming his present position, he
was a study director for five years at the Bureau
of Applied Social Research, Columbia University. He
also holds an appointment as Lecturer in Sociology
at Howard University.